AMERICAN
WOMEN
IN
POVERTY

Recent Titles in
Contributions in Women's Studies

Hard News: Women in Broadcast Journalism
David H. Hosley and Gayle K. Yamada

Faith of a (Woman) Writer
Alice Kessler-Harris and William McBrien, editors

The Language of Exclusion: The Poetry of Emily Dickinson
and Christina Rossetti
Sharon Leder with Andrea Abbott

Seeing Female: Social Roles and Personal Lives
Sharon S. Brehm, editor

A Disturbance in Mirrors: The Poetry of Sylvia Plath
Pamela J. Annas

Women of Exile: German-Jewish Autobiographies Since 1933
Andreas Lixl-Purcell, editor

The Biosocial Construction of Femininity: Mothers and Daughters in Nineteenth-
Century America
Nancy M. Theriot

Good-bye Heathcliff: Changing Heroes, Heroines, Roles, and Values in Women's
Category Romances
Mariam Darce Frenier

The Compassionate Memsahibs: Welfare Activities of British Women in India,
1900–1947
Mary Ann Lind

Against the Horizon: Feminism and Postwar Austrian Women Writers
Jacqueline Vansant

Sealskin and Shoddy: Working Women in American Labor Press Fiction,
1870–1920
Ann Schofield

Breaking the Angelic Image: Woman Power in Victorian Children's Fantasy
Edith Lazaros Honig

Eighteenth-Century Women and the Arts
Frederick M. Keener and Susan E. Lorsch, editors

American Women in Poverty

PAUL E. ZOPF, JR.

Contributions in Women's Studies,
Number 100

GREENWOOD PRESS
New York • Westport, Connecticut • London

Library of Congress Cataloging-in-Publication Data

Zopf, Paul E.
 American women in poverty / Paul E. Zopf, Jr.
  p.   cm. — (Contributions in women's studies, ISSN 0147–104X ;
 no. 100)
  Bibliography: p.
  Includes index.
  ISBN 0–313–25980–1 (lib. bdg. : alk. paper)
  1. Poor women—United States. 2. Women heads of households—
 United States. 3. Cost and standard of living—United States.
 I. Title. II. Series.
 HV1445.Z66 1989
 362.8'3'0973—dc19   88–21348

British Library Cataloguing in Publication Data is available.

Library of Congress Catalog Card Number: 88–21348
ISBN: 0–313–25980-1
ISSN: 0147–104X

First published in 1989

Greenwood Press, Inc.
88 Post Road West, Westport, Connecticut 06881

Printed in the United States of America

♾™

The paper used in this book complies with the
Permanent Paper Standard issued by the National
Information Standards Organization (Z39.48–1984).

10 9 8 7 6 5 4 3 2

Dedicated to
Evelyn

Contents

Figures

Tables

Preface

This book is about those American women who occupy the lowest socio-economic stratum, though it also deals with children in poverty and with several problems of women who are not poor. Since women and children are the focus, the analyses which follow may seem antimale, at least at points. That is not my intention, however, because I mean the book to point up injustices among whatever groups they exist, and I do not argue that any group should suffer deprivation from the efforts to relieve that of another. At the same time, many injustices do result from a gender-segregated social system in which women traditionally have been subordinate and which still adversely affects them in many ways, including low median incomes and high average poverty rates. Therefore, I argue strongly for equity between the sexes in economic justice, political power, participation in decision making, access to health care, and a host of other areas. American society is capable of lifting everyone out of poverty and providing decent work and fair incomes for both sexes. Poverty is a plague on us all, including its victims and the more fortunate among us who agonize over its terrible costs and destructive potential. In short, this book is basically about fairness.

Yet the effort to achieve fairness does reflect a need to give up things: sexism, gender-typing in jobs, undervaluation of women's work, male monopoly of most power systems, and economic inequality. Such sacrifice, however, will help create the caring society of equal opportunity and individual reward we claim to be, and the one we really want to be in our loftiest moments. It also will help improve conditions for persons who cannot be self-sufficient: those elderly who are frail and poor, those disabled who cannot survive without aid, the homeless, children, and others whose care is society's rightful responsibility.

In seeking to understand the questions raised by inequality, I felt compelled to emphasize the unusually high poverty rates, low average incomes, and other conditions which now discriminate against women and children, especially in female-headed families. But I hope both women and men will see a challenge rather than a threat in my emphasis, and that America's action agenda will eliminate unfairness inflicted on any group. Right now, the group of poor women and their youthful dependents, whatever their race and ethnic origin, needs that help more than any other.

Several themes recur in the book, whether one is studying female-headed families or individuals. Those themes are the feminization of poverty, sexist beliefs and the gender discrimination they spawn, persistent racism, a flawed labor market which provides too few good jobs with adequate incomes, educational insufficiency, an archaic welfare system, and the fluctuating nature of poverty. I identify and examine these core aspects of women's poverty as structural flaws in society rather than as character flaws in individuals, and do so at whatever points and in whatever ways they impinge upon women's status. I hope the reader will see how greatly the flaws pervade the socioeconomic system and perpetuate subordinate dependency by the poor, especially women.

The book emphasizes the perspective of social demography, which uses population data as an empirical base to examine both the social causes of specific demographic realities and the social consequences of those realities. The social demography perspective also includes a humanistic component which emphasizes practical problems and the rights and well-being of American women. I have tried to bring these elements together into description, analysis, concern, and proposed action.

I am indebted to the many people who gathered the data and conducted the research which made this book possible. I have tried to treat their work fairly and hope they will accept my gratitude for their important contributions to knowledge.

I am especially grateful to America's poor women for their struggle to surmount the problems I describe, and I fervently hope my efforts will make that struggle a bit easier for them and their children.

As always, I deeply value the support and encouragement of my colleagues at Guilford College, and I am indebted to the college itself for a research grant which helped underwrite the project. I particularly thank Vaneetamarie D'Andrea, Vernie Davis, Sam Schuman, and the students who worked with me to develop and refine many of the ideas in this volume. Moreover, my work owes much to the late T. Lynn Smith, whose own far-ranging sociology and human concern still inspire what I do.

Most importantly, I give my deepest thanks and devotion to Evelyn Zopf, my best friend, who so fully encourages my efforts and inspires so much concern to confront injustice.

Finally, I thank Eric and Mary for their love and enthusiasm.

1

The Concept of Poverty

The poverty problem in the United States disproportionately affects women and children, largely because of substantial increases in the percentage of women who head households with no husband present and who have much smaller average incomes than married-couple families. The condition has become widely known as the *feminization of poverty*.[1] Young women are at particular risk of being poor, though women past 65 also suffer more than most other age groups. The highest poverty rate of all, however, is among young children, a large share of them in female-headed families. These circumstances reflect the burdens imposed on women by high rates of divorce and separation, a rising incidence of births to unmarried women, inadequate employment prospects, lesser work experience and seniority, gender-typing in jobs, wage discrimination, and other socioeconomic conditions.

ORGANIZATION OF THE BOOK

The book explores these conditions in several ways. The balance of chapter 1 discusses the criteria and procedures for measuring poverty, including some conceptual and methodological problems, and explores what the feminization of poverty does and does not mean.

Chapter 2 deals with the realities faced by poor female-headed families and compares their situation with that of married-couple families. It examines the differences by age of the householder (family head) and by race and Hispanic origin, and it discusses the relationship between poverty levels and the presence of dependent children. The chapter also focuses on the amounts and sources of income in poor families and on their income deficits.

Chapter 3 explores the geographic distribution of poor female-headed families by regions, divisions, states, and counties, so as to identify the nation's poverty pockets. It accounts for poverty differences by rural and urban and metropolitan and nonmetropolitan residence and identifies the cities in which female-headed families have the highest and lowest poverty rates. Chapter 3 also traces major trends in the poverty status of female-headed families and how the trends are affected by changing labor-market conditions.

Chapter 4 is an account of *persons* in poverty—a necessary refinement because the data on families do not show the entire picture for individuals. Statistics on persons enable some comparisons by gender, age, race, and other characteristics which the data on families do not. Chapter 4 looks at the poorest of the poor female population—the persons who fall 50 percent or more below the official poverty threshold and who endure society's worst economic conditions. The chapter also concentrates on the near-poor, whose incomes are 0–25 percent above the poverty level. It considers the impact noncash benefits have on poverty and gives trends in the poverty of persons, including children.

Chapter 5 concerns personal income and poverty, and it includes income variations by gender, age, race, and residence. It focuses on the complex relationships between income, levels of education, and work experience. The chapter also discusses sources of income by age groups, income variations by large occupational categories and specific gender-dominated occupations, and the concept of comparable worth. It accounts for income trends by gender, race, educational attainment, work experience, and occupation, and concludes with a brief discussion of long-term unemployment patterns by gender.

Chapter 6 suggests some things which can be done to deal with women's poverty and related problems. It also discusses some other problems and ways to confront them. The major concerns are inequality, economic development, political power, education, family strength, health care, welfare reform, housing, the "invisible" homemaker, and violence. The chapter also looks briefly at prospects for change.

Chapter 7 summarizes the book's principal findings and offers conclusions about poverty among American women.

MEASURING POVERTY

The principal source of data is the U.S. Bureau of the Census, especially its *Current Population Reports* on poverty status, income, and noncash benefits, and the *1980 Census of Population*. Other data and analyses, particularly those which enhance the quality of the official definitions and statistics, come from the sources in the chapter notes. Whenever possible, poverty conditions are portrayed in graphs, maps, and tables, though always with analyses and explanations within the chapter.

Ascertaining demographic realities, including efforts to determine a realistic poverty threshold and who falls below it, is often more difficult methodologically than the large amount of data available would suggest. For example, the Census Bureau estimates poverty status from a population sample subject to error because not everyone can be contacted or because of "definitional difficulties, differences in the interpretation of questions, inability or unwillingness on the part of respondents to provide correct information, inability to recall information," and errors made in collecting, recording, coding, and processing the data or in compensating for missing data and undercoverage.[2] Householders also tend to underreport their income, especially noncash forms, and there is no precise method to quantify the value of some of these resources and make statistical corrections.

The official poverty index also has been revised several times. In addition, the 1984 *Current Population Reports* on poverty reflected a new survey-weighting procedure for the Hispanic population and a revised method for measuring interest income, and those procedures were used in 1985. The sample design also was changed in 1984 and used in the 1985 survey, so recent data are not entirely comparable with earlier data. Furthermore, money income is an incomplete indicator of poverty, for it does not include the goods and services a family provides itself (e.g., child care), noncash benefits, or informal assistance from the extended family, churches, and other groups.[3] Governments and companies supply particularly important noncash benefits, including "employer provided health insurance, food stamps or Medicaid."[4]

These and other methodological problems compromise data reliability and comparability over time. Nevertheless, while some difficulties do stem from refinements in data collection and analysis, the materials generally reflect social realities increasingly accurately as the Census Bureau makes its revisions. Therefore, the statistics which had to be used if the book were to be written at all are those carefully collected and well reported by the Census Bureau. The data in the *Current Population Reports* permit timeliness and those in the *1980 Census of Population,* while not as recent, allow broad coverage and detailed cross-classification. Those comprehensive materials are indispensable if one is to identify the geographic distribution of women's poverty, for the *Current Population Reports* provide little information on that topic.

Poverty Level and the Consumer Price Index (CPI)

The official poverty index was originated in 1964 by Mollie Orshansky at the Social Security Administration, although data collected previously allow an analysis of poverty for as early as 1959. But despite periodic revisions, the index is still based on the U.S. Department of Agriculture's (USDA) economy food plan, meant to reflect the different consumption requirements of families according to size, age of householder, and other criteria.[5] The economy food plan was formulated using nutritional criteria derived by the National Research Council of the National Academy of Sciences. The poverty index, which presents some problems discussed later, originally set different poverty thresholds according to the gender of the householder and farm and nonfarm residence, but those distinctions were eliminated in 1981. In addition, the last threshold in the family-size continuum is now for nine or more persons rather than for seven or more, as it was.

Even though the poverty index is based exclusively on money income and does not reflect the noncash benefits many poor people receive, it is at least a partially flexible response to changing economic conditions, because the dollar amounts of the poverty thresholds for various categories of families, persons, and unrelated individuals are revised each year to reflect changes in the CPI.[6] To illustrate, Table 1–1 shows how the CPI and the poverty threshold for a family of four rose annually between 1959 and 1985. In addition, Table 1–2 indicates that gradations in overall family size and number of children under 18 yield a large number of poverty thresholds. These tables reflect the types of refinements built into the index.

The poverty index is supplemented by data on families and persons who rank at only 50 or 75 percent of the poverty level and on those who place above that level by various increments. The ones who stand 0–25 percent above the poverty threshold are the near-poor. In 1985, for instance, the poverty-level income for a family of four was $10,989, while the figure for a family which ranked 25 percent higher was $13,736. This distinction is especially significant as one identifies those female-headed families which are not quite poor officially, but which also fail to rank much above that level. In many specific cases, relatively minor changes in income convert a family or person from near-poor to poor, and large numbers of modest-income families do move in and out of the poverty class as their members lose or find jobs, separate or form new alliances, and undergo other changes which shift their incomes above or below the poverty level. They make up a far larger group than the families which remain persistently poor for long periods.[7] In fact, both the size of the latter group and the persistence of poverty within it are frequently overestimated, though they are not negligible. Special kinds of help, such as training people for available jobs and creating more well-paying jobs, should be directed to this group to develop self-sufficiency, whereas more temporary kinds of assistance, such as adequate unemployment compensation and periodic assistance with fuel bills, may suffice to lift the temporary poor back above the threshold. Efforts to ameliorate the economic effects of divorce, separation, and widowhood are especially important for women in both categories, because their financial situations usually deteriorate dramatically when a marriage breaks up, particularly if they have dependent children.

Table 1–1

Consumer Price Index and Average Poverty Threshold in Dollars for a Family of Four, 1959–1985

Year	Consumer Price Index (1967=100)	Average Threshold for a Family of Four Persons (Dollars)
1959	87.3	2,973
1960	88.7	3,022
1961	89.6	3,054
1962	90.6	3,089
1963	91.7	3,128
1964	92.9	3,169
1965	94.5	3,223
1966	97.2	3,317
1967	100.0	3,410
1968	104.2	3,553
1969	109.8	3,743
1970	116.3	3,968
1971	121.3	4,137
1972	125.3	4,275
1973	133.1	4,540
1974	147.7	5,038
1975	161.2	5,500
1976	170.5	5,815
1977	181.5	6.191
1978	195.4	6,662
1979	217.4	7,412
1980	246.8	8,414
1981	272.4	9,287[a]
1982	289.1	9,862
1983	298.4	10,178
1984	311.1	10,609
1985	322.2	10,989

Source: U.S. Bureau of the Census, "Poverty in the United States: 1985," Current Population Reports, Series P-60, No. 158 (Washington, DC: Government Printing Office, 1987), p. 162.

[a]Prior to 1981, average thresholds are for a nonfarm family of four.

Types of Money Income

Only certain forms of income figure into the poverty-threshold computations, even though many people receive other benefits which moderate financial stress. The data also report income before payments for personal income taxes, property and other taxes, Social Security, union dues, Med-

Table 1-2

Poverty Threshold in Dollars, by Size of Family and Number of Related Children under 18, 1985

Size of Family Unit	Weighted Poverty Thresholds (Dollars)	Poverty Thresholds (In Dollars) With Related Children Under 18								
		None	One	Two	Three	Four	Five	Six	Seven	Eight or More
One person (unrelated individual)	5,469									
Under 65	5,593	5,593								
65 and over	5,156	5,156								
Two Persons	6,998									
Householder under 65	7,231	7,199	7,410							
Householder 65 and over	6,503	6,498	7,382							
Three persons	8,573	8,410	8,654	8,662						
Four persons	10,989	11,089	11,270	10,903	10,941					
Five persons	13,007	13,373	13,567	13,152	12,830	12,364				
Six persons	14,696	15,381	15,442	15,124	14,819	14,365	14,097			
Seven persons	16,656	17,698	17,808	17,428	17,162	16,667	16,090	15,457		
Eight persons	18,512	19,794	19,969	19,609	19,194	18,847	18,280	17,690	17,540	
Nine or more persons	22,083	23,811	23,926	23,608	23,341	22,902	22,298	21,753	21,617	20,785

Source: U.S. Bureau of the Census, "Poverty in the United States: 1985," Current Population Reports, Series P-60, No. 158 (Washington, DC: Government Printing Office, 1987), p. 163.

icare, and other obligations, so the figures reflect larger amounts than people actually have available to spend on food, housing, and other necessities.

The reported sources of income are "earnings; Social Security and public assistance payments; dividends, interest, and rent; unemployment and workers' compensation; government and private employee pensions; and other periodic income."[8] Certain other kinds of income, such as capital gains, are not included, but most poor people receive little from those sources anyway.

The following are the detailed sources of income used to determine poverty and nonpoverty status: (1) wages or salaries; (2) nonfarm self-employment; (3) farm self-employment; (4) property (interest, dividends, net rent, and estates or trusts); (5) Social Security or railroad retirement; (6) Supplemental Security Income (SSI); (7) public assistance or welfare, including Aid to Families with Dependent Children (AFDC); (8) veterans, unemployment, and workers' compensation benefits; (9) retirement pensions (private, military, federal, state, or local); and (10) other sources (alimony or child support, regular contributions from relatives or others, all other sources).[9] The list is comprehensive but not exhaustive, and some persons who fall into the poverty class according to its items are actually somewhat better off than their official status shows. The difference is noncash benefits.

Noncash Exclusions

Noncash benefits excluded from the poverty-threshold figures do enhance the well-being of most poor households, sometimes significantly. In 1985, for example, if these resources had been counted as income, the official estimate of poverty for the nation as a whole would have been 8–35 percent lower, depending on the range of benefits included and the method used to place a value on them.[10] As a later section shows, however, the poverty rate could just as easily be raised by pushing up the threshold incomes to include everyone who ranks 0–25 percent above the official poverty level. Therefore, the poverty rate depends on which arbitrary criteria are used to measure it.

The noncash benefits fall into two major categories: (1) public noncash transfers, such as food stamps, school lunches, subsidized rental housing, and Medicare, Medicaid, and other health insurance; and (2) noncash benefits provided by unions and employers, such as pension plans and group health insurance plans. Several of the public transfers are means-tested benefits and available only to households with incomes below a specified level. Those benefits are food stamps, free or partially subsidized school lunches, publicly owned or subsidized rental housing, and Medicaid. In 1985 about half of all households which received means-tested benefits were below the poverty level and 59 percent of all poor households had one or more of those benefits. The most frequent was the school lunch program, followed by Medicaid and subsidized housing. This still left well over a third of all poor households with no means-tested benefits, so as helpful as the programs

Table 1–3
**Percent of Female-Headed and Married-Couple Families Classified as
Poor and Receiving Selected Noncash Benefits, 1985**

Noncash Benefit	Percent in Poverty	
	Female-Headed Families[a]	Married-Couple Families
Food stamps	81.7	57.7
Free or reduced-price school lunch	67.9	37.1
Publicly owned or other subsidized housing	76.9	35.8
Medicaid for one or more members	71.2	40.7

Source: U.S. Bureau of the Census, "Receipt of Selected Noncash Benefits: 1985," Current Population Reports, Series P-60, No. 155 (Washington, DC: Government Printing Office, 1987), Tables 5-8.

[a]No husband present.

are, coverage is far from universal. The omissions occur in part because most means-tested noncash transfer payments ascertain eligibility according to not only low income, but also a householder's other assets and resources. Moreover, eligibility for certain programs (e.g., Medicaid) varies from state to state and even by locality. Families which receive no noncash benefits and have poverty-level incomes, therefore, are not necessarily poor by other standards. Even so, many poor are not adequately covered and numerous individual situations are dire indeed, especially among women, minority groups, rural people, and others whose average poverty rates substantially exceed the national norm.

Table 1–3 suggests the degree to which poor families, especially those headed by women, actually receive noncash benefits. It shows the percentages of married-couple and female-headed households classified as poor and also receiving means-tested noncash benefits.

Noncash benefits are not confined to people designated officially as poor, because Medicare, subsidized "regular-price" school lunches under the National School Lunch Program, and pension and health plans provided by employers are non-means-tested resources. Thus, while about 16 percent of all households received at least one means-tested noncash benefit in 1985, 82 percent received at least one non-means-tested noncash benefit.[11]

This spectrum of programs and the large percentage of households covered by one or more of the programs reflects the types of economic protection which have helped reduce the proportions of persons and families in poverty. They are unevenly available, however, and increasingly precarious in the face of budgetary constraints on "social programs," and large numbers of families and persons are still desperately poor. The large majority of that group—77 percent in 1985—consists of women and dependent children, and that fact motivated the analyses in this book.[12]

Shortcomings in the Definitions and Data

Of necessity, offical definitions and data underlie this examination of American women who experience the tragedy of poverty. Those formulations and statistics make it possible to describe, compare, and cross-classify the poor population and to trace trends, but they cannot provide the whole picture and may even create a misleading one. They also have many subjective components influenced by various political considerations. The data cannot show how it feels to be a poor, single teenage mother frustrated by a situation she cannot change; how an aging widow deals with poverty for the first time when her husband dies and her income falls dramatically; or how a poorly educated woman displaced by divorce from her homemaker role struggles by on meager earnings from an undependable, low-status service job. The data reveal some facts about some of the poor, but one must turn elsewhere to comprehend the experience of poverty. Consequently, while the book is basically a demographic analysis of women's poverty, it includes other insights which provide meaning and a human dimension. The study is derived from social demography, which combines the data and methods of formal demography, the insights and interpretations of other social sciences, and the concerns of the humanities.

The interpretations are influenced by contrasts between the nature of poverty in the United States and that in many developing countries. Large proportions of people in poor countries suffer absolute poverty, because they do not get enough food and other necessities to prevent high infant mortality rates, disabling malnutrition and its consequent illnesses, and even starvation. Not many people starve to death in the United States, though perhaps up to 20 million are hungry and chronically malnourished. Most of them are poor people without food stamps; the rest are also poor, but do get food stamps, and still have too little income to afford adequate diets.[13] Some groups experienced rising infant mortality rates in the 1980s, while growing numbers are homeless and depend on handouts and other unreliable sources.

Despite these numerous symptoms of a maldistributive economy, most of America's poor—female and male—suffer relative poverty. Since comparatively few die from the virtual lack of basic necessities, most are poor by comparison with the majority of the population, who not only have enough food to survive, but whose definitions of "necessities" vary along a continuum from modest comfort to extravagant wealth. Thus, the poverty which afflicts most of America's poor is poverty according to a particular set of comparisons with more affluent people, though it may feel no less punitive and excruciating than deprivation among the absolute poor in many developing countries. Furthermore, the structural conditions which create and perpetuate poverty also isolate America's poor as weakly integrated, marginal participants in the system.[14] That marginality and the alienation it often creates are difficult to overcome, especially if one focuses too much on poverty as a result of character flaws rather than social and economic organization. Therefore, the concept of relative poverty should not become a rationalization to minimize the problems of poor Americans. Nor should one accept without question the official designation of who is and is not poor, for with a less parsimonious definition the number would be even greater than it is. Even so, American poverty exists because significant numbers of people do fall below a level of living thought to be "reasonable" or "adequate" or even "minimal" in this society at this time—a level beneath which people cannot obtain the basic necessities of life.[15]

All of those qualifiers are ambiguous: what level is reasonable or minimal and what necessities are basic? Not only are these descriptions difficult to quantify, but government personnel interpret them narrowly so the percentage of people in poverty seems respectably low and declining. As a result, there are serious questions about the accuracy of continuing to base the poverty thresholds on the Department of Agriculture's 1961 economy food plan. The proportion of income people spend on food has fallen from a third to a fifth since 1961, and expenditures for various nonfood items not defined as necessities do not enter directly into the computations. More is "necessary" for a decent life now than was "necessary" in 1961. Furthermore, the economy food plan is the most parsimonious of several the USDA analyzed, and the department itself considers the plan adequate only for temporary use. It is inadequate as a long-term nutritional regimen. The plan also assumes that people are relatively sophisticated in buying and preparing the food and that the family will always eat at home. Actually, a food plan about 25 percent more generous would be a more realistic base for the dollar amounts used as poverty thresholds.[16] Then, of course, a large share of near-poor people would be classified as poor. The argument for higher poverty thresholds opposes the one made by those who feel that excluding noncash benefits causes the poor population to appear too large. Each approach has its merits and faults, and both reflect the difficulty of defining poverty.

Figure 1–1 gives the percentage of female-headed families classified as poor in 1980 and 1985 under the official definition of poverty, the lower percentage which results if the market value of noncash benefits is included, and the higher proportion which occurs when the poverty-income thresholds are increased 25 percent. The diagram shows that the methodological ad-

Figure 1–1
**Poverty Rate in Female-Headed Families According to Various
Definitions of Poverty, 1980 and 1985**

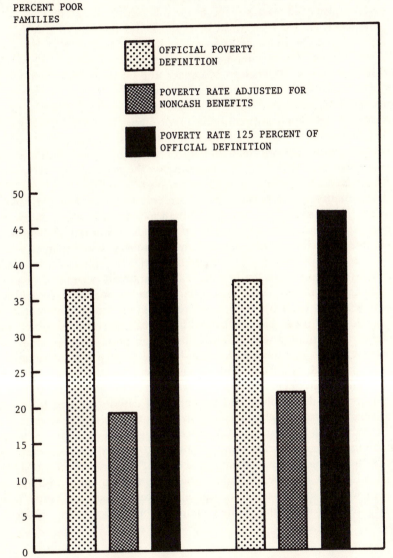

PERCENT POOR
FAMILIES

OFFICIAL POVERTY
DEFINITION

POVERTY RATE ADJUSTED FOR
NONCASH BENEFITS

POVERTY RATE 125 PERCENT OF
OFFICIAL DEFINITION

1980   1985

justments would change the poverty picture substantially, that poverty indexes are arbitrary, and that American poverty as an overall phenomenon is more nearly relative than absolute, though it is absolute in many individual cases.

In order to account for changes in what is accepted as necessary for a decent level of living, the basis for ascertaining poverty needs more dynamic adjustments than those made according to the CPI. The poverty thresholds themselves also need reassessment. Could a family of four really have gotten by adequately in 1985 on an income just above the official threshold of $10,989? Could an individual 65 or over have made it with an income of $5,156? Maybe, but still unable to acquire numerous goods and services widely perceived as necessities. Moreover, the poverty indexes should account more fully for a broader issue: increases or decreases in the proportions of Americans who have equitable access to the system's overall advantages. Are significant economic opportunities becoming more broadly available, or are they concentrating in fewer hands, though perhaps in new ways and by different means than before? The gap between rich and poor does appear to be widening, and in this sense the poor are relatively worse off than they were at various times in the past.[17]

These matters are especially important for women, particularly young women. They are far less represented than men in jobs which pay well; a growing percentage has sole support of dependent children; the burden of economic flaws falls heavily upon them. Moreover, while women's labor force participation rates have increased dramatically in the last few decades, their jobs still tend to concentrate in areas traditionally occupied by women, despite increased entry into male occupational strongholds. In addition, many new jobs filled by women are at the lower end of the status and income levels of the service industries. These realities restrict significant job mobility and, coupled with increases in the proportion of female-headed households with one income, help push more women into marginal economic situations, whether below or just above the official poverty level. This combination of circumstances contributes to the growing feminization of poverty. So do absolute and proportional cuts in funding for "social programs" and tighter eligibility requirements to receive the benefits.

Other personal and structural aspects of poverty include inadequate schooling, limited job skills and opportunities, political powerlessness, vulnerability to exploitation, and anxiety about one's future well-being. Streamlined definitions of poverty could account more for these conditions, too, and for women's "access to resources which are not just family income, but assets, status at work and in the community, and involvement in decision making."[18]

Compromise with Reality

If one is to examine women's poverty but finds the official definitions and data partially flawed and misleading, how then to proceed? Reality demands the use of the official definitions and statistics. They are valuable in many respects, particularly to provide comparative perspectives based on the same definitions applied to all races and other population segments. At the same time, however, maximum accuracy requires that one keep the methodological problems in mind and introduce refinements whenever possible. They show that the extent of poverty is generally underestimated and that women are inequitably represented in satisfactory jobs and have too little control over economic assets of their own.

FEMINIZATION OF POVERTY

It is vital to be clear on what the feminization of poverty does and does not mean. The majority of poor persons are female: 57 percent of the total poverty population of 33 million in 1985 was female; 16 percent of all females and 12 percent of all males fell below the poverty level. But females were 51 percent of the nation's total population, so compared with males, females are not greatly overrepresented in the poor segment. Moreover, these statistical relationships have not changed much since 1959, though the poverty rates did drop significantly for both sexes, at least until the mid–1970s, when they started rising.

What does underlie the feminization of poverty is the huge increase in the percentage of families headed by a woman with no husband present— a woman who is the sole or principal family supporter but whose median income falls far below that of the average married-couple family. Thus, in 1960 about 24 percent of all poor families were maintained by a woman, but by 1985 the figure had jumped to 48 percent. Furthermore, in 1960 about 21 percent of all poor persons in families lived in female-headed units, whereas in 1985 over 45 percent lived in those units.[19] Clearly, the large increase in the number and proportion of families in which a woman is the sole breadwinner, combined with the persistently lower average income received by female than by male householders or married couples, accounts for the feminization of poverty. Previously, poor women were usually the wives of poor men, but now they are much more likely to head families on their own or to be in nonfamily households.[20] Moreover, while poverty rates have declined for both married-couple and female-headed families, after 1959 the drop was faster for the former than for the latter, leaving the female-headed units at an even greater relative disadvantage. Part of the difference is due, ironically, to the large number of wives who entered the paid labor force in the past two decades, because their earnings, though still only about two-thirds those of men, reduced the incidence of poverty among married-couple families. At the same time, increases in the rates of divorce, separation, and births to unmarried women added greatly to the number of female-headed families forced to get by on the woman's lower average income, even though the divorce rate leveled off and even fell a bit after 1981. The incidence of premarital sexuality and unmarried childbearing among teenagers grew dramatically after 1970, and they and their children are especially susceptible to poverty because of the young woman's usually meager resources and the deficient child-support contributions by most young unmarried fathers.[21] The feminization of poverty, therefore, reflects the marked income difference between one-earner and two-earner households, no matter how they come into being.[22]

It also reflects the insufficiency of well-paying jobs for women and the financial problems which result from relying only on their own incomes within that structurally disdvantageous context. More specifically, some industries which provide the jobs women fill pay wages which force a woman to seek other sources of income if she and her dependents are to stay above the poverty level. Those industries also produce many part-time and part-year jobs which pay especially low wages.[23] Since expansion of the service sector and loss of many manufacturing jobs which pay better wages have been central features of recent occupational change, poverty among working women is also a major feature of that change.

The children of divorce are far more likely to remain with their mothers than their fathers, and in 1985 over 90 percent of all children under 18 and living with one parent resided with their mothers. Therefore, when divorce occurs, a family usually loses the earner with the largest wage but none of the nonearning dependents. The decrease in the family's expenses because of the husband's departure is usually minor compared with the loss of his income, even in those relatively rare cases in which alimony and child support are both substantial and regular. Furthermore, while remarriage ordinarily improves a woman's economic status significantly, the remarriage rate of divorced and widowed men is much higher than that of women who lost their mates, so a woman is far more likely to continue relying on her smaller average wage and/or public assistance. Even when children are not involved, divorce usually leaves the woman in a poorer economic situation than the man, though she does have greater freedom than a mother to remain in or enter the labor force without spending time and money on child care and some other domestic responsibilities. On balance, these kinds of changes in family composition ordinarily have little effect or even a positive one on men, but they usually have significant negative consequences for women and children.[24]

Given the importance of these conditions, chapters 2 and 3 turn to poverty in the female-headed family and its contrasts with the married-couple unit.

NOTES

1. One account of the process is Hilda Scott, *Working Your Way to the Bottom: The Feminization of Poverty* (London: Pandora Press, 1984).
2. U.S. Bureau of the Census, "Poverty in the United States: 1985," *Current*

Population Reports, Series P–60, No. 158 (Washington, DC: Government Printing Office, 1987), p. 172.

3. Greg J. Duncan, Richard D. Coe, and Martha S. Hill, "The Dynamics of Poverty," in Greg J. Duncan, Richard D. Coe, Mary E. Corcoran, Martha S. Hill, Saul D. Hoffman, and James N. Morgan, *Years of Poverty, Years of Plenty* (Ann Arbor, MI: Institute for Social Research, 1984), p. 36.

4. U.S. Bureau of the Census, "Poverty in the United States: 1985," p. 1.

5. The terms *family* and *household* do not mean the same. A family refers to a group of two or more persons (one of whom is the householder) related by birth, marriage, or adoption and residing together. A household consists of all persons who occupy a housing unit, and can include not just related family members, but lodgers, foster children, wards, employees, and others who share the household. See ibid, p. 154.

6. U.S. Bureau of the Census, *Statistical Abstract of the United States: 1987* (Washington, DC: Government Printing Office, 1986), p. 415.

7. Martha S. Hill, "The Changing Nature of Poverty," in Yeheskel Hasenfeld and Mayer N. Zald, eds., "The Welfare State in America: Trends and Prospects," *Annals of the American Academy of Political and Social Science* 479 (May 1985), pp. 40–41.

8. U.S. Bureau of the Census, "Poverty in the United States: 1985," p. 9.

9. U.S. Bureau of the Census, "Money Income of Households, Families, and Persons in the United States: 1985," *Current Population Reports,* Series P–60, No. 156 (Washington, DC: Government Printing Office, 1987), Table 38.

10. U.S. Bureau of the Census, "Poverty in the United States: 1985," p. 10.

11. U.S. Bureau of the Census, "Receipt of Selected Noncash Benefits: 1985," *Current Population Reports,* Series P–60, No. 155 (Washington, DC: Government Printing Office, 1987), Tables A, D.

12. For an account of nonmoney resources, see Hill, "The Changing Nature of Poverty," pp. 33–34.

13. See the Physician Task Force on Hunger in America, *Hunger in America: The Growing Epidemic* (Cambridge, MA: Harvard University School of Public Health, 1985).

14. Victor Fuchs, "Redefining Poverty and Redistributing Income," *The Public Interest* 8 (Summer 1967), p. 92.

15. Scott, *Working Your Way to the Bottom,* p. 6.

16. Hill, "The Changing Nature of Poverty," p. 34; and Duncan, Coe, and Hill, "The Dynamics of Poverty," pp. 42–43.

17. George Ritzer, *Social Problems,* 2nd ed. (New York: Random House, 1986), p. 343.

18. Scott, *Working Your Way to the Bottom,* p. 13.

19. U.S. Bureau of the Census, "Poverty in the United States: 1985," Table 1.

20. Hill, "The Changing Nature of Poverty," p. 38.

21. For a discussion of this matter, see Sandra L. Hofferth, Joan R. Kahn, and Wendy Baldwin, "Premarital Sexual Activity Among U.S. Teenage Women Over the Past Three Decades," *Family Planning Perspectives* 19:2 (March/April 1987), pp. 46–53.

22. For accounts of several of these factors, see Hill, "The Changing Nature of Poverty," pp. 37–38; and William P. O'Hare, "Poverty in America: Trends and

New Patterns," *Population Bulletin* 40:3 (Washington, DC: Population Reference Bureau, 1985), pp. 31–34.

23. Joan Smith, "The Paradox of Women's Poverty: Wage-earning Women and Economic Transformation," in Barbara C. Gelpi, Nancy C. M. Hartsock, Clare C. Novak, and Myra H. Strober, eds., *Women and Poverty* (Chicago: University of Chicago Press, 1986), pp. 137–138.

24. Mary Corcoran, Greg J. Duncan, and Martha S. Hill, "The Economic Fortunes of Women and Children: Lessons from the Panel Study of Income Dynamics," in Gelpi and others, *Women and Poverty*, pp. 14–15.

2

Families in Poverty:
Realities and Variations

FAMILY FUNCTIONS AND POVERTY

The family institution performs numerous functions for individuals and the system at large. Chief among the societal tasks is *socialization,* or the process by which persons learn and generally accept the features of a society well enough to participate in it adequately as adults.[1] The process also provides major aspects of the personality and the self-concept. In the United States, tradition prescribed a family consisting of husband, wife, and children, and while the presence of both parents did not guarantee adequate socialization, it was thought to provide the best prospects. Moreover, the two-parent unit was supposed to be best able to ensure emotional support for children and spouses and to generate sufficient income for the family's material needs.

However realistic these expectations were, until the past few decades most families were husband-wife-children units in which the couple had been married only once. As late as 1960, for example, there were only 1.9 million female-headed families and they made up just 7 percent of all families.[2] By 1985 the number had risen to 10.2 million, the proportion to 16 percent of the nation's total. Two-thirds of those families contain at least one child under 18, and all female-headed families account for 12.5 million children, or 20 percent of the nation's total. In addition, about 63 percent of the women who head families work, so that group of 6.4 million women has to reconcile paid employment with primary responsibility for child care. In the 3.5 million female-headed families below the poverty level, 1.4 million (40 percent) of the women work, and they face especially exhausting efforts to balance job and family responsibilities.[3]

The statistics inspire some basic questions which pertain to much of the poor population, but especially to persons who live in female-headed families with no husband present.

1. How much does the socialization process in the poor, one-parent family help propagate poverty and futility as a mindset? Or, to what degree does it embue children with the will to overcome obstacles and rise above the parent's poverty?

2. To what degree are poor adolescents alienated from a system in which they rank at the bottom economically, and to what extent does that help push them into illegal behavior?

3. How do young people in poverty perceive education, work, personal relationships, and their prospects? What do those perceptions portend for adulthood? Is this poor group a fatalistic "generation of shrinking horizons," diverted increasingly into "hustling" and "getting by"? Do structural constraints in the society keep them from full integration into the system regardless of the incentives they may have? Do they contribute to or detract from cohesion in the system?

4. What are the effects of peer relationships and pressures on children and adolescents who grow up in poverty?

5. To what extent do poverty and its concomitants diminish tenacity, creativity, and hope among poor parents as they and their offspring confront barriers to full social participation and economic justice?

6. What are the racial and ethnic variations in poverty rates and in the content, quality, and effect of socialization in a poverty setting?

7. What are the effects of being newly poor, often because of divorce or other conditions which force a woman and her children below the poverty line for the first time? What are the consequences of moving in and out of poverty as jobs are lost or obtained, a second family wage earner leaves or reappears, or fortunes rise and fall for other reasons?

8. How can young adults in poverty best find rewarding places in the enlarging service and information economy, given their lower than average levels of education and limited job skills? How are they to contend with the decrease in manual labor and other types of jobs which often have been their only employment protection against destitution or public assistance? Can they hope to escape poverty in the plethora of low-wage jobs (e.g., janitor, fast-food worker) available to them?

9. How much is poverty perpetuated by living in a neighborhood (e.g., an inner-city ghetto) where few jobs of any kind and virtually no good ones are nearby?

10. What efforts are necessary for the poor population to achieve self-sufficiency and end their subservient dependency relationship with the society and its agencies? How much does that dependency result from the characteristics of the poor and how much from basic flaws in the social system?

11. To what degree are Americans, especially the political power holders,

committed to provide ample well-paying jobs and improve educational, occupational, and child-care opportunities, and, thus, income levels? How strong is the national will to eliminate poverty?[4]

Some of these questions have obvious answers, others do not. Research has dealt extensively with some, less with others. Some obvious answers may not be implemented because the poor are perceived as too unimportant to justify the expense or because they have little collective power. No matter what the responses, the questions reflect the sociocultural context in which to examine the facts on poor families.

Some Words of Caution

One needs to be careful about stereotyping in using the preceding or any other set of queries. For example, two-thirds of all mother-only families are not poor; family socialization can be inadequate at any level of the class system. Married-couple and female-headed families both have their share of children and adolescents with low-quality parenting. Many of the problems some poor female-headed families face, such as alcoholism, drug dependency, physical and mental abuse, and inadequate job opportunities, also afflict many married-couple units. Teenage pregnancy, a growing phenomenon which helps explain the high poverty rates of female-headed families, affects nonpoor groups as well. The one-parent family can be strong because of helpful relatives and friends, intrafamily harmony, and determination. Nevertheless, most major problems which children, adolescents, and their families suffer are disproportionately likely in the poor female-headed units created by divorce, desertion, widowhood, and births to unmarried mothers.[5]

The notion of a permanently poor subculture which passes on the problem from generation to generation also needs to be treated cautiously. A group of persistently poor does exist, but many more people in poverty at any given time occupy that status temporarily, though perhaps moving in and out of it repeatedly over longer periods. Moreover, the features of the persistently poor group partially refute the argument that the poor remain so because of character flaws which leave them unmotivated to improve. In fact, about a third of those who are persistently poor are elderly and have few options, and the other two-thirds live in female-headed families. Most persistently poor family heads must care for dependent children while they contend with the single parent's lesser opportunities for work and income.[6]

FEMALE-HEADED AND MARRIED-COUPLE FAMILIES

In 1985 there were 64 million American families: 51 million (80 percent) were married-couple units, 10 million (16 percent) had a female householder

Table 2-1

Percent of Families below the Poverty Level, by Type of Family, Age of Householder, and Race, 1985

Type of Family and Age of Householder	Percent in Poverty		
	All Races	White	Black
All families			
All ages	11.4	9.1	28.7
Under 25	30.2	24.7	62.1
25-44	13.1	10.5	30.3
45-64	8.1	6.4	21.2
65 and over	7.0	5.6	22.0
Married-couple families			
All ages	6.7	6.1	12.2
Under 25	14.7	13.9	26.0
25-44	7.1	6.6	9.8
45-64	5.8	5.2	11.6
65 and over	5.7	4.8	17.9
Other families, male householder			
All ages	12.9	11.2	22.9
Under 25	23.5	23.5	a
25-44	11.3	10.8	13.5
45-64	11.7	10.0	24.3
65 and over	12.4	5.6	a
Other families, female householder			
All ages	34.0	27.4	50.5
Under 25	74.2	68.0	86.0
25-44	40.5	33.9	55.1
45-64	21.1	15.3	36.6
65 and over	13.3	10.6	24.9

Source: U.S. Bureau of the Census, "Poverty in the United States: 1985," Current Population Reports, Series P-60, No. 158 (Washington, DC: Government Printing Office, 1987), Table 15.

aBase less than 75,000.

and no husband present, and 2 million (2 percent) had a male householder and no wife present.[7] If existing patterns of family formation continue, by 2000 there will be about 72 million families, 18 percent of which will have a female householder and 78 percent of which will be married-couple units.[8]

Every comparison among types of families shows the female-headed unit to have a much higher poverty rate than other families. (See Table 2-1.) Furthermore, while the proportion of all families below the poverty threshold fell 37 percent between 1960 and 1985, the figure for female-headed families dropped only 20 percent, so the group with the worst initial disadvantage improved least. The female-headed unit is still anywhere from two to five times as likely as other families to be poor, the precise ratio depending on the age and race of the householder. Consequently, while poverty rates have fallen for all groups, the progress for female-headed units as a whole has been modest. It has been especially slow for young householders, as reflected in a poverty rate of 74 percent for families headed by a woman under 25. The worst case of all is young black female householders, 86 percent of whose families were ranked as poor in 1985.[9]

The poverty trends between 1978 and 1983 proved fairly discouraging for various family types; all but a few of the categories in Table 2–1 had higher rates in 1983 than five years earlier. There were some changes in the ways to measure poverty during that period, but they generally made the rates appear lower. Therefore, the increases—substantial for certain groups—represent economic deterioration for many families because of recession, unemployment, and reduced governmental support for various programs which help the poor. However, the poverty rate did fall some after 1983.

During the late 1970s and early 1980s the poverty rates of black and white married-couple families also increased, except in those with a householder 65 and over. In that group the rates fell significantly for both races. In families headed by a woman the only group whose poverty rate fell was elderly blacks. The most significant increases were among women aged 45–64, even though they have the lowest poverty rates. Many of them were less successful than younger women in finding or retaining jobs during the economic downturn because their levels of education are lower and their work experience is more likely to be as housewives. In addition, the work force in some industries, such as textiles, contains large proportions of middle-aged women, and those industries lost many jobs in the 1970s and early 1980s. Some women in their early 60s and even late 50s also retired, and most experienced income reductions in the process. Divorced women aged 45–64, who now number almost 4 million, also have smaller chances than younger ones for remarriage and the economic improvement which usually goes with it, especially if the older women have children at home.[10] Female family heads under 25, with the highest poverty rates by far, also lost considerable ground in the late 1970s and early 1980s. That was true for blacks and whites, but the situation of blacks, already much worse, deteriorated faster. Those aged 25–44 had relatively small increases in poverty rates. Elderly white householders experienced a slight increase; blacks had a decrease, though their rates are still nearly three times those of elderly whites. (See Table 2–1 for the situation in 1985.)

Unemployment is particularly significant for the female householder with no husband present. In 1985, 10.5 percent of that group was unemployed, compared with 5.6 percent of married women with a husband present and 4.3 percent of married men with a wife present.[11]

The most significant conclusion from the data on family poverty is that the presence or absence of a wage-earning male is crucial in determining a family's probability of being poor.[12] It is more striking than racial variations, though they are important, and it is more influential than age differences, though they too matter. Furthermore, the departure of a husband is more critical to a family than if he was not present to begin with: The Michigan longitudinal Panel Study of Income Dynamics (PSID) found that female-headed families with no husband present and not on welfare at the beginning of the study (1968) were less likely to go on it than those with a male householder who left during the study.[13] But many women on their own because of divorce marry again, especially if they are relatively young, and their economic situation generally improves. Therefore, one should not confuse divorce as a status occupied by persons at the time survey data are gathered with divorce as a permanent condition, because the poverty implications of the two can be quite different.[14]

The presence or absence of a husband per se is not the critical factor affecting poverty, but rather that men's average income is significantly higher than women's and that in the majority of married-couple families both spouses work for wages. Those are the principal safeguards against poverty. In 1985, for example, married-couple families had a median income of $31,100, compared with only $13,660 in female-headed families. Among whites the median incomes of the two types of families were $31,602 and $15,825, respectively; among blacks the figures were $24,570 and $9,305; among Hispanics they were $22,269 and $8,792.[15] The discrepancies between married-couple and female-headed families are somewhat less in the youthful ages because of more nearly uniform economic disadvantages regardless of gender, and for people 65 and over because when men retire they experience a larger percentage income drop than women. Nevertheless, very significant differentials in incomes and poverty rates separate married-couple and female-headed families regardless of race, age, education, rural or urban residence, or any other characteristics. That gender difference is the most pronounced feature of America's present poverty problem.

The average poverty rates of both sexes are raised by inadequate education, poor job skills, too few job prospects, insufficient wages, low work commitment, poor health, and racism. But some of the causes of poverty are peculiar to women. Generally only they are pushed into poverty by divorce, socialization into traditional gender roles, sexism, and childrearing. Therefore, not only do women accept most of the constraining responsibility for child care, but their opportunities are further limited by occupational gender-typing, sex discrimination, and sexual harassment.[16] So, many of the causes of women's poverty differ from those which affect men, and policies to treat poverty without accounting for these variations will not solve more than a portion of women's problems.

DIFFERENCES BY AGE OF HOUSEHOLDER

The discussion has already covered some variations in family poverty rates by large age groups, but it must account for differences by narrower age ranges than appear in Table 2–1. Figure 2–1 uses that refinement, showing poverty rates for householders in female-headed and other families. The data are for five-year age ranges and for whites, blacks, and Hispanics (who may be of any race).

The changes in poverty rates by age are more striking for women than for men. Female householders aged 15–24 experience rates of well over 50 percent, reaching a peak of 71 percent for young black and Hispanic women. The rates fall dramatically for blacks, whites, and Hispanics until about age 50 or 55, after which the decline is gradual. Poverty rates of married-couple families, in contrast, are only somewhat higher in the ages 15–24 than in those 30–59, and at no point up to age 60 are the rates nearly as high or the change nearly as spectacular as for female heads. Young women householders are far more likely than young men householders to fall into poverty, and women of other ages up to 55 or 60 are not much better off relative to men. The older women do compare favorably with young women, because the latter have lower incomes and heavier childrearing responsibilities.[17]

Figure 2–1 also shows a strong gender convergence in poverty after age 60 or so, until there is little or no difference between men and women 75 and over in the white, black, and Hispanic groups. In all three cases, however, the convergence results from poverty rates which continue to fall or at least level out for the oldest women, combined with increases among the oldest men. In fact, the increases begin in the early 50s and coincide with the retirement patterns among men. Those who leave the labor force with income from Social Security, private pensions, and other sources generally experience a cash income drop of a third to a half, and some become newly poor. Thus, the incomes of elderly men come to resemble more closely those of elderly women, who earlier received less on the average but whose financial status changes less. In addition, widows make up 67 percent of the female population 75 and over, and in most cases the elderly widow's income and many of her needs (e.g., mortgage payments) both decrease and her net economic situation changes relatively little.[18] Therefore, poverty afflicts roughly equal percentages of elderly men and women, though the rates do vary considerably by race and Hispanic origin. The average incomes of the elderly also have increased faster than those of the total population and the proportion protected from destitution by one or more income sources has grown.[19]

VARIATIONS BY RACE AND HISPANIC ORIGIN

Everywhere in the age spectrum white female householders have much lower poverty rates than blacks and Hispanics. (See Figure 2–1.) Moreover,

Figure 2–1
**Percent of Female-Headed and Other Families below the Poverty Level,
by Age, Race, and Hispanic Origin of Householder, 1980**

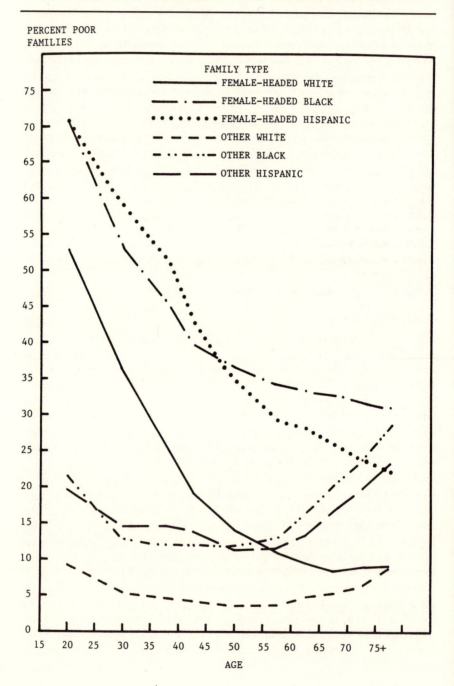

poverty rates decrease with age more rapidly for whites than for the two minority groups. For example, the poverty rate of white women house-holders aged 15–24 is 75 percent of the rate among both blacks and His-panics, but by age 75 the rate for whites is only 29 percent of that for blacks and 40 percent of the one for Hispanics. Thus, while the average poverty situation of all women improves with age, at least until 65, the pace of improvement among disadvantaged minority-group members is consider-ably less than in the more favored white group. Despite a minor convergence after 65 because the rate among white women rises slightly, the widening racial and ethnic gap at most ages calls for more attention to the needs of elderly black and Hispanic female householders.[20]

The difference in poverty rates between blacks and Hispanics is not great until age 55 or so, but then the rate drops more for Hispanics than for blacks. This is partly because Cubans are heavily represented in the older Hispanic population, and they have higher averge levels of affluence than Puerto Rican, Mexican, Central American, and other Hispanic groups. In 1985 about 39 percent of the Puerto Rican population 65 and over, 23 percent of the Mexicans in those ages, and 21 percent of all other elderly Hispanics, who include Cubans, fell below the poverty level. Many of the Cubans were middle- and upper-class refugees from the Cuban Revolution in the early 1960s, and though some arrived in the United States with few resources, they now have significantly higher average incomes than other elderly Hispanics. In fact, virtually every social indicator shows the Cuban population to enjoy greater material well-being than the other groups which make up the Hispanic population.

Black female family heads experience unusually high poverty rates for several reasons. First, they are nearly four times more likely than white women to have births out of wedlock; in 1985 about 60 percent of all black births were to unmarried women, compared with 14 percent of all white births.[21] Young women are especially affected, for 90 percent of births to black women aged 15–19 (and 45 percent among whites) were out of wedlock. Both races in those ages are extremely likely to fall below the poverty line, but blacks are especially vulnerable as they try to support children alone.

Second, separated black women spend an average of seven years apart from their husbands before they reconcile or divorce, compared with an average of one year for white women.[22] Black women also have a higher divorce rate and a lower remarriage rate than white women; blacks are more likely to remain single. Therefore, a larger share of black women must depend exclusively on their own financial resources.[23] Some of these racial differences in marital status are due to the lower average income of black than white men, because black women are faced with a relative shortage of prospective mates who can help support a family, especially since the interracial marriage is still quite uncommon. The scarcity leads many black women to avoid marriage, while others abandon financially strained unions.

Third, women of both races are more likely now than in earlier generations to enter the labor force and to get by on their own earnings. The average earnings are far lower for black women than for any other race and gender group, however, so they are the most likely to be poor.[24]

In all these respects, young black women in inner-city ghettos are at a particular disadvantage, and their fate is inseparable from that of young black men. About 40 percent of black teenage males are jobless, so a large share of young fathers cannot help support their offspring, who often end up in female-headed families with meager resources and a high probability of persistent welfare dependence. Thus, the ghetto imposes isolation from economic opportunity; separation from black middle-class role models, most of whom have left; weak family formation and support; and a strong tendency to rely on illegal ways to survive, especially drug dealing and prostitution. "Significant racial differences persist in education, occupational status, personal and family income, unemployment and labor force participation."[25] These differences contribute to higher poverty rates among blacks than among whites and to much higher rates and slower improvement for women than for men. Jobs, job training, and education are at least part of the agenda needed to rescue women and men from the poor inner-city islands of despair.

PRESENCE OF DEPENDENT CHILDREN

After 1970, women's entry into the labor force created dramatic changes in the American family. The distinction between male breadwinner and female homemaker diminished, but because the proportion of female-headed families also rose, the entry of women into the labor force did not reduce childrearing responsibilities—the working mother is still usually the housewife who cares for the home and children whether or not a husband is present.[26] Therefore, a complex relationship exists between poverty levels and the presence or absence of children under 18. In 1985, for instance, 10 percent of the female-headed families without related children under 18 were below the poverty level, compared with 33 percent of those with one child. In the families with a male present the figures were 5 and 6 percent, respectively, so while the poverty status of those units is slightly affected by the presence of children, the impact is much greater in families headed by a woman. These patterns apply to blacks and whites, and for both races children are significantly associated with how far below the poverty level a female-headed family falls and even whether it places in the poor category at all.[27]

The methodological use of progressively higher poverty thresholds as family size increases has only a minor effect: In 1985 the difference between the poverty threshold for a two-person family with no children and that for a two-person family with one child was just $211—an amount far too small to account for much of the higher poverty rate in the family with the child. The constraints children impose on a woman's work opportunities and the cost of their support are much more influential in raising the poverty rate. Moreover, the effects are far more important for a woman than for a man, because while a husband may share some domestic tasks, the wife generally assumes most household and childrearing duties. In the female-headed family she carries them alone, and if she holds a paying job the woman must make day-care arrangements which may consume a sizable share of her income. Some low-income women can use relatives in this capacity, but most pay for child care, which is provided by baby-sitters or group centers costing $50 to $100 per week.[28] While this and other expenses are not included in the official measurement of poverty status, child-care costs can subtract a substantial amount from the overall income of a poor working mother and may even prohibit her from working. Moreover, formal child-care arrangements are still insufficient to the need. California, Connecticut, Massachusetts, Minnesota, and New York devote significant resources to child care, but 33 states recently lowered their standards for day-care centers and reduced enforcement of those standards. In 23 states fewer children were under care in 1986 than in 1981.[29] But even if significantly better child care were available, a large share of poor women would still be unable to find jobs which pay enough to raise them above the poverty level.[30]

The problem has gotten worse for women, because the increase in female-headed families has raised the proportion of all poor children who live in them. In 1985, for example, 13 million children were below the poverty level, and 6.7 million (52 percent) of them were in female-headed families. In 1960 there were 17.3 million children in poverty, but only 4.1 million (24 percent) lived in families headed by a woman. Thus, while the number of poor children fell by over 4 million in 25 years, the percentage living in female-headed families more than doubled. In addition, the 1985 poverty rate for children in those families was 54 percent, compared with only 12 percent in other types of families.

The changes are especially striking in the black population. In 1985 there were 4.2 million poor black children under age 18, and 77 percent were in families with a female head. In 1960 there were about 6 million poor black children, but only 28 percent lived in female-headed families, so the proportion has nearly tripled. In 1985 the poverty rate for black children in female-headed units was 67 percent, compared with 19 percent in other types of black families. Furthermore, the younger the child, the greater the likelihood she/he will be poor. The poverty rate for those under 3 in black female-headed families was 77 percent, and it dropped progressively to 52 percent for those aged 16 and 17. Part of the reason is the youthfulness of mothers with very young children, for their median income is far lower than that of somewhat older women. In 1985, 86 percent of the families headed by a black woman aged 15–24 were poor, compared with 54 percent of those with a householder aged 25–44.[31]

These patterns reflect the massive shift of children in poverty to the female-headed family, especially in the black population. In fact, the magnitude of that change dwarfs some others, including fluctuations in general poverty rates over time. As noted in chapter 1, "The real change has been that poor women in the past were likely to be the wives of impoverished men. Today, however, they are much more likely to be head of their own household."[32] Those with children under 3 also have inordinately high unemployment rates and are likely to hold part-time rather than full-time jobs, which compounds the problem.[33]

The relationship between numbers of dependent children and poverty is shown in Table 2–2. The most striking feature is the significant jump in poverty rates from families with no children to those with one child. Then, among both major races, the more dependent children, the higher the poverty rate. That trend is particularly pronounced in female-headed families, where there is a major difference in income and family responsibilities between women with no children and those with even one child. For both races the increments of increase are more substantial with each additional child in female-headed families than in other types.

These patterns lend scant support to the notion that women bear children in order to benefit from the welfare system, especially Aid to Families with Dependent Children (AFDC). Generally, a woman can receive AFDC payments only if she has no legal husband, though more than half the states do have provisions to aid poor two-parent families in which the father is the principal wage earner, is out of work, and has exhausted his unemployment insurance. Such households make up only about 10 percent of all AFDC families, however, so women are the vast majority of recipients.[34] Presumably, AFDC benefits could prompt a woman not to marry and instead allow the program to support her and her carelessly or deliberately conceived offspring. If the benefits really were sufficient to provide a strong incentive to remain unmarried and reproduce, however, the poverty rates would likely not be as high as they are, particularly among people in the early childbearing years, and they probably would not rise so much with each successive child. The payments would provide a reasonably comfortable level of living and no stigma would attach to using them. But the percentages of families receiving AFDC benefits are highest in states with the lowest payments (e.g., $160 a month for a family of four in Mississippi) and lowest in states with the highest payments (e.g., $563 in New York and California). For this and other reasons welfare does not seem to generate much incentive for the large majority of poor women to create single-parent families or to produce more children.[35] Instead, it provides only modest assistance, and AFDC payments

Table 2–2

Percent of Female-Headed and Other Families below the Poverty Level, by Number of Children under 18 and Race, 1985

Family Type and Number of Children	Percent in Poverty		
	All Races	White	Black
All families			
Total	11.4	9.1	28.7
No children	5.5	4.7	13.7
1 child	12.2	10.2	25.7
2 children	15.3	12.8	32.9
3 children	23.1	18.0	46.2
4 children	33.7	25.8	56.5
5 children[a]	47.7	33.5	76.9
Female householder[b]			
Total	34.0	27.4	50.5
No children	10.3	8.3	19.1
1 child	33.2	29.3	44.1
2 children	46.5	42.0	56.1
3 children	65.4	59.2	73.9
4 children	77.6	69.1	82.9
5 children[a]	84.5	73.9	90.9
Other families[c]			
Total	7.0	6.3	13.1
No children	4.8	4.3	11.7
1 child	6.1	5.7	9.6
2 children	8.3	7.9	11.3
3 children	13.5	12.4	17.4
4 children	20.5	19.2	23.8
5 children[a]	33.6	25.8	55.1

Source: U.S. Bureau of the Census, "Poverty in the United States: 1985," *Current Population Reports*, Series P-60, No. 158 (Washington, DC: Government Printing Office, 1987), Table 4.

[a]Families with more than 5 children were too few to report.

[b]No husband present.

[c]Married-couple and male-headed families.

alone are not high enough in any state to lift a family above the poverty level. In addition, the federal guidelines for AFDC (and Medicaid) payments were made more stringent in 1981 and the actual payments per family were sharply reduced, though the benefits do vary widely because AFDC is administered by states and local areas.

These and other cutbacks, however, seem not to have been the major cause of poverty increases in the early 1980s.[36] The difficulty many poor people had in finding and keeping adequately paid work was more important, because earnings are the principal income source for a sizable share of the poor. Therefore, improvements in the overall economy, opportunities for rewarding employment, programs to equip the able-bodied poor with better job skills, and suitable day-care arrangements for children and disabled family members seem better ways to tackle poverty than are unrealistic increases in AFDC and other transfer payments. Indeed, the significant drop in poverty after 1959 occurred before the major transfer programs were implemented, but during a period of high employment and low inflation. Conversely, poverty rates leveled out in the 1970s when unemployment rose and the OPEC oil crisis and other forces raised prices, even while better programs for the poor were implemented. Other economic problems between 1979 and 1982 also helped raise poverty rates despite increases in the amount of transfer payments. Thus, public assistance has less impact on poverty rates than do the health of the economy, the extent and nature of job opportunities in it, and the intensity of competition for those jobs.[37]

Better, more streamlined and rational AFDC programs would help, of course, provided they actually met the needs of the poor and did not create work disincentives. But improved opportunities to become self-sufficient are more strategic over the long run, and they are better able to lift poor women above the poverty level as full participants in the economy and as positive role models for their children.[38] As matters stand now, most of the jobs available to welfare mothers do not pay enough to allow them to escape poverty, so many mothers must rely on public assistance.[39] But that reliance is a rational response to a structural reality, not a personal defect.

Poverty rates vary not just according to the number of children, but also by their ages, because the younger the child, the younger the mother and the smaller her chance to provide an adequate income.[40] Table 2–3, which reports data for female-headed families only, shows the major patterns in 1985.

The highest poverty rates of all are among women with at least one child under 6 plus one or more aged 6–17, regardless of the mother's age and race. Their average family size is comparatively large and the official poverty thresholds under which they are classified are relatively high as a result, but their incomes may be little better or even worse than those of women with few or no children. A childless woman has more freedom to enter the labor force, remain in it full time, and enjoy the resultant income, pay raises, and progress toward seniority. Even if she is working in a low-status service job, the single, widowed, or divorced woman who is free of childrearing is much better able to avoid poverty than is a mother in any of those marital categories. In addition, the presence of children under 6 is more likely than the presence of those aged 6–17 to be associated with poverty for householders up to age 44. For women aged 45–64, however, the relationship

Table 2–3

**Percent of Female-Headed Families below the Poverty Level, by Race
and Age of Householder and Children, 1985**

Age of Householder and Number of Children	Percent in Poverty		
	All Races	White	Black
Householder all ages			
No children under 18	10.3	8.3	19.1
Children under 6 and 6–17	66.3	60.2	73.3
Children under 6 only	55.9	51.6	65.5
Children 6–17 only	34.0	28.3	47.4
Householder under 25			
No children under 18	a	a	a
Children under 6 and 6–17	92.7	97.6	88.9
Children under 6 only	79.0	75.8	85.0
Children 6–17 only	a	a	a
Householder 25–44			
No children under 18	8.7	7.0	14.1
Children under 6 and 6–17	67.5	60.8	76.5
Children under 6 only	42.5	38.2	55.6
Children 6–17 only	34.7	29.6	46.9
Householder 45–64			
No children under 18	11.4	8.6	22.8
Children under 6 and 6–17	49.4	39.4	54.5
Children under 6 only	28.8	24.8	34.7
Children 6–17 only	31.8	25.3	47.1

Source: U.S. Bureau of the Census, "Poverty in the United States: 1985,"
Current Population Reports, Series P-60, No. 158 (Washington, DC:
Government Printing Office, 1987), Table 15.

aPoor families fewer than 25,000.

reverses, partly because some look after grandchildren with financial help from their mothers, many of whom work.

Whether or not mothers work strongly affects their chance of being poor. In 1985, 33 million women of all financial statuses had children under 18. About two-thirds of them worked, most full time. In addition, keeping house was the reason 85 percent of the nonworking mothers gave for not holding jobs. Women with children under 6 plus 6–17 were least likely to work, and those with only the older group of children were most likely to do so, because parenting needs and day-care costs for young children kept more mothers at home. Ten percent of the working mothers were also below the poverty level—significantly less than the 16 percent for all women. Only 41 percent of the poor mothers worked, but the majority did so full time. They averaged only 29 weeks per year, however, compared with 41 weeks for all working mothers, and poverty rates were affected accordingly. Thus, not only does the presence of children affect a woman's prospect to be poor, but so does her work experience. When single parenthood and care for children, particularly those under 6, combine with nonwork or sporadic employment, the poverty rate rises to more than twice the average for women as a whole.[41]

These problems are especially acute for teenagers who give birth. They are more likely to suffer health problems than older mothers, to produce a comparatively large number of total births in relatively rapid succession, to have low levels of educational attainment and low earnings, and to be disproportionately dependent on welfare. Their children are unusually likely to suffer birth defects, low birth weight, illness, abuse, and neglect, and the young women tend to be relatively ineffective as mothers. Furthermore, if they give birth out of wedlock, teenage mothers who then marry have unusually high rates of marital breakup.[42] Since about 59 percent of all births to mothers aged 19 and under in 1985 were out of wedlock, these problems are of substantial magnitude. In a large share of cases, the young mother becomes head of a single-parent household, beset by the problems which both induce and reflect poverty. The one-parent family—black and white—also has some tendency to replicate itself, because "female offspring who live in single-parent families at some point between the ages of 12 and 16 are more likely to form single-mother households in early adulthood than their counterparts from two-parent families."[43]

LEVELS OF EDUCATION AND POVERTY RATES

With some exceptions, the more formal schooling a female family head obtains, the less likely she is to be poor. There are significant differences by age and race, however, so controls for those characteristics are necessary. Poverty rates are also greater at some educational levels than at lower ones, and those variations need explanation. The data in Table 2–4 enable several conclusions.

1. Regardless of age and race, female householders who fall at the bottom of the educational scale—functional illiterates with four or fewer years of schooling—have far higher poverty rates than high-school graduates or those who attended at least one year of college. Since functional illiteracy means that one has not obtained "the reading and writing skills to function effectively" in a complex industrial society, it often produces or perpetuates poverty.[44] Part of the problem results from the attitudes of some middle-class teachers toward poor children. Many times they are expected to perform poorly, the student-teacher relationship becomes adversarial, and the

Table 2–4
Percent of Female Family Heads below the Poverty Level, by Years of Schooling Completed, Age, Race, and Hispanic Origin, 1980

Years of Schooling Completed and Race	Percent in Poverty			
	All Ages	15–24	25–64	65 and Over
White				
Elementary school				
0–4 years	32.1	67.4	45.8	18.4
5–7 years	28.4	78.0	40.1	13.2
8 years	23.9	80.4	32.7	9.6
High school				
1–3 years	32.6	71.5	32.4	7.9
4 years	20.7	44.7	20.1	5.4
College				
1 or more years	13.9	31.1	14.1	4.0
Black				
Elementary school				
0–4 years	49.2	72.5	56.9	39.9
5–7 years	49.7	88.6	55.3	34.5
8 years	53.5	87.1	56.5	31.0
High school				
1–3 years	58.2	84.1	55.4	29.3
4 years	43.4	65.4	40.0	24.2
College				
1 or more years	27.4	49.3	25.1	17.4
Hispanic[a]				
Elementary school				
0–4 years	51.9	76.5	56.6	30.8
5–7 years	54.0	79.1	55.8	24.2
8 years	55.7	86.1	53.5	22.9
High school				
1–3 years	60.3	79.8	56.2	19.7
4 years	38.9	56.6	36.9	14.2
College				
1 or more years	26.6	46.6	24.7	14.7

Source: U.S. Bureau of the Census, 1980 Census of Population, Detailed Characteristics, United States Summary, Section A: United States (Washington, DC: Government Printing Office, 1984), Table 306.

[a]May be of any race.

expectation of failure becomes a self-fulfilling prophecy. Thus, relatively large proportions of children from poor families abandon education as threatening or as an irrelevant antidote to poverty.[45] This is often the case for young women who become pregnant while still in school.

2. At every educational level black and white women aged 15–24 have

higher poverty rates than those aged 25–64, and the latter have higher rates than women 65 and over. The contrast between the youngest and the oldest women is especially striking. The presence or absence of children is one reason for the high rate among young women, because only about 8 percent of high-school-age women who do not marry or have children drop out of school, compared with 25 percent of those who have a child out of wedlock and over 75 percent of the ones who marry *and* have a child. Given the high divorce rate in the last group, its members are very likely to end up heading one-parent families, to be undereducated, and to be poor.[46] In addition, society provides fewer financial protections for young adults and their children than for elderly people.

3. At every age and educational level black women have substantially higher poverty rates than white women. Therefore, high overall poverty rates among black females cannot be attributed primarily to their lower median age or level of schooling. More instrumental factors include black women's greater representation in low-status jobs, their larger average number of dependent children, their greater chances never to have married and to be divorced or separated, and their lesser likelihood to receive help from absent fathers of their children, though women of both races have serious problems in that respect.

4. Hispanic women have much higher poverty rates than all white women in all educational categories and age groups. In some categories, however, they do fare better than blacks. Among Hispanics aged 15–24 the poverty rates are quite high at the elementary school level, but a bit better than those for blacks at higher levels of schooling. Hispanics aged 25–64 have lower poverty rates than blacks at most educational levels, and those 65 and over have lower rates than blacks at all levels. The patterns are partly due to the different age and economic profiles of the Puerto Rican, Mexican, and Cuban groups which make up much of the Hispanic contingent. For example, a large share of the more affluent Cuban population is 65 and over, whereas the percentage of young people in the poorer Puerto Rican population is exceptionally high.

5. The levels of education and poverty rates of young female householders are not always inversely related; at some levels of schooling the poverty rates are greater than at lower levels. For example, among blacks, whites, and Hispanics aged 15–24, the poverty rates *rise* from 0–4 years of schooling, to 5–7 years, to 8 years. Among the youngest members (15–17) of that age group the proportion who left school before reaching the eighth grade is exceptionally low, but the percentage who quit school just after the eighth grade is abnormally high. The women aged 15–17 are less likely than those aged 22–24 to have children and are more apt to receive some financial help from families, often still being perceived as dependent children themselves even though they head families. Thus, they have not quite reached the age when, as householders, they incur the greatest poverty risks. The

youngest women are also a tiny minority of those aged 15–24 with less than eighth-grade educations, so they have little statistical impact on the overall age group. Finally, very young women who conceived before marriage are now much more likely to marry than were their counterparts in the mid–1960s. Their levels of education are still apt to be low, but marriage takes more of them out of the category of female householder, leaving the somewhat older and somewhat better-educated women more likely to be on their own and therefore poor.[47]

6. In every race, ethnic, and age group poverty rates are substantially higher among female family heads who ended their educations with 1–3 years of high school than among those who graduated. Many of the women who dropped out before graduating had unwanted or mistimed pregnancies and are unmarried; some were never married, while other married young and divorced or separated. Many do not have the credentials and minimal job skills to be employable at income levels which exceed AFDC payments. They tend to be part of the "expendable" labor force whose work is undervalued and underpaid and who are apt to be last hired, first fired. In a time when a 6 or 7 percent unemployment rate is "acceptable," joblessness is most easily tolerated by the society if the unemployed are women, minorities, and others least able to fight back but for whom unemployment means poverty.

7. Elderly female householders have relatively low poverty rates at all educational levels. Some, mostly widowed or divorced women, are poor, but the poverty rate of elderly people fell significantly in the 1970s because of transfer payments and regardless of educational status. They also carry smaller average support burdens than young and middle-aged female householders. Over 90 percent are not in the labor force and are independent of unemployment problems, though the retirement incomes of many are relatively small, often because they get only a fraction of their late husbands' retirement incomes. Other elderly women were effectively excluded from labor unions during their working years and were easily exploited with low wages which later became the basis for computing pensions.[48] With controls for educational status, however, the elderly are now less susceptible to poverty than most other age groups, especially young women who receive AFDC, which came within 62 percent of the poverty line in 1970, but only 44 percent in 1985.

The National Alliance of Businesses estimates that three of every four jobs requires education or training beyond high school. As new job-seeking cohorts become smaller because of lower birth rates after the baby boom, job competition should diminish and there should be more opportunities for women to enter rewarding careers, a larger share of them nontraditional. Workers will have to prepare for those careers, however, or many women who seek work to evade poverty will still be locked into low-paying, dead-end positions. Moreover, post–high school training will not guarantee a high wage, because many of the jobs requiring specific expertise will still be created in the service industries, retail trade, and state and local government at the lower end of the pay scale.[49] Thus, a move from the welfare rolls to the tax rolls will not ensure that a woman householder can escape poverty or rise more than slightly above it. In addition, as the number and percentage of elderly people grow, young women may find the programs to meet their educational needs are less well funded than various projects for older people.

In summary, despite some variations in the correlation between poverty rates and levels of education, as a rule the more the schooling, the lower the poverty rate. The causes of women's poverty are too complex to reduce to this one relationship or to eliminate only by improving educational achievement and quality, however, though such improvements are one of several crucial steps in that direction.

FAMILY INCOME

Relative Amounts of Income

The striking difference between the median incomes of married-couple families, even with one earner, and female-headed families with no husband present contributes to the feminization of poverty. Table 2–5, which gives the dollar income per member in various types of families, illustrates the situation.

For all races collectively and for blacks, whites, and Hispanics separately, families with both spouses present have a much higher per capita income than other types of families, whether the householder is male or female. In most cases the crucial factor is having either two earners or only one in the family. For example, in 1985 married-couple families with a male householder (wife present) and families with a female householder (husband present) had per capita incomes of $11,062 and $11,605, respectively. In male-headed units with the wife absent, however, the income per member was lowered by almost a quarter and in female-headed families with the husband absent it was reduced by nearly two-thirds.

Families with divorced male householders also do relatively well economically. While divorce may lower income to some degree because the wife's earnings are lost, those earnings average much less than the husband's and his financial loss is fully offset by decreased responsibility for some of his wife's expenses and, ordinarily, those of any dependent children. They usually become the mother's responsibility. "Most men who divorce or separate are immediately better off because they retain most of their labor incomes, typically do not pay large amounts of alimony and child support to their ex-wives, and no longer have to provide for the level of needs associated with their former families."[50] The average divorced woman, on the other

Table 2–5
Income per Family Member, by Marital Status, Race, and Hispanic Origin, 1985

Marital Status	Per Capita Income (Dollars)			
	All Races	White	Black	Hispanic[a]
Male householder	11,024	11,397	7,578	6,642
Married, wife present	11,062	11,412	7,716	6,558
Married, wife absent	8,568	9,237	b	b
Widowed	9,429	10,758	4,890	b
Divorced	11,463	11,878	7,241	b
Single	9,840	10,738	6,343	8,063
Female householder	7,186	8,419	4,233	4,272
Married, husband present	11,605	12,665	7,179	6,489
Married, husband absent	4,045	4,449	3,285	2,540
Widowed	7,496	8,681	4,047	5,171
Divorced	6,305	6,792	4,665	4,402
Single	4,552	6,256	3,238	3,404

Source: U.S. Bureau of the Census, "Money Income of Households, Families, and Persons in the United States: 1985," Current Population Reports, Series P-60, No. 156 (Washington, DC: Government Printing Office, 1987), Table 14.

[a]May be of any race.

[b]Base less than 75,000 families.

hand, suffers a substantial loss of income as the victim of these conditions. In fact, per capita income in families with a divorced female householder is little more than half that in units with a female householder and a husband present.

Widower-headed families have a somewhat lower per capita income than those headed by married men with a wife present, but the difference is not great and is largely attributable to the lower average income of the elderly population where widowers are concentrated. Widow-headed families, while better off than those headed by a divorced, single, or married woman with an absent husband, have a per capita income sharply lower than that of married-couple families.

Finally, families headed by a single man have a slightly higher per capita income than those headed by a widower and a somewhat lower one than those headed by a married man with a wife present, but the differences are not great. Per capita income in families headed by a single woman, however, is only 39 percent of that in units headed by a woman with a husband present.

The gender differences are striking: Per capita income in families headed by a man is not greatly affected by variations in marital status; income in units headed by a woman is drastically lower in every marital situation except where a husband is present. One comparison shows why. In 1985 per capita income in families headed by a male with a wife present was $11,062, the average number of family members was 3.27, the average number of related children under 18 was 0.94, and the average number of wage earners was 1.73. In contrast, per capita income in female-headed families with the husband absent was only $4,045, but the average number of family members was 3.38, the average number of related children was 1.76, and the average number of wage earners was only 1.14.[51] It is difficult to find a clearer illustration of how poverty has become feminized!

The situation is exacerbated because most mothers with absent husbands receive no help from those men, either because they cannot be found or they are unwilling or unable to pay. In 1985, for instance, 8.8 million women aged 18 or over were living with one or more children under 21 whose fathers were absent. Forty percent received no help at all from those fathers. About 39 percent of the women without help had never been officially awarded child support and 26 percent of the ones who had were unable to collect any of the amount granted. Another 26 percent received only part of what was awarded. Most of the women either could not locate the father or could not establish paternity. Never-married mothers were far less likely than separated or divorced mothers to receive help from the fathers.[52] In all, only 24 percent of the 8.8 million women were awarded support payments and actually received the full amount.[53] The other three-quarters either received no award, collected none of what was owed them, or received only partial payment. So the feminization of poverty includes a persistent double standard of family responsibility, despite the minority of divorced, separated, or unmarried fathers whose children live with them or who conscientiously help support the ones living with their mothers.

Income in female-headed families also varies by marital status, reflecting the diversity among female householders. In 1985, for example, the per capita income in families headed by a married but separated woman was only $3,929; it rose to $4,552 for single heads, $6,305 for those who were divorced, and $7,496 for widowed householders. Clearly, marital status beyond whether or not a husband is present is associated with significant variations in income, the support burden the householder must carry, and her prospects of being poor.

Income Deficits in Poor Families

"Income deficit is the difference between the total income of families and unrelated individuals below the poverty level, and their respective poverty thresholds."[54] This dollar figure is the amount necessary to raise the median incomes of poor families to just their poverty thresholds.

Table 2–6

Median Income Deficit of Families below the Poverty Level, by Family Type and Race, 1985

Family Type	Income Deficit (Dollars)		
	All Races	White	Black
All families			
Female-headed, no husband present	4,138	3,700	4,973
Other	3,359	3,454	2,924
Families with related children under 18			
Female-headed, no husband present	4,379	3,869	5,000
Other	3,930	4,037	3,780
Families without related children under 18			
Female-headed, no husband present	2,364	2,159	2,753
Other	2,254	2,347	1,764

Source: U.S. Bureau of the Census, "Poverty in the United States: 1985," Current Population Reports, Series P-60, No. 158 (Washington, DC: Government Printing Office, 1987), Table 29.

Reported in Table 2–6, the income deficits show that the average female-headed family below the poverty threshold falls deeper beneath that level than the typical poor married-couple family. The average deficit in 1985 was $779 greater for female-headed units than for other types of families; for whites the difference was $246, and for blacks it was $2,049. While poor black female-headed families have significantly larger deficits than poor white ones, however, the reverse is true among married-couple and male-headed units, largely because of the income improvements black men experienced after 1960. As a result, the greatest deficit is for black female-headed families, followed by white female-headed units. Poor black families with a married couple or male head push upward closest to the poverty threshold, followed by poor white families with a male present. Among poor black and white families of all types collectively, it would take $3,800 just to raise the median income to the official poverty level. The white female-headed units would need $3,700, the black ones $4,973. Thus, that half of all poor families below the median deficits would require substantially more than these amounts just to reach the poverty level.

The poor are also getting poorer as measured by the median income deficit. Between 1977 and 1985 the deficit in poor female-headed families grew from $3,429 to $4,090 (in constant 1985 dollars), so not only has the number of poor persons living in female-headed families grown, but these individuals have fallen even deeper into poverty.[55] But this trend should not obscure the volatility of family income and the individual family dynamics which impel significant drops and rises in levels of living over time, causing numerous families to move in and out of poverty.[56]

Taxation increases the income deficits further, for in 1985 nearly two-thirds of all households with incomes below the poverty level paid one or more of four taxes (federal income, state income, FICA payroll, own-home property). Their average income fell 8 percent as a result, and the mean tax per poverty household was about $360.[57] Nor do these figures include state and local sales taxes, which fall especially heavily on the poor.

Source of Income in Poor Families

Almost all families below the poverty line have some officially listed money income, often from a combination of wages, Social Security, public assistance (especially AFDC in female-headed households), and other sources. In fact, in 1985 only 0.9 percent of all female-headed families reported having no money income. That group did number 96,000, however, and all were poor. These figures compare with 84,000 (0.2 percent) of all other families, so even in the group with no money income woman-headed families are significantly overrepresented.

The relative importance of the various sources of income differs between the average female-headed family and the typical married-couple family, and between the average poor and nonpoor female-headed unit, so it is useful to identify the differences. (See Table 2–7.)

A major reason why poor female-headed families are poor, regardless of householder age, is that the percentage with earnings is little more than half that of nonpoor female-headed units. On the other hand, a far larger share of poor female-headed units than any other families have income from public assistance. The proportion is highest among householders under 25, largely because of their reliance on AFDC, and welfare as an income source diminishes significantly with age. But in families with female heads under 65, public assistance and earnings are both major sources of income, so a sizable segment of the welfare population is also a working population. The minority dependent on welfare over the long term is a fairly small segment of all recipients in any given year, and while some children in welfare-dependent families become addicted when they establish their own families, the proportion is not large.[58]

Supplemental Security Income (SSI) goes to a third of the poor households headed by an elderly woman and a fifth of the ones with an elderly male householder, but SSI is a minor source for the younger poor and all age groups above the poverty level, given its primary focus on poor people 65 and older.

Table 2–7

Percent of Families Receiving Income from Specified Sources, by Poverty Status, Gender, and Age of Householder, 1985

Source of Income	Female Householder[a]			Other Householder		
	Under 25	25–64	65 and over	Under 25	25–64	65 and over
Income above poverty level						
Earnings	94.1	96.0	66.6	99.9	97.2	42.8
Social Security	10.4	19.2	95.9	1.8	8.6	94.7
Public assistance	16.3	6.2	3.9	4.1	1.2	0.8
Supplemental Security Income (SSI)	3.0	4.7	17.5	0.6	1.2	3.1
Other transfer payments	7.4	13.5	15.6	16.4	15.6	8.6
Dividends, interest, rent	52.5	57.2	62.9	62.1	75.4	80.5
Pensions and other[b]	31.0	43.8	39.0	16.9	19.4	54.9
No income	0.0	0.0	0.0	0.0	0.0	0.0
Income below poverty level						
Earnings	43.2	53.1	35.4	84.2	79.7	20.7
Social Security	1.9	11.6	89.1	3.2	12.1	82.2
Public assistance	70.0	58.2	16.7	22.2	18.5	5.6
Supplemental Security Income (SSI)	1.2	7.2	33.9	2.7	5.9	20.2
Other transfer payments	3.6	7.0	8.9	10.4	16.3	4.5
Dividends, interest, rent	8.1	11.4	19.3	16.3	27.1	32.9
Pensions and other[b]	22.8	23.0	15.1	9.9	12.3	14.5
No income	4.5	2.6	0.5	5.1	1.8	2.7

Source: U.S. Bureau of the Census, "Poverty in the United States: 1985," _Current Population Reports_, Series P-60, No. 158 (Washington, DC: Government Printing Office, 1987), Table 28.

[a]No husband present.

[b]Includes private pensions, government employee pensions, alimony, annuities, and other sources.

Other transfers, such as food stamps and subsidized school lunches, are a more important source to female heads above the poverty level than to those below it, partly because of the ways eligibility is determined, and partly because the poorest women may be less familiar with the programs or ways to deal with their administrators.

Dividends, interest, and rent, not surprisingly, accrue to very few poor female householders, although older women are more likely than younger ones to have income from these sources. In most cases poor women simply lack the savings, investments, and real property which would yield such income. Poor or not, female-headed households have substantially less net worth than married-couple households, and a smaller share of it comes from income produced by financial assets.

Private pensions also play a relatively small role for poor female heads, especially those 65 and over who might be expected to receive them. Poor elderly women fare slightly better than poor elderly men in this respect, though neither group is well covered by private or governmental employee pensions, and the average amounts they do receive are small. Both sexes below the poverty threshold contrast sharply with the nonpoor elderly, for whom pensions are a relatively important source. Even so, only 55 percent of the male-headed and married-couple families with an elderly householder have private pension income. The percentage in female-headed families is much lower and underscores the need to provide better and wider coverage, because inadequate pension income is one reason why the elderly poor are poor.

The poor aged 65 and over do rely heavily on Social Security, because 89 percent of the female-headed families and 82 percent of the other families have income from that source. They are less well covered than the nonpoor, however, 95 percent of whom in all types of families have income from Social Security.

Cash welfare income also has different results for the persistently poor and the temporarily poor, helping people in the first category but having limited usefulness for those in the second. Thus, welfare does not adequately cover the "new" poor or people who move in and out of poverty as their economic conditions deteriorate and improve. In some cases, even when public assistance could be helpful, participation rates are relatively low. This is less true, however, for AFDC than for other programs, such as SSI and food stamps. The relatively low participation rates are due to transportation and other access costs, problems in dealing with the welfare bureaucracy, the stigma attached to reliance on welfare, and misinformation about the programs and eligibility for them.[59]

But even if all eligible families and persons participated fully in the present programs, welfare as now constituted would not eradicate poverty, and alone it helps few families rise above the poverty level.[60] The benefits are quite small in many states and the programs generally do not lead to self-sufficiency, despite the controversial "workfare" approach used in some places. In fact, the goals of assisting the temporarily poor and preventing long-term welfare dependency are partly contradictory, and the dilemma remains unresolved.[61]

NOTES

1. Ian Robertson, *Sociology*, 3rd ed. (New York: Worth, 1987), p. 115.
2. Philip K. Robins and Katherine P. Dickinson, "Child Support and Welfare

Dependence: A Multinomial Logit Analysis," *Demography* 22:3 (August 1985), p. 367.

3. See Chaya S. Piotrkowski and Mitchell H. Katz, "Women's Work and Personal Relations in the Family," in Phyllis W. Berman and Estelle R. Ramey, eds., *Women: A Developmental Perspective* (Washington, DC: National Institutes of Health, 1982), p. 223.

4. Several of these questions about the poor, especially young people and their prospects, were inspired by ethnographic studies reported in Terry M. Williams and William Kornblum, *Growing Up Poor* (Lexington, MA: Lexington Books, 1985); and Jay McLeod, *Ain't No Makin' It: Leveled Aspirations in a Low Income Neighborhood* (Boulder, CO: Westview Press, 1987).

5. For an analysis of divorce trends, see Paula England and George Farkas, *Households, Employment, and Gender* (New York: Aldine, 1986), pp. 59–65.

6. Mary Corcoran, Greg J. Duncan, and Martha S. Hill, "The Economic Fortunes of Women and Children: Lessons from the Panel Study of Income Dynamics," in Barbara C. Gelpi, Nancy C. M. Hartsock, Clare C. Novak, and Myra H. Strober, eds., *Women and Poverty* (Chicago: University of Chicago Press, 1986), p. 19.

7. U.S. Bureau of the Census, "Poverty in the United States: 1985," *Current Population Reports*, Series P–60, No. 158 (Washington, DC: Government Printing Office, 1987), Table 3.

8. For the projections, based on Series B assumptions, see U.S. Bureau of the Census, "Projections of the Number of Households and Families: 1986 to 2000," *Current Population Reports*, Series P–25, No. 986 (Washington, DC: Government Printing Office, 1986), Table 1.

9. U.S. Bureau of the Census, "Poverty in the United States: 1985," Table 15.

10. Paul C. Glick and Arthur J. Norton, *Marrying, Divorcing, and Living Together in the U.S. Today* (Washington, DC: Population Reference Bureau, 1979), p. 19.

11. U.S. Bureau of the Census, "Population Profile of the United States: 1984–85," *Current Population Reports*, Series P–23, No. 150 (Washington, DC: Government Printing Office, 1987), p. 46.

12. England and Farkas, *Households, Employment, and Gender*, p. 70.

13. Nancy Smith Barrett, "Data Needs for Evaluating the Labor Market Status of Women," in U.S. Bureau of the Census, Barbara B. Reagan, ed., "Issues in Federal Statistical Needs Relating to Women," *Current Population Reports*, Series P–23, No. 83 (Washington, DC: Government Printing Office, 1979), p. 15. See also Thomas J. Espenshade, "The Economic Consequences of Divorce," *Journal of Marriage and the Family* 41:3 (August 1979), pp. 615–625.

14. Greg J. Duncan and Saul D. Hoffman, "A Reconsideration of the Economic Consequences of Marital Dissolution," *Demography* 22:4 (November 1987), p. 485.

15. U.S. Bureau of the Census, "Money Income of Households, Families, and Persons in the United States: 1985," *Current Population Reports*, Series P–60, No. 156 (Washington, DC: Government Printing Office, 1987), Table 9.

16. Hilda Scott, *Working Your Way to the Bottom: The Feminization of Poverty* (London, Pandora Press, 1984), p. 23.

17. For a discussion of the relationship between age and income, see Beth J. Soldo, "America's Elderly in the 1980s," *Population Bulletin* 35:4 (Washington, DC: Population Reference Bureau, 1980), pp. 21–23; Jacquelyne J. Jackson, *Mi-*

norities and Aging (Belmont, CA: Wadsworth, 1980), pp. 166–169; and Philip Janson and Karen Frisbie Mueller, "Age, Ethnicity, and Well-Being," *Research on Aging* 5:3 (September 1983), pp. 353–367.

18. Corcoran, Duncan, and Hill, "The Economic Fortunes of Women and Children," p. 16.

19. R. Meredith Belbin, "Retirement Strategy in an Evolving Society," in Frances M. Carp, ed., *Retirement* (New York: Behavioral Publications, 1972), p. 177.

20. Fred C. Pampel, *Social Change and the Aged* (Lexington, MA: D.C. Heath, 1981), p. 18.

21. U.S. National Center for Health Statistics, "Advance Report of Final Natality Statistics, 1985," *Monthly Vital Statistics Report* 36:4 (Washington, DC: Government Printing Office, July 17, 1987), Table 18.

22. William P. O'Hare, "Poverty in America: Trends and New Patterns," *Population Bulletin* 40:3 (Washington, DC: Population Reference Bureau, 1985), p. 32.

23. For data supporting these observations, see U.S. Bureau of the Census, "Marital Status and Living Arrangements: 1985," *Current Population Reports,* Series P-20, No. 410 (Washington, DC: Government Printing Office, 1986), Table 1.

24. O'Hare, "Poverty in America," p. 32. See also William J. Wilson and Kathryn M. Neckerman, "Poverty and Family Structure: The Widening Gap Between Evidence and Public Policy Issues," paper presented at the Conference on Poverty and Policy: Retrospect and Prospects (Williamsburg, VA: Institute for Research on Poverty and U.S. Department of Health and Human Services, December 6–8, 1984).

25. Melvin E. Thomas and Michael Hughes, "The Continuing Significance of Race: A Study of Race, Class, and Quality of Life in America, 1972–1985," *American Sociological Review* 51:6 (December 1986), pp. 830, 839–840. See also William J. Wilson, *The Declining Significance of Race: Blacks and Changing American Institutions,* 2nd ed. (Chicago, University of Chicago Press, 1980).

26. Annegret S. Ogden, *The Great American Housewife* (Westport, CT: Greenwood Press, 1986), p. 221. See also U.S. Bureau of Labor Statistics, "Families at Work: The Job and the Pay," *Monthly Labor Review* 106:12 (Washington, DC: Government Printing Office, December 1983), pp. 16–22.

27. Greg J. Duncan and James N. Morgan, "An Overview of Family Economic Mobility," in Greg J. Duncan, Richard D. Coe, Mary E. Corcoran, Martha S. Hill, Saul D. Hoffman, and James N. Morgan, *Years of Poverty, Years of Plenty* (Ann Arbor, MI: Institute for Social Research, 1984), pp. 18–22.

28. Martin O'Connell and David E. Bloom, *Juggling Jobs and Babies: America's Child Care Challenge,* occasional paper no. 12 in the series Population Trends and Public Policy (Washington, DC: Population Reference Bureau, 1987), p. 1.

29. Claudia Wallace, "The Child-Care Dilemma," *Time* (June 22, 1987), p. 58.

30. Greg J. Duncan, Richard D. Coe, and Martha S. Hill, "The Dynamics of Poverty," in Duncan and others, *Years of Poverty,* p. 63.

31. Parts of this analysis are adapted from O'Hare, "Poverty in America," p. 32.

32. Martha S. Hill, "The Changing Nature of Poverty," in Yeheskel Hasenfeld and Mayer N. Zald, eds., "The Welfare State in America: Trends and Prospects," *Annals of the American Academy of Political and Social Science* 479 (May 1985), p. 38.

33. U.S. Bureau of the Census, Cynthia M. Taeuber and Victor Valdisera,

"Women in the American Economy," *Current Population Reports,* Series P–23, No. 146 (Washington, DC: Government Printing Office, 1986), p. 17.

34. O'Hare, "Poverty in America," p. 33.

35. Ibid.

36. Ibid, pp. 36–37.

37. Ibid, p. 12.

38. Sheila B. Kamerman, "Women, Children, and Poverty: Public Policies and Female-Headed Families in Industrial Countries," in Gelpi and others, *Women and Poverty,* pp. 60–61.

39. Scott, *Working Your Way to the Bottom,* p. 24.

40. Richard A. Easterlin, "The New Age Structure of Poverty in America: Permanent or Transient?" *Population and Development Review* 13:2 (June 1987), p. 200.

41. For the data, see U.S. Bureau of the Census, "Poverty in the United States: 1985," Table 23.

42. John O. G. Billy, Nancy S. Lansdale, and Steven D. McLaughlin, "The Effect of Marital Status at First Birth on Marital Dissolution among Adolescent Mothers," *Demography* 23:3 (August 1986), pp. 329, 340.

43. Sara S. McLanahan, "Family Structure and Dependency: Early Transitions to Female Household Headship," *Demography* 25:1 (February 1988), p. 14.

44. Henry S. Shryock and Jacob S. Siegel, *The Methods and Materials of Demography,* Vol. 1 (Washington, DC: Government Printing Office, 1973), p. 325.

45. Jeremy Larner, "Crisis in the Schools," in Ben B. Seligman, ed., *Aspects of Poverty* (New York: Crowell, 1968), p. 129.

46. Arleen Leibowitz, Marvin Eisen, and Winston K. Chow, "An Economic Model of Teeenage Pregnancy Decision-Making," *Demography* 23:1 (February 1986), pp. 74–75.

47. U.S. National Center for Health Statistics, "Trends in Marital Status of Mothers at Conception and Birth of First Child: United States, 1964–66, 1972, and 1980," *Monthly Vital Statistics Report* 36:2 (Washington, DC: Government Printing Office, May 29, 1987), pp. 3–4.

48. For analyses of women's role in the labor movement, see Ruth Milkman, ed., *Women, Work, and Protest: A Century of U.S. Women's Labor History* (Boston, MA: Routledge & Kegan Paul, 1985).

49. U.S. Bureau of the Census, Taeuber and Valdisera, "Women in the American Economy," p. 27.

50. Duncan and Hoffman, "A Reconsideration of the Economic Consequences of Marital Dissolution," p. 495.

51. U.S. Bureau of the Census, "Money Income of Households, Families, and Persons in the United States: 1985," Table 14.

52. Andrea H. Beller and John W. Graham, "Child Support Awards: Differentials and Trends by Race and Marital Status," *Demography* 23:2 (May 1986), p. 231.

53. For the data and an analysis, see U.S. Bureau of the Census, "Child Support and Alimony: 1985," *Current Population Reports,* Series P–23, No. 152 (Washington, DC: Government Printing Office, 1987). See also U.S. Bureau of the Census, Taeuber and Valdisera, "Women in the American Economy," p. 36; and U.S. Bureau of the Census, "Population Profile of the United States: 1984–85," p. 33.

54. U.S. Bureau of the Census, "Poverty in the United States: 1985," p. 163.

55. William P. O'Hare, "The Eight Myths of Poverty," in Leroy W. Barnes, ed., *Social Problems 87/88* (Guilford, CT: Dushkin, 1987), p. 122.

56. Greg J. Duncan, "The Volatility of Family Income Over the Life Course," paper presented at the Annual Meetings of the Population Association of America (Chicago: April 30–May 2, 1987), p. 3.

57. U.S. Bureau of the Census, "Household After-Tax Income: 1985," *Current Population Reports*, Series P–23, No. 151 (Washington, DC: Government Printing Office, 1987), pp. 1–2.

58. Greg J. Duncan, "Welfare Use in America," *ISR Newsletter* (Winter, 1986–87), p. 5.

59. Greg J. Duncan and Richard D. Coe, "The Dynamics of Welfare Use," in Duncan and others, *Years of Poverty*, pp. 84–88.

60. Hill, "The Changing Nature of Poverty," p. 43.

61. Duncan and Coe, "The Dynamics of Welfare Use," p. 89.

3

Families in Poverty:
Distribution and Trends

The nation's poor female-headed families are much more heavily concentrated in some regions, divisions, states, and counties than in others. To acquire data on this uneven distribution of poverty one must turn to the *1980 Census of Population*, because the more recent *Current Population Reports* do not supply the necessary data, though they do enable some updating.

GEOGRAPHY, RACE, AND ETHNICITY

There are relatively small variations among the four regions in the poverty rates of female-headed families of all races collectively. The South fares worst, the West best, but the difference of 6 percentage points is not startling. (See Table 3–1.) In 1960 the regional differences were considerably greater, but because poverty rates declined more in the South than in the other three regions, those differences have diminished.[1] After 1978 and during the recessions of the early 1980s, however, the rates rose in all regions, including the thriving Sunbelt states of the South and West, though not as much as they did in the Northeast and Midwest with their older traditional industries susceptible to high unemployment rates.[2]

These same patterns prevail in the nine census divisions which make up the four regions, although the differences among the divisions are somewhat greater. Thus, 12 percentage points separate the East South Central division, with the highest poverty rate, from the West North Central division, with the lowest. That variation pales, however, beside much greater differences among the races in every region, division, and state. Therefore, the rest of this section focuses on those racial differences in the geographic units.

Table 3–1

Percent of Female-Headed Families below the Poverty Level in Regions, Divisions, and States, by Race and Hispanic Origin, 1980

Region, Division, and State	Percent in Poverty					
	All Races	White	Black	American Indian[a]	Asian[b]	Hispanic[c]
United States	30.3	22.3	46.3	46.4	25.7	48.2
Northeast	30.4	22.5	44.6	44.8	23.3	61.8
New England	27.4	23.9	44.2	49.6	21.8	67.3
Maine	30.8	30.6	d	61.2	d	d
New Hampshire	24.6	24.3	d	d	d	d
Vermont	28.2	28.0	d	d	d	d
Massachusetts	27.5	24.1	43.0	45.2	21.3	68.8
Rhode Island	29.3	26.6	53.1	51.4	d	56.9
Connecticut	26.2	19.2	44.5	47.0	d	67.9
Middle Atlantic	31.3	22.0	44.6	42.8	23.5	61.1
New York	34.2	24.0	44.0	43.9	22.5	60.4
New Jersey	29.2	19.5	44.6	33.1	20.6	62.4
Pennsylvania	27.4	20.6	46.1	47.4	32.2	67.6
Midwest	28.6	21.9	45.8	52.4	27.6	48.0
East North Central	29.4	21.8	46.3	46.0	25.1	49.3
Ohio	29.5	23.2	46.5	44.8	36.1	50.2
Indiana	26.8	22.2	43.2	50.5	32.7	46.7
Illinois	30.8	19.1	48.6	43.5	17.1	50.3
Michigan	30.7	23.8	43.9	46.6	27.9	46.5
Wisconsin	25.1	20.3	47.6	45.7	34.9	48.9
West North Central	25.8	21.9	42.7	57.1	35.4	39.6
Minnesota	22.8	20.7	44.9	51.7	33.6	47.9
Iowa	25.8	24.4	45.6	67.4	38.8	38.0
Missouri	27.0	21.5	41.1	38.8	29.9	32.5
North Dakota	26.6	23.5	d	59.0	d	d
South Dakota	34.4	27.4	d	64.8	d	d
Nebraska	25.2	20.9	49.4	57.2	d	42.2
Kansas	25.6	21.0	44.5	49.6	55.4	40.2
South	33.1	22.3	48.4	42.6	35.9	43.3
South Atlantic	31.1	20.0	45.6	43.9	33.3	33.7
Delaware	30.1	20.2	46.0	d	d	69.7
Maryland	25.4	16.2	35.7	49.5	21.3	30.3
District of Columbia	28.5	8.4	30.5	d	d	30.7
Virginia	29.5	20.0	44.2	33.8	15.6	34.4
West Virginia	30.3	29.3	41.0	d	d	30.4
North Carolina	31.6	19.8	46.0	47.8	37.0	47.3
South Carolina	35.8	20.1	49.2	d	42.8	53.9
Georgia	35.5	20.0	49.7	33.3	38.5	43.2
Florida	30.4	19.5	52.6	38.1	34.7	30.9

48

Table 3–1 (continued)

Region, Division, and State	Percent in Poverty					
	All Races	White	Black	American Indian[a]	Asian[b]	Hispanic[c]
East South Central	37.3	26.2	53.7	44.6	36.7	50.8
Kentucky	35.0	31.3	51.7	47.9	d	50.0
Tennessee	33.8	24.7	50.5	42.6	38.5	49.1
Alabama	38.9	23.2	54.4	43.3	36.3	48.5
Mississippi	43.6	23.6	56.8	45.5	d	57.1
West South Central	38.3	23.6	50.5	41.5	40.0	47.1
Arkansas	38.1	27.2	57.2	30.4	46.9	63.5
Louisiana	41.5	21.3	56.8	53.5	48.9	41.2
Oklahoma	31.1	25.3	48.8	43.2	39.3	47.5
Texas	30.7	23.2	44.4	34.7	37.6	47.3
West	26.9	22.7	39.0	45.8	23.9	39.2
Mountain	28.2	23.8	42.9	53.4	32.0	44.0
Montana	30.4	27.5	d	53.0	d	47.8
Idaho	33.1	31.8	d	71.3	d	54.4
Wyoming	23.6	22.4	d	38.4	d	37.4
Colorado	26.0	22.1	41.4	45.0	33.7	46.5
New Mexico	37.2	30.4	61.9	54.6	d	44.2
Arizona	27.7	21.2	44.6	54.2	34.1	42.6
Utah	28.0	26.4	47.3	54.9	29.7	48.3
Nevada	18.6	14.3	36.9	42.2	22.7	24.5
Pacific	26.5	22.3	38.6	39.4	23.5	37.7
Washington	28.2	26.6	38.3	49.3	24.9	45.3
Oregon	28.0	26.7	45.5	46.5	34.3	39.5
California	26.1	20.9	38.6	35.5	22.1	37.4
Alaska	26.5	21.0	30.3	39.7	d	d
Hawaii	28.0	32.1	d	d	25.1	45.1

Source: U.S. Bureau of the Census, 1980 Census of Population, General Social and Economic Characteristics, reports for states (Washington, DC: Government Printing Office, 1983), Tables 72, 82, 92, 98.

[a]Includes Eskimo and Aleut.

[b]Includes Pacific Islander.

[c]May be of any race.

[d]Fewer than 100 female-headed families below the poverty level.

In the South the poverty rate of black female-headed families is 117 percent higher than that of white units, and even in the West, where black families are least likely to be poor, their poverty rate is 72 percent above that of the white families. In the Northeast the black-white variation is 98 percent, and in the Midwest 109 percent. By comparison, the highest regional poverty rate among blacks (in the South) is only 24 percent greater than the lowest (in the West). Thus, poverty is far more evenly distributed *within* each racial group than it is *between* them, and black female-headed families are more than twice as likely as white ones to be poor in three of the four major regions.

Part of the racial difference is due to the larger average number of children in the black female-headed family, part is the result of lower average levels of schooling attained by black than white women, and part stems from the larger percentage of black women who are unemployed or locked into low-status jobs.[3] But even with controls for these factors, black women still have higher poverty rates as a consequence of racism and other socioeconomic derivatives of slavery and sharecropping in southern agriculture before World War II. Despite the progress black women have made in education and job status, improvements in their median income lag and the percentages in poverty and on welfare remain very high. Cutbacks in federal programs for education and job training, along with competition with the rapidly growing Hispanic population, also help slow the progress of black women out of poverty, and many of them could be an "underclass" for decades more.[4]

One could argue that this is solely the result of growing separation between poor blacks and middle- and upper-class blacks, and that the most affluent groups are either holding their own in comparison with whites or are improving more rapidly.[5] There is some truth to this "bifurcation thesis," especially when one compares black married-couple and female-headed families. But even with such variables as education and work experience controlled, the median income of black female family heads is significantly lower than that of whites and their poverty rate is much higher.[6] So throughout the nation, being black in and of itself still carries major economic disadvantages.

The patterns by census divisions are similar to those in the regions, with black female-headed families trapped in poverty at least twice as often as white units in six of the nine divisions. The exceptions are New England and the Mountain and Pacific divisions, but even there black families headed by a woman have poverty rates at least 73 percent greater than white units.

Native Americans ("American Indian, Eskimo, and Aleut," according to the Census Bureau) have a national poverty rate of 46 percent for female-headed families—the same as that for black units. Regional rates for native Americans vary from 52 percent in the Midwest to 43 percent in the South. The differences among the nine census divisions range from 57 percent in the West North Central division to 39 percent in the Pacific division. Thus, the range is greater than the one for blacks because of more variable advantages available to Indian groups in the several geographic areas, but the poverty difference between native-American and Caucasian families is much more significant than the variations within the Indian group. In some sections, native Americans also compare poorly with blacks, especially in the West North Central and Mountain divisions. In others, blacks fare worse, particularly in the East South Central and West South Central divisions. Overall, however, native Americans "statistically remain among the poorest economically, the least employed, the unhealthiest, the lowest in educational and income level, and the worst-housed ethnic group in America."[7]

Asians include Chinese, Filipinos, Japanese, Asian Indians, Koreans, Vietnamese, Hawaiians, Samoans, Guamanians and other Pacific Islanders. Female-headed families in the Asian group as a whole have a poverty rate only slightly above that of white female-headed families, and by this index they fare much better than blacks and native Americans. There are, however, significant variations within the Asian contingent. In the Northeast and the West Asians have poverty rates below the national norm; in the Midwest Asian rates are somewhat above average; in the South they are significantly higher. The lowest rates for Asians in the nine census divisions are in New England and the Pacific division; the highest are in the West South Central and East South Central divisions. Those two also have the highest percentages of poor white and black families, so the overall poverty conditions of an area affect all racial groups.

Hispanic female-headed families have a higher national poverty rate than any other group listed in Table 3–1, even blacks and native Americans. In part this pattern prevails because since 1973 (the first year for which data on Hispanics are available) Hispanic median family income has not changed as a proportion of the median for all white families, even though there is evidence of overall improvement in the occupational status of Hispanics.[8] The variations by divisions, however, are greater for Hispanics than for the other groups just discussed because of the variable economic well-being of Hispanic groups of different national origins. The poverty rates of Hispanic female-headed famlies in nearly all the states of the Northeast exceed 60 percent, because the Hispanic contingent consists heavily of Puerto Ricans— the poorest of the Spanish-origin groups. The rates are lowest in the South Atlantic and Pacific divisions. The first is strongly influenced by Florida's Cuban population, which has the highest average level of affluence among Hispanics.[9] The largest Hispanic group has Mexican ancestry; they make up about 60 percent of the Spanish-origin total, and California and Texas together contain about three-quarters of them. In some sections, such as the Pacific division, their poverty rates are relatively low because many of the Mexican-background people are descendants of families who long have lived north of the Rio Grande. In other areas the rates are high because many Mexicans are recent arrivals starting at the bottom of the status and income hierarchy.

Collectively, people with Mexican, Puerto Rican, and Cuban backgrounds make up about 80 percent of the nation's total Hispanic population, but in certain areas other groups (Dominicans, Colombians, Spaniards, Ecuadorans, Nicaraguans, Salvadorans, Panamanians, etc.) do have some impact on the percentages of Spanish-origin female-headed families below the poverty level.

DIFFERENCES BY STATES

The poverty patterns in the divisions reflect those in the component states, so many of the conclusions about the larger units apply to the smaller ones. As expected, racial composition plays an important role. While there are notable state variations in the poverty rates of white female-headed families, from 8 percent in the District of Columbia to 33 percent in Hawaii, the black-white difference within each state is generally much greater than the state-to-state differences within each race. This is true even in Nevada, Minnesota, Wyoming, New Hampshire, and Wisconsin, where overall poverty rates in female-headed families are quite low. Table 3–1 shows that the usual pattern is poverty rates in black families about twice as high as those in white ones, although in some states the ratios are a bit lower, in others a little higher. Even in Maryland, where poverty rates are far below the national averages for both races, the rate for black families is over twice that for white ones. Florida has one of the greatest discrepancies and so does the District of Columbia. In Florida, however, the black rate is well above the national norm for blacks, while in the nation's capital it is significantly below.

There also are fairly wide variations in black family poverty among the states, from relatively low rates in Alaska, the District of Columbia, Maryland, Nevada, and Washington to unusually high ones in New Mexico, Arkansas, Mississippi, Louisiana, and Alabama, all with 54 to 62 percent of their black female-headed families below the poverty line.

The native-American population exceeds 50,000 in only seven states, which account for 52 percent of all poor female-headed Indian families. Among the seven, poverty rates are over 54 percent in New Mexico and Arizona, followed in descending order by Washington, North Carolina, Oklahoma, Alaska, and California (36 percent). The variations are due to differences in levels of living among various tribal groups, the proportions of people who are rural and urban, and the poverty rates for all persons collectively in a state. New Mexico, for instance, ranks among the five states with the highest poverty rates for whites, blacks, and native Americans.

The proportions of Asian female-headed families in poverty vary widely among the states. Those with high rates have relatively large proportions of Vietnamese, who were torn fairly recently from their cultural settings and plunged into entirely different ones. Many have problems with family disruption, cultural conflict, language differences, prejudice, and the need to begin working and earning near the bottom of the socioeconomic ladder. Some Vietnamese families are headed by a woman widowed by the war. Others originated as married-couple units containing a former American soldier now divorced or separated from his wife. But significant differences also prevail between the early and more recent Vietnamese refugees and among those who originated in different sections. Many of the early arrivals were politicians and other affluent persons who fit into the system relatively easily, whereas the later arrivals were more apt to be peasants for whom acculturation is more difficult. In addition, the ethnic Vietnamese are more likely than the sino-Vietnamese to be employed, to have high incomes, and to be independent of government support.[10]

The states with relatively large Japanese, Filipino, Chinese, and Korean populations have comparatively few Asian female-headed families in poverty, partly because these groups have had much more time to make cultural and economic adjustments, and partly because the emphasis on family ties and achievement provides economic protection. That protection, however, may make family income look relatively high and thereby reduce official poverty rates, while it conceals significant numbers of individuals with low incomes.[11]

As in the regions and divisions, the poverty rates of Hispanic female-headed families in the states are affected by the distribution of Puerto Ricans, Cubans, and Mexicans. Thus, the highest rates are in Delaware, Massachusetts, Connecticut, and Pennsylvania, where Puerto Ricans are two-thirds or more of the Hispanic population. New York and New Jersey also have large Puerto Rican populations whose poverty rates are far above the national average for Hispanics. The lowest rates are in Nevada, Maryland, West Virginia, and the District of Columbia, all of whose Hispanic populations have high proportions of Mexicans, and in Florida, where Cubans are nearly two-thirds of the Hispanic total.

Even though Hispanics now have higher poverty rates than non-Hispanic whites in every state except Louisiana, Hispanics in the United States are generally better off than those in the countries of origin, and the opportunities to improve should produce a widespread reduction in poverty rates, at least in rising generations. The process may be slow, however, for although Puerto Rican migrants in the 1980s are better educated than those who came in the 1950s and 1960s and are more likely to settle in different areas, their employment status is not much better.[12]

In summary, while the poverty rates of female-headed families vary according to overall levels of poverty in the 50 states, the differences among the races are more striking than the differences among the states for any one race. Geographic variations are important, especially at the local level, and differential poverty is at least partly a state and community problem, but the more significant racial and ethnic variations are essentially a national problem. They show that even with many other characteristics held constant, some groups still suffer persistent racism and its attendant problems of low esteem, subordinate status, and the special disabilities imposed on minority populations.[13] These are structural matters which affect the whole society.

COUNTY COMPARISONS: THE POVERTY POCKETS

The state is still a large unit by which to study the geographic distribution of poverty, which differs from county to county and even among smaller groups. In fact, in some ways poverty is principally a local problem because of variable employment prospects and other conditions. The county is the most practical subdivision to use in pinpointing the areas of severe poverty and in emphasizing other geographic variations in proportions of poor families. Figure 3–1 shows the percentages of female-headed families below the poverty level in each of the nearly 3,100 counties. The map and some data not reflected on it enable several conclusions.

1. Every county except 26 (seven in South Dakota; four each in Montana, Nebraska, and Texas; three in North Dakota; two in Kansas; and one each in Missouri and Wyoming) has a higher poverty rate for female-headed than for other families, usually two or three times higher, but sometimes four to six times greater. In some cases the rates for all types of families are relatively high; in others the rates for female-headed families are far above those in other families; in a few the rates are low and similar. But apart from the 26 exceptional counties, woman-headed families everywhere are much more likely than other types to be poor.

2. Large parts of the South still suffer more than their fair share of poverty despite progress in the region as a whole, and the counties with large proportions of black female-headed families have abnormally high rates. Many are concentrated in the Mississippi Delta portions of Mississippi, Arkansas, and Louisiana, and in central and southern Mississippi, Alabama, and Georgia, while others blanket the eastern parts of South Carolina, North Carolina, and Virginia. Often they are in old plantation sections, where a small landowning elite and a large mass of landless agricultural laborers made up two-class systems, though a small middle class was sometimes present, as were numerous yeoman and tenant farmers.[14] In quite a few of these areas industries still provide too few jobs, and many which are available pay poorly. Organized labor also is generally weak in these places, and much of the income from agriculture is low.

3. The areas of coal mining and small farming in eastern Kentucky and western West Virginia also have high poverty rates, as do the southern parts of Oklahoma and Texas. The last two cases are influenced by recent Hispanic migrants, among whom the female-headed family is particularly common

Figure 3-1

Percent of Female-Headed Families below the Poverty Level in Counties, 1980

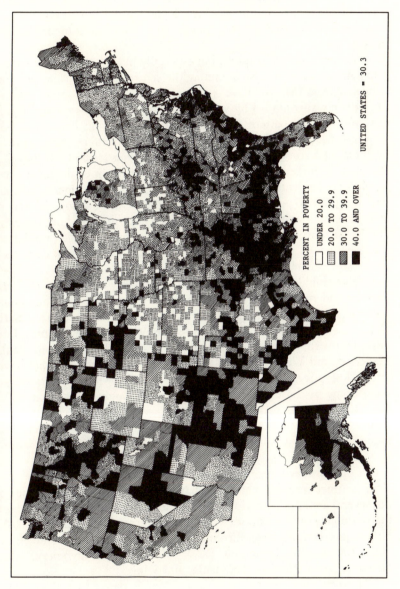

PERCENT IN POVERTY

	UNDER 20.0
	20.0 TO 29.9
	30.0 TO 39.9
	40.0 AND OVER

UNITED STATES = 30.3

because of the widespread consensual union in Latin America, where one in five households is estimated to have a female head.[15] Poverty pockets also appear in north Georgia, east and west Tennessee, west Florida and parts of that state's central ridge, and the Texas panhandle. In some of the states of the census South, such as Oklahoma and North Carolina, a few counties contain large percentages of poor native-American families headed by a woman.

4. Throughout the country, but especially in the older urban concentrations, numerous counties containing the central cities of Metropolitan Statistical Areas (MSAs) have relatively high poverty rates. Many are immediately surrounded by suburban counties with very low rates. Some examples of this pattern are the counties containing Baltimore, Boston, Chicago, Cleveland, Denver, Detroit, Gary, Milwaukee, New York, Philadelphia, and several New Jersey cities, including Jersey City, Passaic, and Paterson. In these and other cities at least 30 percent of the female-headed families are below the poverty level, but each city is contiguous to counties with less than 20 percent. Several cities with the most serious poverty problems have high unemployment rates which contribute to both poverty and family breakup, which are reciprocals. Some have sizable populations of the "new poor," including many homeless families living in cars, shelters, or the streets.

5. Some highly urbanized counties have poverty rates below the national average and roughly the same as those in contiguous suburban counties. Some examples are the counties which contain Albany (NY), Charlotte, Columbus (OH), Dallas, Des Moines, Fort Worth, Grand Rapids, Greensboro, Hartford, Houston, Minneapolis, Nashville, Pittsburgh, St. Paul, San Francisco, and Winston-Salem. Other heavily urbanized counties have relatively low poverty rates but border on counties with comparatively high ones. Some of those urbanized units contain Boise, Charleston (WV), El Paso, Las Vegas, Los Angeles and other coastal California cities from Santa Cruz southward to San Diego, Salt Lake City, Santa Fe, Tulsa, and the numerous cities on Florida's east coast from West Palm Beach southward to Miami.

6. Certain heavily urbanized counties have high poverty rates and are close to other counties which also have high rates. Many are in the South, but several are in other regions and divisions with higher poverty rates than the national norm. Counties with this pattern contain Albany (GA), Albuquerque, Baton Rouge, Birmingham, Charleston (SC), Fresno, Jacksonville, Kalamazoo, Lexington (KY), Memphis, Montgomery, Muncie, Newport News, Norfolk, Pensacola, and Selma.

7. Poverty rates in the most rural counties depend on several factors. Black people still living in the old plantation areas have already been mentioned, and while outmigration has greatly thinned their ranks, the high poverty rate among the female-headed families which remain affects some

patterns in Figure 3–1. But the problem also afflicts relatively large numbers of white families in many of those same areas, because rural rates, especially in small towns and villages, are higher than urban rates. In 1980, for example, 26 percent of the rural female-headed white families and 52 percent of the black ones were below the poverty level, compared with urban rates of 21 percent for whites and 46 percent for blacks.

Nor is rural poverty confined to the South, for the rates are relatively high in many rural counties of such states as Arizona, Idaho, Maine, Nevada, New Mexico, North Dakota, South Dakota, Utah, and Washington. Conversely, rates are relatively low in the rural areas of such Midwestern states as Illinois, Indiana, Iowa, Kansas, Minnesota, Nebraska, and Wisconsin. There the rural populations are largely white and middle-class, and the farmers among them grow grain crops, engage in dairying, or operate the corn-cattle-hog production complex. These enterprises produce a relatively high level of living, although poverty rates did rise in the mid–1980s because of the farm cost-debt-price crisis.

Female-headed families also have comparatively low poverty rates in a group of rural counties in the Piedmont sections of North Carolina and South Carolina and in the mountains of North Carolina, Virginia, and part of West Virginia. Some of these Appalachian and other rural counties have lost large proportions of young women (poor and nonpoor) seeking better economic opportunities in urban areas. Consequently, the poor migrants among them raise the poverty rates of the cities while they decrease the rates of their rural home counties. In addition, traditional family solidarity and emphasis on the husband as provider in some of these rural sections help keep rates of breakup relatively low, and this minimizes the percent of female-headed households, poor or not.[16] Pooling income also keeps some of these families above the poverty level.

8. The poverty rates in some counties, many of them rural, also are affected by their proportions of native Americans and Hispanics. For example, female-headed families in Lasalle County, Texas, have a 78 percent poverty rate, and 74 percent of its people are Hispanic, nearly all Mexican. In San Juan County, Utah, 51 percent of the female-headed families are poor and 45 percent of its people are native American.[17] These patterns are repeated elsewhere, such as the Texas counties just across the border from Mexico.

In summary, county data on the percentages of poor female-headed families show the nation's worst poverty pockets as well as its more fortunate sections. The variations are associated with race, ethnicity, discrimination, rural or urban residence, economic conditions of particular cities, and the nature of suburbs around central cities. The most frequent variations, however, result from local differences in the types of industries which predominate and the number and kinds of jobs they provide. While certain personal characteristics, such as low educational attainment, may contribute to pov-

Table 3–2
Percent of Female-Headed Families below the Poverty Level, by
Residence, 1980

Residence	Percent in Poverty			
	All Races	White	Black	Hispanic[a]
All residence forms	30.3	22.3	46.3	48.1
Urban	30.1	21.5	45.7	48.2
Rural	30.9	25.8	52.1	47.4
Farm	17.8	15.4	49.2	42.9
Nonfarm	31.5	26.4	52.2	88.5
Metropolitan	29.4	20.9	44.7	48.0
In central cities	35.3	23.7	46.4	52.4
Outside central cities	22.4	18.7	38.9	37.9
Nonmetropolitan	33.8	27.2	54.6	49.5

Source: U.S. Bureau of the Census, 1980 Census of Population, General Social and Economic Characteristics, United States Summary (Washington, DC: Government Printing Office, 1983), Tables 96, 108, 119, 129, 139, 149, 159.

[a]May be of any race.

erty, the occupational structure of local areas has a far more significant effect on the percentage of female householders below the poverty line. Therefore, if an area has ample well-paying jobs with security and good fringe benefits, the poverty rates are relatively low.

DISTRIBUTION OF POVERTY BY RESIDENCE

The differences in poverty rates by counties urge a closer look at variations between rural and urban residents, rural-farm and rural-nonfarm groups, metropolitan and nonmetropolitan populations, and central-city and suburban residents in MSAs.

Rural and Urban Differences

Rural female-headed families, both black and white, have somewhat higher poverty rates than do urban families, though the difference is not great. (See Table 3–2.) Within the overall rural category there is substantial variation between the poverty rates of farm and nonfarm female-headed families. Thus, about 18 percent of the rural-farm families but 32 percent of the rural-nonfarm units are poor. This seems inconsistent with the fact that 13 percent of *all* farm families and only 11 percent of *all* rural-nonfarm families are poor. Several factors account for the discrepancy.

1. The social norms which still prevail in the farm population, often reinforced by the dynamics of the patriarchal family, pressure young women not to form one-parent families in the first place, whether by divorce or birth out of wedlock.[18] This contrasts with the conglomeration of small towns, villages, sparsely settled nonmetropolitan areas, and other population segments which make up the heterogeneous rural-nonfarm population where behavioral constraints are more diverse and often less restrictive.

2. The farm population has a significant deficiency of young adult women (and men) because of outmigration.[19] In 1985 only 12 percent of the nation's female farm population was aged 20–29, compared with 18 percent in the nonfarm group. In fact, farm women appear with less frequency than nonfarm women in every age group from 20 to 40, and with greater frequency in all older ages except 75 and over.[20] Thus, the female farm population is older on the average than the urban and rural-nonfarm groups, and because young female householders are most susceptible to poverty, their relative scarcity on farms reduces poverty rates there. Many of the outmigrants are unencumbered single women seeking urban opportunities, but others divorce or give birth out of wedlock and then leave, because of either social pressure or limited opportunities. Others may move when either divorce or unmarried birth is imminent, partly because many farm areas provide inadequate welfare benefits for the female-headed family and outmigration is a logical response. In any case, a higher percentage of farm than nonfarm women can be found in married-couple families, and relatively few farm women are divorced.[21]

3. Owing largely to the age profile, farm female householders are much less likely than their nonfarm sisters to have charge of children under 6 and aged 6–17.[22] About 24 percent of the rural-nonfarm female householders have children under 6, compared with only 10 percent of the rural-farm women. The figures for those with children under 18 are 66 percent and 38 percent, respectively. Inasmuch as the presence of dependent children is directly correlated with poverty rates, their much smaller representation in female-headed farm families is associated with lower poverty rates.

4. Patterns of family structure and solidarity are such in many farm areas that a woman who becomes a family head with no husband present is absorbed into another family unit. This is especially likely for a widow. She then would not appear in the data on female-headed families and her chances of being poor because she was isolated would diminish. Poor or wealthy, she would not be reported separately as a householder. Even if a widow or other female householder is not taken into another family unit, she is more likely than her urban counterpart to live with an income-pro-

ducing male, especially an adult son. Whatever the reasons, the female-headed family with income provided solely by that head is less common in the farm population than in other groups, just as the nonfamily household is less common in the farm population.[23]

5. The gender balance tips toward men in the farm segment. In 1985, for all ages 15 and over, there were 108 males for each 100 females in the farm population, compared with 93 in the nonfarm group.[24] Therefore, a woman's statistical chance for marriage or remarriage is greater in the farm population, and to the extent women are more likely to be married, the proportion of female-headed families is reduced, especially among young and middle-aged women. That spares some women the risk of poverty as a householder.

6. Farm women who become widows and therefore householders often move to small towns and villages. To the degree the loss of a husband's earning power pushes a woman and her family into poverty, this migration represents the transfer of poverty from the farm population to the rural-nonfarm group, where underemployment is also relatively severe.[25] In other cases, a widow who has sole possession of a working farm after her husband's death may continue to operate it, perhaps with the help of an adult offspring, and she, as an official householder with no husband present, may have enough financial protection to stay above the poverty line.

7. Part of the recorded lower poverty rate of female-headed farm families in 1980 was the result of methods used to measure poverty. Prior to 1981, the official poverty threshold for farm families was lower than that for nonfarm units, on the assumption that farm families had gardens, livestock, and other subsistence commodities which justified using a smaller cash threshold to determine poverty status. Thus, a four-person, female-headed nonfarm family was labeled poor below $8,382 cash income, whereas a comparable farm family was designated poor below $7,152. That lower threshold reduced the number of female-headed farm families classified as poor. The farm-nonfarm distinction was dropped, partly because only about half the farm population is engaged principally in agriculture and only about 70 percent of all farm operators and managers actually live on farms.[26] For 1980 and earlier, however, the different poverty thresholds decreased the percentage of farm families below the poverty line and concealed some actual poverty problems. In addition, until 1981 the poverty threshold for a female householder was set lower than that for a male householder—another methodological maneuver which caused women's poverty rates to seem lower than they actually were.

8. Farm women aged 15–19 and 65 and over are more likely than nonfarm women to be in the labor force. Since those are the ages when the poverty risk is greatest, the higher rates of labor force participation produce some protections against poverty. In addition, the unemployment rates of farm women are about half those of the nation's total female labor force. Furthermore, in 1985 about 71 percent of the employed female farm labor

force worked in nonagricultural industries, principally the service industries, retail trade, and manufacturing.[27] While many of those jobs do not provide a high wage, the income is sufficient to protect some farm women against poverty, especially if combined with an income from farming.

9. The nation's largest farm population is located in the Midwest, where the types of farming generally provide middle-class status and greater protection against poverty than in the South, parts of New England, and some other sections. Consequently, both female-headed and other farm families are less likely to be poor in the Midwest than in other areas, and that region's relatively large farm population has considerable statistical influence on the nation's total farm group.

10. There is little difference in the poverty rates of rural-farm and rural-nonfarm black female householders. This contrasts sharply with the situation for whites, among whom the rate is considerably higher in the rural-nonfarm population. Therefore, poverty by residence is more uniformly distributed and much greater for black than for white women, and the relatively low overall rate of women's poverty in farm areas results from the advantages enjoyed by whites. Blacks are also such a small percentage of the farm population that their characteristics have little statistical influence on it. In 1985 they made up 12 percent of the nonfarm population but only 2 percent of the farm group, so the impact of their higher poverty rates is greatly diluted in the latter. Only about 120,000 blacks are left on farms, contrasted with over 5 million whites. Poverty among blacks is heavily concentrated in urban centers, basically because of the massive migration of blacks out of rural areas prior to 1970 or so. As a result, only 11 percent of all poor black female-headed families are in rural areas, compared with 23 percent of the white units. Among Hispanics the poverty problem is even more an urban one, for only 5 percent of all poor Hispanic female-headed families are rural.

None of these observations should obscure the higher overall poverty rate in the farm than in the rural-nonfarm population.[28] They simply demonstrate that poor women in farm areas are more likely than others to be the wives of poor men or to be living in other families which they do not head. The fact that they are less likely to be householders without a husband present is no guarantee they are less likely to be poor. Indeed, many local rural economies are seriously underdeveloped and poorly diversified, and they provide low wages and limited employment options which keep abnormally large proportions of families in poverty.[29] This is a major reason why poverty rates among female-headed rural-nonfarm families are so high.[30]

Metropolitan and Nonmetropolitan Differences

Table 3–2 shows that for blacks, whites, and Hispanics the poverty rates in the metropolitan population are lower than in the nonmetropolitan segment, though the difference among Hispanics is small. These variations correspond in part to the rural-urban differences already discussed, although "metropolitan" is not synonymous with "urban," nor does "nonmetropolitan" mean the same as "rural." On the contrary, many MSAs contain sizable rural populations, and there are many small cities in nonmetropolitan sections.

Within the metropolitan population as a whole and for blacks, whites, and Hispanics alike, the poverty rates of female-headed families are significantly lower in the areas outside central cities of MSAs than inside those cities, which have unusually high proportions of poor female-headed families. For example, 54 percent of all female-headed families in the nation but 65 percent of its poor ones live in the central cities of MSAs. Conversely, 38 percent of all female-headed families but only 29 percent of the poor ones live outside central cities. A large share of that population is suburban and has a higher median income than the central-city population, although there are many poor suburbanites as well, and the number of poor people in white suburban populations is growing especially rapidly.[31]

The concentration of women's poverty in central cities is greater for blacks than whites. About 66 percent of all black female-headed families live in central cities, as do 66 percent of those below the poverty level. Only 32 percent of all white female-headed families and 34 percent of the poor ones reside in those centers. Poor white families are more heavily represented than black ones in the suburbs of MSAs and in the smaller cities and towns in nonmetropolitan areas.

Hispanic female-headed families are more evenly dispersed among central cities, suburbs, and nonmetropolitan areas, mostly smaller cities. The central-city population, however, does have more than its fair share of poor Hispanic families. They are underrepresented in suburbs; the nonmetropolitan areas, except for rural sections, have about their proportional share. As noted earlier, the specific patterns of Hispanic poverty vary widely by the distribution of the Puerto Rican, Mexican, Cuban, and other contingents.

Extremes among the Cities

The nation's smaller cities, not the largest ones, have both the highest and lowest poverty rates among female-headed families, mainly because of their racial and ethnic composition, industrial base, occupational structure, proximity to large cities with their particular features, and other local characteristics. Thus, all ten cities with the highest poverty rates and all ten with the lowest rates have 25,000–85,000 people. Table 3–3 shows these poverty patterns in woman-headed families, along with some other social indicators. For comparison, it provides data for the United States as a whole.

Highest Poverty Rates. Many of the poorest cities are just outside large

Table 3–3

Selected Social Indicators for Cities with 25,000 or More Inhabitants and the Ten Highest and Ten Lowest Poverty Rates in Female-Headed Families, 1980

City and Rank	Percent in Poverty			Percent High School Graduates	Per Capita Income (Dollars)
	Female-Headed Families	All Families	Children Under 18		
United States	30.3	9.6	16.0	66.5	7,298
Highest poverty rates					
Prichard, AL	61.2	35.1	48.8	42.2	3,432
East St. Louis, IL	60.5	38.9	54.9	46.3	3,681
Camden, NJ	55.6	32.3	51.9	41.4	3,966
Del Rio, TX	54.7	26.4	40.8	47.7	4,324
Monroe, LA	53.4	23.8	42.3	59.0	5,817
West Memphis, AR	52.7	20.4	36.1	54.0	5,619
Fayetteville, NC	52.2	18.7	32.2	65.5	6,166
Fort Pierce, FL	51.4	20.8	41.4	52.5	5,592
Greenville, MS	51.3	25.6	40.2	50.6	4,663
North Charleston, SC	50.9	17.3	27.9	64.0	5,737
Lowest poverty rates					
Raytown, MO	4.1	1.7	1.9	79.1	9,221
Elk Grove, IL	4.5	1.2	1.4	84.3	9,729
Saratoga, CA	5.0	1.4	1.5	92.5	15,059
Overland Park, KS	5.4	2.1	2.7	91.1	10,623
Menomonee Falls, WI	5.5	0.9	1.3	78.8	9,097
Fair Lawn, NJ	6.2	2.9	4.2	74.6	10,019
Tamarac, FL	6.6	3.3	6.4	67.0	8,979
Allen Park, MI	7.0	1.8	2.1	71.9	10,163
Shaker Heights, OH	7.8	2.2	3.9	90.7	15,668
Merrillville, IN	9.2	2.5	3.1	72.3	9,130

Source: U.S. Bureau of the Census, County and City Data Book, 1983 (Washington, DC: Government Printing Office, 1983), Tables A, C.

urban centers, and in nearly every case they contain unusually high proportions of black people, ranging from 26 percent in North Charleston, South Carolina, to 96 percent in East St. Louis, Illinois. (The national average is 12 percent.) The one standout is Del Rio, Texas, which has very few blacks but whose proximity to the Mexican border has raised its Hispanic population to 70 percent of the total. Thus, the cities with the highest percentages of female-headed families in poverty all have heavy concentrations of minority groups with their relatively high poverty rates. In fact, some of the cities are places into which poorer minorities have been segregated because of economic status, traditional housing patterns, earlier avoidance behavior, and persistent racism.

The cities with high poverty rates for female-headed families also have rates for all families and for children under 18 which are two or three times the national average. Conversely, the percentages of high school and college graduates and average per capita income are well below national norms in nearly every case. Nine of the ten cities also have unemployment rates above the U.S. figure. In short, the problem of poverty in female-headed families is not isolated from the social milieu, but is simply one serious, integral symptom of a network of structural defects which exacerbate each other and force some of the nation's cities to confront multiple problems simultaneously. Moreover, in virtually every case female-headed families in the counties containing the ten cities also have poverty rates of 40 percent or more.

Lowest Poverty Rates. The ten cities with the lowest poverty levels in female-headed families represent the reverse of most conditions just described. Like the ones with high rates, however, they also are generally located near large metropolises, and many serve as affluent suburbs for those centers. For example, Elk Grove, Illinois, is close to Chicago; Menomonee Falls, Wisconsin, is near Milwaukee; Allen Park, Michigan, is just south of Detroit; and Shaker Heights, Ohio, is southeast of Cleveland. All of the low-poverty cities except Shaker Heights are at least 94 percent white, and while a quarter of the population of Shaker Heights is black, in no other case does any minority group make up more than 5 percent of the population.

These cities also have no more than 3 percent of all families and fewer than 7 percent of all children under 18 below the poverty level. The percentages of high school graduates are above the national norm except in Tamarac, Florida, with a relatively large population of elderly people whose average educational attainment is below the national figure. In every low-poverty city per capita income exceeds the national average by at least 23 percent, and it is at least 46 percent higher than in the high-poverty cities. Unemployment rates in the ten affluent cities are also well below the national average, except for Allen Park, Michigan, where unemployment patterns were affected by the economic problems suffered in the late 1970s and early 1980s by its large neighbor, Detroit.

These smaller cities with relatively minor poverty problems also are parts of large metropolitan networks, and most of them reflect the process of residential sorting by race and class—a process which keeps poverty rates low in some cities, high in others. In some cases the low-poverty cities are part of relatively affluent counties and MSAs. In others they are islands of affluence in counties and/or MSAs with serious poverty problems. Often the difference depends on the conditions in a nearby metropolis and the highly diverse cluster of "megacounties" in which it is enmeshed.

Large Urban Centers. A look at the cities with 500,000 or more inhabitants shows that most also have relatively high poverty rates and compare poorly with the national average on other social indicators. (See Table 3–

Table 3–4
Selected Social Indicators for Cities with 500,000 or More Inhabitants, 1980

City and Rank by Size of Population	Percent in Poverty			Percent High School Graduates	Per capita Income (Dollars)
	Female-Headed Families	All Families	Children Under 18		
United States	30.3	9.6	16.0	66.5	7,298
New York	41.0	17.2	31.8	60.2	7,271
Chicago	40.2	16.8	30.8	56.2	6,933
Los Angeles	29.4	13.0	23.7	68.6	8,408
Philadelphia	38.2	16.6	30.0	54.3	6,053
Houston	26.5	10.0	17.0	68.4	8,793
Detroit	41.0	18.9	31.5	54.2	6,215
Dallas	29.0	10.8	20.2	68.5	8,612
San Diego	27.3	9.2	16.6	78.9	8,016
Pittsburgh	32.0	11.9	24.3	61.1	6,845
Baltimore	39.8	18.9	32.5	48.4	5,877
San Antonio	39.6	16.9	28.9	58.6	5,671
Indianapolis	27.5	8.8	15.6	66.7	7,585
San Francisco	24.0	10.3	19.4	74.0	9,265
Memphis	42.1	17.1	31.6	63.3	6,466
Washington	28.5	15.1	27.0	67.1	8,960
San Jose	21.0	6.3	10.0	76.4	8,379
Milwaukee	34.5	11.2	22.5	63.6	7,028
Cleveland	43.7	18.8	31.3	50.9	5,770
Columbus	33.3	12.1	21.3	68.9	6,783
Boston	37.1	16.7	30.9	68.4	6,555
New Orleans	46.8	21.8	38.7	59.2	6,463
Jacksonville	38.3	12.9	22.2	66.2	6,767

Source: U.S. Bureau of the Census, County and City Data Book, 1983 (Washington, DC: Government Printing Office, 1983), Tables A, C.

4.) In 1980 there were 22 cities ("urban places") with at least a half million people, and 12 ranked worse than the national average on all of the selected social indictors. That is, they had above-average poverty rates for female-headed and other families and for children under 18; they had below-average percentages of high school and college graduates and per capita incomes. Those cities, in descending order of size, are New York, Chicago, Philadelphia, Detroit, Pittsburgh, Baltimore, San Antonio, Memphis, Milwaukee, Cleveland, New Orleans, and Jacksonville. Most were particularly hard hit by long-term changes in the country's industrial complex and by the recessions and related problems of the late 1970s and early 1980s.

Only two of the cities—Indianapolis and San Jose—ranked better than the national average on all five social indicators, although Los Angeles and San Diego did so on all but one. Houston, Dallas, and San Francisco ranked better on three of the five. There is also a wide range between the extremes on some of the indicators, reflecting broader variations among the cities. For example, New Orleans had the highest proportion (47 percent) of female-headed families in poverty, San Jose the lowest (21 percent). However, a low rank on one indicator usually accompanies a low rank on several others, which again shows that certain cities have complex constellations of severe problems. In this sense, high percentages of female-headed families in poverty are both a problem per se and a symptom of much more extensive difficulties, usually so interwoven that progress in solving one is difficult without a comprehensive attack on the others. The efforts to solve a problem—women's poverty in this case—are complicated by weak consensus about the nature, magnitude, and causes of the problem, and even by disagreement over whether it is a problem at all.[32] Consequently, women's poverty ranks differently on the priority lists of various cities and states. It also shifts periodically as an object of federal concern. Some cities are better able than others to grapple with the problem, and some have conditions which attract or generate relatively high proportions of poor female-headed families. Hence the variations in Table 3–4.

TRENDS IN FAMILY POVERTY

The poverty rates of all groups in American society fell significantly after 1959, but the fall was far greater for some groups than others and female-headed families lagged in this process. Figure 3–2 shows what happened between 1959 and 1986, although three methodological alterations affected the trend lines somewhat: (1) Prior to 1970 blacks were in the category "Negro and other races," and the apparent increase in their poverty rate in 1970 over 1969 reflects the change which separated blacks from Asians and other groups. (2) The Census Bureau refined the methodology for measuring poverty, especially in 1966, 1974, 1979, 1981, and 1983. Consequently, relatively minor changes in poverty rates around each of those years reflect the revisions along with actual changes in poverty. (3) The designations "head of household" and "head of family" were replaced in 1980 by the term "householder," and some families which might have been listed earlier as having a male head were shifted out of that category.[33] The refinement "female householder, no husband present" minimizes the impact of this change, however, because the residual category has a male present. This study is less concerned with who is "head" than with how the presence or absence of two earners, ordinarily receiving quite different incomes because of gender, affects poverty levels.

The designation "other" in Figure 3–2 refers to a combined group of married-couple and male-headed families. Some of the latter have no wife present, but they are a small minority and in 1985 over 95 percent of the "other" families were married-couple units.

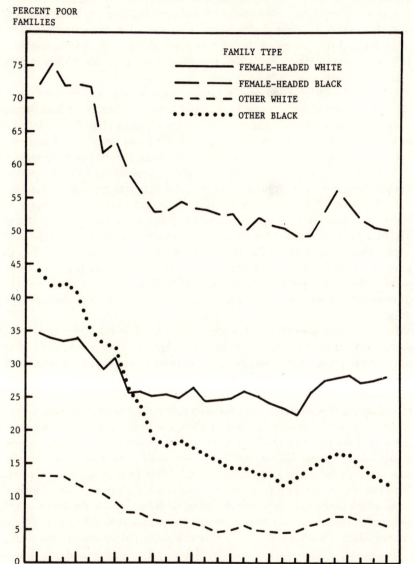

Female-Headed Families Improve Relatively Slowly

Three features stand out in the trend lines in Figure 3–2.

1. The poverty rates in families of all kinds declined sharply during most of the 1960s, changed relatively little between 1968 and 1978 or so, rose significantly in the recessionary late 1970s and early 1980s, and decreased at variable paces after 1983. White female-headed families were an exception after 1984, because their poverty rate rose. The increases after 1978 or so pushed the poverty rate for white female-headed families higher in 1983 than at any time since 1965. For black families it was higher in 1982 than in any year since 1966.

2. Over the 1959–86 period, female-headed families experienced slower rates of movement out of poverty than did other families, regardless of race. At the same time, the percentage of all persons living in female-headed units increased dramatically.[34] As a result, in 1959 a female-headed family was 2.4 times more likely than a married-couple family to be poor, whereas by 1986 the ratio had risen to 4.2. In 1959 about 26 percent of all poor persons lived in female-headed families, but in 1986 that was true of 48 percent.

3. Between 1959 and 1986 the black married-couple family made the fastest progress out of poverty, followed by the white married-couple unit. The black female-headed family improved much more slowly and the white female-headed unit made the slowest progress of all.[35] Black families did have the worst initial disadvantage, so their more rapid progress helped narrow the racial gap in poverty rates, though it remains substantial. The difference between black and white married-couple families decreased the most.

Despite some improvement women who head families are now much more likely than male heads to be poor than they were when all of the poverty rates were substantially above current levels, and even with major changes in the economy since the mid–1960s, the poverty rate for female-headed families has remained all too stable.[36] This situation reflects the feminization of poverty and results from substantial increases in the number and proportion of female-headed families, the larger percentage of persons living in those families, the large income drop a woman usually incurs when a male wage earner leaves the family, the poor record of men's financial assistance to ex-wives and children, and other factors already discussed. No-fault divorce plays a particularly insidious role, because when property is divided evenly and the man has been receiving either the larger or the only wage, his economic situation usually improves as he relinquishes family support duties, while conditions for his wife and children usually deteriorate. This is especially true when a division of family assets substitutes for alimony payments to the wife, because the "community property" of most couples who divorce has modest value compared to an ongoing wage. It represents

Table 3–5

Ratio of Poverty Rates in Female-Headed Families to Those in Other Families, by Race and Hispanic Origin, Selected Years, 1959–1985

Year	Ratio		
	White	Black	Hispanic[a]
1959	2.62	1.63	b
1960	2.62	1.79	b
1965	3.37	1.97	b
1970	4.03	2.97	b
1975	4.71	3.53	3.03
1980	4.59	3.45	3.33
1981	4.49	3.39	3.45
1982	3.99	3.43	2.93
1983	4.04	3.32	2.96
1984	4.23	3.52	3.20
1985	4.35	3.83	3.11

Source: U.S. Bureau of the Census, Current Population Reports, Series P-60, various issues (Washington, DC: Government Printing Office).

[a]May be of any race

[b]Data not available.

a one-time disbursement to each party, and the wife's share rarely provides an adequate continuing income.[37]

Table 3–5 shows the degree to which differential declines in family poverty rates have eroded the relative position of the average female-headed unit. Using selected years, the table presents the ratio between poverty rates in female-headed families and those in other families. If the rates of the two types of families were the same in a given year, the index would be 1.00, so a higher figure represents the degree to which poverty rates for female heads exceed those for male heads. The data are for white, black, and, beginning with 1975, Hispanic families.

While all race and gender groups have lower poverty rates now than in 1959 (1975 for Hispanics), the situation of black, white, and Hispanic female-headed families has gotten worse relative to other family types. In 1959 the poverty rate for white female-headed families was 2.6 times that of other family types, but by 1985 the ratio was 4.4. In the black population the ratio rose from 1.6 to 3.8. It is important to note, however, that the ratios for whites were even higher in 1975 and 1980 than in 1985, as they were for Hispanics in 1980 and 1981, so women in those groups have made a certain amount of progress recently. Among blacks the ratio was higher in 1985 than at any prior time, so the position of the black woman-headed family has consistently eroded by this particular comparison.

The gender discrepancies of the 1980s reveal pervasive and continuing neglect of the plight of women attempting to manage families by themselves. To deal with that problem, existing programs need to be revised and new ones created to move many more female-headed families out of poverty and prevent the slide of others into it. One such effort is fair alimony and child-support payments to prevent the plunge of many women and children toward the poverty line while ex-husbands experience little financial hurt. For the older divorced woman, who may be unemployable or unable to enter the labor force at a decent wage, redistribution of the ex-husband's income should probably be long term. For the younger woman with small children, redistribution should help her provide adequately for her family and acquire skills to enter and move up in the work force, and it should help finance suitable day care for the children. If we are to have no-fault divorce, it should not impose substantial disadvantages on the wife and require no sacrifice by the husband. In most cases she has contributed to the family's resources, including the husband's earning power, and she should share equitably in the returns.

In addition, cuts in benefits to the poor, beginning largely with the 1981–82 budget and tax reductions and the 1981 Omnibus Budget Reconciliation Act to reform welfare, need to be reexamined and altered where necessary. For example, the food stamp program was reduced heavily and benefits were ended for nearly 1 million recipients and reduced for all others. AFDC payments and Medicaid stopped for 500,000 low-income working families when the AFDC guidelines were tightened in 1981. Low-income housing rents have risen so that shelter represents a growing percentage of income. The Comprehensive Employment and Training Act (CETA) was terminated in 1983 and about 500,000 public-sector jobs disappeared with it. Some were replaced by private-sector positions, but overall job-training programs for low-income and unskilled people were reduced by two-fifths. The Work Incentive Program to help welfare mothers get private-sector jobs was also cut by a third, even though many welfare mothers want work and could get it with some assistance. In all, from 1982 to 1985 about $57 billion got cut from programs which mainly help the poor. The effects of these cuts fall disproportionately on women and children. Perhaps new programs to foster self-sufficiency and diminish welfare dependency will result in better, more workable and well-funded programs to accomplish those goals, but at this writing the plight of many poor is growing worse, not better. Chapter 6 looks at some additional ways in which public efforts can reverse that trend.[38]

There is more to the story than government funding cuts, which may play a smaller part than other factors in poverty rate increases. The number of poor has grown significantly because huge job losses and other economic problems created recessions after the mid–1970s. Consequently, there are too few jobs for the poor, and many which do exist pay poverty-level wages. Many new jobs are at the lower end of the wage and status scale in the service industries, and while there are good ones too, most are inaccessible to those poor people who lack appropriate skills. Government can help provide people with the skills to compete for the better alternatives. Over the long run, such expenditures make for a more productive population and reduce the proportion on welfare, although it, including AFDC, should be strengthened for people who are unemployable for various reasons.

More broadly, efforts to reduce inequality call for major changes in social structures and human relations. Given their weak economic and political position, the poor are often subject to subtle and even blatant coercion of various kinds. In addition, many employers, social workers, and other members of higher socioeconomic classes expect the poor to behave according to certain stereotypes, and social interaction, especially power relationships, may create behavior which conforms to the stereotypes and has predictable outcomes. Society may even manipulate the allocation of jobs and status to guarantee a supply of cheap workers when they are needed, but who become the unemployed poor when they are not. Conversely, reducing inequality would make poor workers a scarce commodity. People could not be hired and fired at will, because their scarcity would give them more bargaining power and make them more competitive with middle-class workers. The latter and employers who would be forced to pay higher wages both have vested interests in keeping the poor available but low on the status scale. The indoctrination process also perpetuates these relationships, ensures that the powerless acquiesce to the powerful, and retards the development of solidarity among the poor. These constraints on the poor are often reflected in the argument which attributes poverty to character flaws and blames the poor for being poor.[39]

Changing Effects of Labor-Market Conditions

Though the focus of this book is the poverty status of women and children, that condition exists in a broader context and is related to other trends. In particular, the poverty rate of children has risen for reasons besides the increased proportion living in female-headed families. That situation would not explain the rise in poverty of persons under 18 living in married-couple families, from a low of 7.6 percent in 1973 to a peak of 13.5 percent in 1983. Richard Easterlin suggests that the increase among this group, especially children under 6, and growth in the percentage of female-headed families resulted from "the trend in labor market conditions by age."[40] That is, the poverty rates of young children rose because their young-adult parents suffered higher unemployment rates and greater decreases in real income than older adults.[41] In addition, as labor-market and income conditions deteriorated in the late 1970s and the early 1980s, they increased marital strains in young families with young children and raised the divorce and separation rates. That process increased the proportion of female-headed families vulnerable to poverty. Fewer unmarried couples who conceived were financially able to marry, and another group of young women and children was added to the category of female-headed families. Thus, adverse labor-market conditions increased unemployment, decreased real income, caused higher rates of marital breakup, and raised the illegitimacy rate. The net result was higher poverty rates among young families and children, whether married-couple or female-headed units.[42]

Why the deterioration in labor-market conditions, especially after the late 1960s? Easterlin offers two reasons: First, the growth of aggregate demand for products and services decreased and resulted in higher unemployment rates, especially among vulnerable young workers. Second, the supply of young workers increased as the baby boom moved into adulthood.[43] Some became a substantial "surplus" for whom there were too few good jobs— or no jobs at all—and they encountered the stress of unemployment or settled for low-wage, low-status positions. Entry-age workers also tend to be less productive than experienced workers, and the stagnant productivity which resulted also worsened poverty. Given the low birth rates of the 1970s and 1980s, however, the relative supply of young workers will decline in the 1990s and that should ease job competition and reduce unemployment rates, provided the demand for goods, services, and the workers to produce them does not slip and young workers can compete successfully with older ones. Easterlin believes demand is not likely to fall, because with a decrease in the proportion of young workers the unemployment rate can drop without escalating wages and prices into a new inflationary spiral. Therefore, policies to increase aggregate demand could provide employment for a larger share of young workers and decrease their poverty rates.[44]

On the other hand, because poverty rates among householders of both sexes and their children are an integral part of how the entire social system is organized, those rates will recede only if the structure and its internal dynamics are changed deliberately.[45] It is currently unclear that such deliberate changes will be made or even attempted in the foreseeable future. Other changes, such as an increased number of retiring older workers, an even higher percentage of female-headed families, and the aging of the population, are virtually inevitable. Future poverty rates will be affected by those and other dynamics, and because of these forces the rates could either fail to drop or actually increase toward 2000.[46]

NOTES

1. Martha S. Hill, "The Changing Nature of Poverty," in Yeheskel Hasenfeld and Mayer N. Zald, eds., "The Welfare State in America: Trends and Prospects,"

Annals of the American Academy of Political and Social Science 479 (May 1985), p. 37.

2. William P. O'Hare, "Poverty in America: Trends and New Patterns," *Population Bulletin* 40:3 (Washington, DC: Population Reference Bureau, 1985), p. 15.

3. John Reid, "Black America in the 1980s," *Population Bulletin* 37:4 (Washington, DC: Population Reference Bureau, 1982), pp. 30–31.

4. Ibid, pp. 30, 31–32.

5. William J. Wilson, "The Black Community in the 1980s: Questions of Race, Class, and Public Policy," in Norman R. Yetman, ed., *Majority and Minority* (Boston, MA: Allyn and Bacon, 1985), p. 497.

6. Denys Vaughn-Cooke, "The Economic Status of Black America: Is There a Recovery?" in James D. Williams, ed., *The State of Black America, 1984* (New Brunswick, NJ: Transaction Books, 1984), p. 13.

7. Michael E. Dorris, "The Grass Still Grows, the Rivers Still Flow: Contemporary Native Americans," *Daedalus* 110:2 (Spring 1981), p. 63.

8. Cary Davis, Carl Haub, and JoAnne Willette, "U.S. Hispanics: Changing the Face of America," *Population Bulletin* 38:3 (Washington, DC: Population Reference Bureau, 1983), p. 36. See also Dennis M. Roth, "Hispanics in the U.S. Labor Force: A Brief Examination," in Congressional Research Service, *Hispanic Population of the United States: An Overview* (Washington, DC: Government Printing Office, 1983), pp. 69, 72.

9. Davis, Haub, and Willette, "U.S. Hispanics," p. 37.

10. Jacqueline Desbarats, "Ethnic Differences in Adaptation: Sino-Vietnamese Refugees in the United States," in Dennis Gallagher, ed., "Refugees: Issues and Directions," *International Migration Review* 20:2 (Summer 1986), p. 406.

11. Harry H. L. Kitano, *Race Relations* (Englewood Cliffs, NJ: Prentice-Hall, 1985), p. 226.

12. Vilma Ortiz, "Changes in the Characteristics of Puerto Rican Migrants from 1950 to 1980," *International Migration Review*, 20:3 (Fall 1986), p. 625.

13. Rudolph Gomez, "Introduction," in Rudolph Gomez, Clement Cottingham, Jr., Russell Endo, and Kathleen Jackson, eds., *The Social Reality of Ethnic America* (Lexington, MA: D.C. Heath, 1974), p. x.

14. For a discussion of early agrarian class systems, see T. Lynn Smith and Paul E. Zopf, Jr., *Principles of Inductive Rural Sociology* (Philadelphia, PA: F. A. Davis, 1970), pp. 267–278. See also Frederick A. Bode and Donald E. Ginter, *Farm Tenancy and the Census in Antebellum Georgia* (Athens, GA: University of Georgia Press, 1986).

15. Thomas W. Merrick, "Population Pressures in Latin America," *Population Bulletin* 41:3 (Washington, DC: Population Reference Bureau, 1986), pp. 20, 21.

16. William E. Philliber, "Wife's Absence from the Labor Force and Low Income among Appalachian Migrants," *Rural Sociology* 47:4 (Winter 1982), pp. 708–709.

17. For a study of the historical antecedents of poverty among three Indian groups, see Richard White, *The Roots of Dependency: Subsistence, Environment, and Social Change among The Choctaws, Pawnees, and Navajos* (Lincoln, NE: University of Nebraska Press, 1983).

18. John Hagan, John Simpson, and A. R. Gillis, "Class in the Household: A Power-Control Theory of Gender and Delinquency," *American Journal of Sociology* 92:4 (January 1987), pp. 788, 812–813.

19. U.S. Bureau of the Census, "Population Profile of the United States: 1984–85," *Current Population Reports,* Series P–23, No. 150 (Washington, DC: Government Printing Office, 1987), p. 16.

20. Ibid, pp. 16–17.

21. Ibid, p. 17.

22. Rachel Ann Rosenfeld, *Farm Women: Work, Farm, and Family in the United States* (Chapel Hill, NC: University of North Carolina Press, 1985), p. 49.

23. U.S. Bureau of the Census, "Population Profile of the United States: 1984–85," p. 17.

24. U.S. Bureau of the Census, "Farm Population of the United States: 1985," *Current Population Reports,* Series P–27, No. 59 (Washington, DC: Government Printing Office, 1986), Table 4.

25. Daniel T. Lichter and Janice A. Costanzo, "Nonmetropolitan Underemployment and Labor-Force Composition," *Rural Sociology* 52:3 (Fall 1987), p. 329.

26. U.S. Bureau of the Census, "Farm Population of the United States: 1985," p. 2.

27. U.S. Bureau of the Census, "Population Profile of the United States: 1984–85," p. 17.

28. Ibid.

29. Southeast Women's Employment Coalition, *Women of the Rural South: Economic Status and Prospects* (Lexington, KY: Southeast Women's Employment Coalition, 1986), p. 17.

30. For a 10-year anthropological investigation of the economic conditions in the households of one rural-nonfarm hamlet, see Janet M. Fitchen, *Poverty in Rural America: A Case Study* (Boulder, CO: Westview Press, 1981).

31. William P. O'Hare, "The Eight Myths of Poverty," in Leroy W. Barnes, ed., *Social Problems 87/88* (Guilford, CT: Dushkin, 1987), p. 122.

32. Paul B. Horton, Gerald R. Leslie, and Richard F. Larson, *The Sociology of Social Problems,* 9th ed. (Englewood Cliffs, NJ: Prentice-Hall, 1988), p. 3.

33. For the procedure now used to identify the householder, see U.S. Bureau of the Census, "Money Income of Households, Families, and Persons in the United States: 1985," *Current Population Reports,* Series P–60, No. 156 (Washington, DC: Government Printing Office, 1987), p. 168.

34. Hill, "The Changing Nature of Poverty," p. 38.

35. James P. Smith and Finis R. Welch, *Closing the Gap: Forty Years of Economic Progress for Blacks* (Santa Monica, CA: Rand Corporation, 1986), pp. 104–106.

36. U.S. Bureau of the Census, Cynthia M. Taeuber and Victor Valdisera, "Women in the American Economy," *Current Population Reports,* Series P–23, No. 146 (Washington, DC: Government Printing Office, 1986), p. 38.

37. For a comprehensive analysis of this matter, see Lenore J. Weitzman, *The Divorce Revolution: The Unexpected Consequences for Women and Children in America* (New York: Free Press, 1985).

38. Parts of this paragraph are adapted from O'Hare, "Poverty in America," pp. 35–36.

39. Several of the foregoing points are adapted from Murray Milner, Jr., "Theories of Inequality: An Overview and a Strategy for Synthesis," *Social Forces* 65:4 (June 1987), pp. 1063–1068. One influential work emphasizing poverty as a result of constraints in the social system is Michael Harrington, *The Other America* (New

York: Macmillan, 1962). See also his later *The New American Poverty* (New York: Holt, Rinehart & Winston, 1984).

40. Richard A. Easterlin, "The New Age Structure of Poverty in America: Permanent or Transient?" *Population and Development Review* 13:2 (June 1987), p. 198.

41. Ibid, p. 199.

42. Ibid, pp. 200–201.

43. Ibid, p. 202.

44. Ibid, pp. 204–205.

45. O'Hare, "Poverty in America," pp. 37–39.

46. Hill, "The Changing Nature of Poverty," p. 46.

4

Persons in Poverty

The analysis of family poverty provides only a partial impression of how individuals fare in the struggle to get along financially. "The family" also changes in many ways over its life cycle, as individuals leave and enter, economic fortunes deteriorate and improve, and the members rise above or fall below the poverty level at any given time.[1] Those changes make the family a complex and sometimes difficult unit for anlaysis, so the data on *persons in poverty* can be used to add to the portrait of America's poor female and child populations. Some parts of the analysis of poverty, such as the situation of poor children, do require reference to family types. But other aspects, such as the educational levels and work experience of women, can be examined outside the family context. Therefore, this chapter focuses on persons, though often as members of certain types of families.

Three basic conditions influence the poverty status of women as individuals: (1) A larger number of women than ever must rely entirely on their own incomes, mostly from earnings with *some* public assistance and other sources in *some* cases. (2) Many of the new jobs available to women, largely in the service industries, provide only limited opportunities to escape poverty.[2] (3) Most of the poor are in that situation only temporarily, though women are more likely than men to be among the significant minority of persistently poor.[3]

FEMALE-MALE VARIATIONS

As in the case of family householders, individual females have higher poverty rates than males no matter what their age or race. (See Table 4–1.) But for persons the gap is not nearly as wide at most ages as it is when types of family heads are compared. Nor are the rates for individual females

Table 4–1

Percent of Persons below the Poverty Level, by Gender, Age, Race, and Hispanic Origin, 1985

Gender and Age	Percent in Poverty			
	All Races	White	Black	Hispanic[a]
Female				
All ages	15.6	12.6	34.8	30.6
Under 15	21.9	17.2	45.6	39.4
15–17	17.1	13.1	36.3	40.1
18–21	19.3	16.6	34.3	32.0
22–24	18.2	15.2	37.1	27.1
25–34	14.2	11.2	32.4	28.4
35–44	11.1	9.1	24.9	23.8
45–54	9.7	7.6	24.7	17.8
55–59	11.5	9.5	28.5	18.6
60–64	12.3	10.6	29.4	24.2
65 and over	15.6	13.8	34.8	27.4
Male				
All ages	12.3	10.1	27.4	27.4
Under 15	21.0	16.5	44.2	41.5
15–17	17.1	13.2	37.9	38.3
18–21	14.9	12.4	30.1	28.6
22–24	13.0	11.8	20.9	23.8
25–34	8.5	7.6	12.8	19.0
35–44	8.2	7.1	16.4	18.1
45–54	7.1	6.4	12.1	12.6
55–59	8.0	6.9	18.6	11.3
60–64	10.0	8.5	25.6	21.5
65 and over	8.5	6.9	26.6	19.1

Source: U.S. Bureau of the Census, "Poverty in the United States: 1985," Current Population Reports, Series P-60, No. 158 (Washington, DC: Government Printing Office, 1987), Table 7.

[a]May be of any race.

as high as those for female householders. For example, in 1985 the poverty rate for female householders under age 25 was 74 percent, compared with 15 percent for married-couple families with a male head that age. But for individual females under 25, the poverty rate was 20 percent, compared with 18 percent for males. In fact, in all age groups under 65, the poverty rates of female-headed families are several times those of married-couple units, whereas for persons the gender discrepancies are not nearly as great. They are still important enough, however, to examine carefully, using controls for age and other characteristics.

POOR WOMEN ACROSS THE AGE SPECTRUM

Poor persons of both sexes are disproportionately concentrated at the lower end of the age scale. Among females the highest rate is for those under 15, because so many are members of poverty-stricken families, while some are on their own to cope with oppressive socioeconomic conditions. Both groups under 15 produce only negligible income. (See Table 4–1.) The poverty rate drops for those aged 15–17, because more women in these ages do earn some income, although most are still in families, poor though many of those units may be.

The poverty rate then rises for females aged 18–21, though conspicuously not for males. The women are now more likely to be on their own, some as householders with one or more young children. Sizable numbers have not completed college or even high school and are either unemployed, working at jobs with low earnings, or dependent on public assistance. But problems in the socioeconomic system, such as segregation in employment and gender discrimination, overshadow personal attributes as causes of poverty. In 1985, for example, year-round, full-time female workers at all ages had much smaller median incomes than males, even with educational attainment and type of job held constant. The gender discrepancy is even greater when all persons rather than just year-round, full-time workers are compared, because women are more likely to work part time or part year, to hold low-paying jobs regardless of weeks and hours worked, to be first fired during recessions, and not to work for wages at all. Compared with men, they are still the more exploited and expendable segment of the labor force.

The decline in poverty rates with age lasts until about 55 for women, after which the rates rise. By age 65 and over the poverty index is back to that for women in their mid–20s. It also rises for men after 55, but more slowly than for women, and among males 65 and over it even falls slightly below that in the ages 60–64. Women experience no such drop, and in the older ages their poverty rate is over 80 percent higher than that of men. The difference results largely from the substantial advantage in retirement benefits which older men enjoy and their much lesser tendency to be widowers and alone.

At any age several life events can impel women toward poverty. Becoming divorced or widowed or a single mother provides particular impetus, but other events are also instrumental. For instance, women are more susceptible than men to unemployment in the manufacturing industries where their wages typically have been fairly high. They are also more apt to leave jobs because of homemaking responsibilities, including childbearing and childrearing and caring for infirm elders, and to exit and reenter the labor force periodically. They are particularly likely to have to settle for part-time and/or low-wage jobs which men would not take.[4]

Table 4-2
Median Age of the Poor and Total Populations, by Gender, Race, and Hispanic Origin, 1985

Population Type and Gender	Median Age (Years)			
	All Races	White	Black	Hispanic[a]
Poor population				
Female	26.3	27.9	23.6	20.2
Male	20.0	22.2	15.5	16.3
Total population				
Female	32.7	33.5	28.2	25.6
Male	30.7	31.5	25.5	24.5

Source: U.S. Bureau of the Census, "Poverty in the United States: 1985," Current Population Reports, Series P-60, No. 158 (Washington, DC: Government Printing Office, 1987), Table 7.

[a]May be of any race.

Poor Young Women

Despite the relatively high poverty rates among elderly women and the problems they face, the poverty population is significantly younger on the average than is the nonpoor group. Two comparisons illustrate the situation.

First, Table 4-2 shows the median age of the poverty population and the total population in 1985, cross-classified by gender and race and Hispanic origin. The female population in poverty has a median age 6.7 years below that of the total female population because of the relatively large proportion of girls and young women in the poverty group. The difference for males— 10.5 years—is even greater, because boys and young men outnumber girls and young women, although this statistical relationship reverses in the early 20s because of differential mortality and produces a growing "surplus" of women as age increases. Regardless of that pattern, however, the relative youthfulness of the poverty population stands out, because 39 percent of the entire poor population is under age 18, compared with only 27 percent of the nonpoor group. By gender, 32 percent of the poor female population is under 18, contrasted with 23 percent of the nonpoor females; 42 percent of the poor males and 24 percent of the nonpoor males are below that age. Part of this young poverty population consists of teenagers who have left the parental home and who have a much lower median income than persons who remain in the home, while they also often have much higher expenses than they would have had in the family. Many are the products of family

Figure 4–1
**Age-Sex Pyramids Comparing the Poor and Nonpoor Populations, by
Gender, 1985**

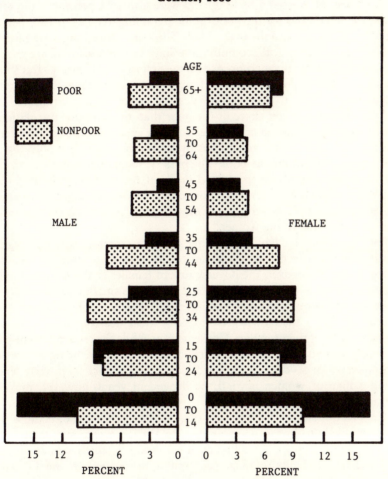

breakup, so changes in family composition have a profound impact not
only on family economic status, but on that of persons as well.[5] Other poor
teenagers, of course, are still dependents living in poor families.

Second, a comparison of the age-sex pyramids for the poor and nonpoor
populations also reflects the disproportionate concentration of poor persons
in the younger ages. (See Figure 4–1.) The pyramid is constructed as follows:
The population below the poverty level—males and females of all ages—is
used as the total (100 percent). Then, the females in each specific age group
are computed as a percentage of the numerical total; the males in each
specific age group are calculated as a percentage of the same total. For

example, in 1985 the total poverty population was 33,064,000. Females aged 0–14 numbered 5,547,000 and were 16.8 percent of the total; males in those ages numbered 5,563,000 and were also 16.8 percent of the total. Thus, the lowest bar for the poor on the pyramid stretches to 16.8 percent on both the female and the male sides.[6] The same procedure is used for the nonpoor population. After computations have been made for all age groups, the second pyramid is superimposed on the first to yield Figure 4–1. It shows the ages in which poor females and males are overrepresented and underrepresented relative to nonpoor females and males.[7]

A substantially larger share of the poor than the nonpoor population is under 15 years of age, gender aside. Females aged 15–24 also are overrepresented in the poverty group, but by those ages males are only slightly overrepresented among the poor. The bars symbolizing the poor show that they are generally underrepresented in all of the ages past the mid–20s, except for women 65 and over. Those older persons are slightly overrepresented as part of the poverty population, though to a much smaller extent than children and young women.

Both measures (median age and the age-sex pyramid) show how significantly poverty affects the young, especially dependent children but also young adults. Moreover, the poverty rate of females is above that of males at every age, even under 15. The difference then is small, however, because these are still largely dependent children and whether or not they are poor depends little on their own gender and a great deal on the income and poverty status of their families. Consequently, while the tendency to be poor is greatly increased by living in a female-headed family, being a boy or a girl under 15 or so does not in itself have much impact on poverty levels. Being a man or women beyond the dependent years, however, makes a considerable difference.

The greatest risk of poverty is among children under age 6, because they are most likely to live in poor families. In 1985, for example, the poverty rate for children under 6 in all types of families collectively was 26 percent. The rate fell gradually to 15 percent among those aged 16 and 17, partly because their chances of being in nonpoor families were greater, and partly because they had reached the ages at which they themselves might produce some earnings, although the routine, low-paying jobs which teenagers tend to get are no guarantee against poverty and may even use up much of the time they need to explore, experience, contemplate, learn, and mature.[8]

But whether or not teenagers bring in some income, the most crucial factor affecting their tendency to be poor is whether the family has a female head with no husband present or has both parents (or a male head) present. The same is true for children of all ages.[9] This is demonstrated by the data in Table 4–3, which shows the poverty rates of children under 18 according to several age categories and the two principal types of family structure.

Table 4–3
Poverty Rate of Children under 18, by Family Type, Age, Race, and Hispanic Origin, 1985

Children by Family Type and Age	Percent in Poverty			
	All Races	White	Black	Hispanic[a]
Female-headed families[b]				
Ages 0–18	53.6	45.2	66.9	72.4
Under 3	70.0	63.7	77.2	80.1
3–5	62.2	54.7	73.5	76.8
6–13	53.5	45.3	66.9	73.8
14 and 15	41.8	33.3	58.0	60.5
16 and 17	37.3	29.0	51.7	61.9
Other families				
Ages 0–18	11.7	10.4	18.8	27.4
Under 3	13.3	12.2	20.4	28.7
3–5	13.4	12.5	18.7	30.4
6–13	11.5	10.1	19.1	26.8
14 and 15	9.7	8.7	15.5	24.9
16 and 17	8.8	7.1	19.0	23.8

Source: U.S. Bureau of the Census, "Poverty in the United States: 1985," Current Population Reports, Series P-60, No. 158 (Washington, DC: Government Printing Office, 1987), Table 7.

[a]May be of any race.

[b]No husband present.

Poor Elderly Women

The elderly poor are something of a special category, because their poverty rates have fallen more dramatically than those of most other age groups, and because the elderly who remain poor have some unique problems. Most important, about a third of all persistently poor persons are elderly, so older people are greatly overrepresented in the group whose escape from poverty has proven virtually impossible.[10] To account for the situation of poor elderly women, this section briefly compares some of their circumstances with those of elderly men and poor women of other ages, especially the young.[11]

Women aged 65 and over are more likely to be poor than those in any other age group above 24, though women under 24 are considerably worse off than the elderly. (See Table 4–1.) On the average and despite many individual exceptions, older women are much more likely than very young women to benefit from governmental programs which raise their incomes, such as Social Security, cost-of-living increases in those benefits, Medicare and Medicaid, and Supplemental Security Income (SSI). The programs for young women are fewer, less generous, and more stigmatized, and young women were more subject to funding cutbacks in the 1980s. In addition, labor-market conditions for women in the family-forming ages deteriorated in recent recessions, so they and their children are especially beset by poverty.[12] Elderly women do not usually form families, though some may remarry and many care for grandchildren and very elderly relatives. Nor is a recession likely to have as much impact on them as on younger women. Inflation is usually the greater enemy of the elderly.

Despite certain advantages in the older years, however, the poverty indexes of women begin to rise in the mid–50s, when the rates are about 30 percent higher than those of men, and they keep rising into the later years, when they are more than 70 percent higher than those of men. In fact, after 55 the rise for women continues uninterrupted, whereas for men there is very little change, partly because men are more likely than women to get attractive jobs after they retire from original ones, especially if they retire relatively young (e.g., career military personnel).[13] Men also enjoy much wider private pension coverage and more generous average benefits, though they do suffer an average drop in income by a third or more when they retire. Even so, far smaller percentages of men than women plunge into poverty as a result of the financial conditions which accompany aging. For women, becoming widowed is one of the most crucial conditions.

In order to make the comparisons clearer, more refined age categories than "65 and over" are necessary. Table 4–4 provides those refinements, not just for people past 64, but beginning with those aged 60. Their poverty rate is already rising because some workers 60–64 have to retire as a result of disability or work force reductions, and their average private pensions, if any, are lower than those of persons who work until age 65. So are the Social Security benefits of people 62–64, who also are not eligible for Medicare until they reach 65. These and other factors help explain why the poverty rates of both men and women are higher in their early 60s than they are between 65 and 71, when full Social Security benefits, Medicare, and other advantages are available and retirement is less likely to result involuntarily from disability or work force reductions.

In the group 72 and over the poverty rates for both sexes jump significantly, though the relative disadvantage of women persists. Thus, the nation's oldest women have poverty rates roughly the same as those of women aged 15–17, though the elderly do fare better than persons in the ages under 15 and 18–21. On balance, while elderly women have made important progress out of poverty since the early 1960s and are no longer the nation's poorest group, their average position is well below those of women in most other age categories and of elderly men. In 1985 this translated into 2.5

Table 4–4
Percent of Persons Aged 60 and Over below the Poverty Level, by
Family Status, Age, and Gender, 1985

Family Status and Age	Percent in Poverty		
	Both Sexes	Female	Male
All family statuses			
Ages 60 and over	12.3	14.7	9.0
60 and 61	10.9	12.0	9.6
62–64	11.5	12.5	10.4
65–71	10.2	12.4	7.5
72 and over	14.8	18.0	9.5
Living in families			
Ages 60 and over	6.9	7.2	6.6
60 and 61	8.0	8.1	7.8
62–64	8.0	7.6	8.4
65–71	6.1	6.5	5.7
72 and over	6.7	7.2	6.2
Living alone			
Ages 60 and over	25.1	26.8	18.7
60 and 61	23.4	25.7	16.9
62–64	24.8	27.7	17.3
65–71	22.5	24.0	17.7
72 and over	26.7	28.2	20.1

Source: U.S. Bureau of the Census, "Poverty in the United States: 1985," Current Population Reports, Series P–60, No. 158 (Washington, DC: Government Printing Office, 1987), Table 11.

million women 65 and over living below the poverty level; two-thirds were 72 and over. As noted earlier, the group which stands the greatest chance of being persistently poor is elderly (and black, rural, and southern), not an underclass of young people living in large cities, deprived though many of them are.[14]

Well over two-thirds of all elderly women below the poverty level are *unrelated individuals*. They are persons "not living with any relatives," though some may "be part of a household including one or more other families or unrelated individuals or [they may] reside in group quarters such as a rooming house."[15] The large majority, however, lives alone. In 1985, for example, 71 percent of all elderly women below the poverty level were unrelated individuals living alone, even though unrelated individuals made up only 43 percent of the total female population 65 and over. By comparison, only 36 percent of the nonpoor women 65 and over were living by themselves. Thus, solitude is one of the principal features of a large majority of poor elderly women. They differ substantially from poor elderly men in this respect, for in 1985 only 34 percent of them were classified as unrelated individuals living alone. A mere 13 percent of the nonpoor men 65 and over lived alone. Put differently, 80 percent of all elderly persons living alone are women and 85 percent of all poor elderly persons living alone are women.[16]

Other Age Groups

The most significant poverty characteristic in the age group 25–64 is the drop in poverty rates with increasing age, at least until 55. The lowest rate for women is in the ages 45–54, which are the years when the proportion of women married with a husband present (72 percent) is the highest. These are also the ages when the rate of widowhood is well below half that of women aged 55–64 and when the proportion divorced is lower than in the ages 35–44.[17] Women's median income is not at its highest in the ages 45–54, however; it is exceeded by the incomes of the several groups between 25 and 44. Among year-round, full-time workers, the median income is higher in the ages 25–44, 55–64, and even 65–69 than it is in the ages 45–54. Thus, those women have exceptionally low poverty rates because they are more likely than any other age group to be part of an intact married couple. Conversely, when age is held constant, a woman's prospects to avoid poverty are worse when she is independent of a male wage earner, whether because of nonmarriage, widowhood, divorce, or separation. That price many women still must pay for being on their own reflects the extent to which their poverty status stems from institutional arrangements and traditional role expectations. This is not to ignore the many individuals who thrive economically on their own, but is to suggest that great numbers of women are still bound economically to men, even though the women may contribute earnings and other tangible assets to their relationships. This dependency pattern and its ramifications must change if the poverty rates of women are to drop to the levels experienced by men and married-couple families. Better public assistance programs would help, but they do not get at the basic problem of dependency. In order to solve it we need more pervasive changes in work opportunities, social structures, cultural values, attitudes, and male-female relationships.

VARIATIONS BY RACE AND HISPANIC ORIGIN

As with female family heads, black and Hispanic women as individuals have far higher poverty rates than white women. (See Table 4–1.) Of the two minority groups, blacks have the higher rate at every age, though the gap is far less than the one between whites and the two minorities. For all three groups, persons under 15 are most likely to be poor, reaching 46 percent for blacks, 39 percent for Hispanics, and 18 percent for whites. In all three cases the rates generally decrease with age to lows in the 45–54 group, and then rise in the older years. Well over a third of all black women 65 and over are poor, as are more than a quarter of Hispanic women and 14 percent of the whites.

The poverty rates of black, white, and Hispanic children in female-headed families are commonly three, four, or even five times higher than those in families with a male present. (See Table 4–3.) Moreover, the youngest children fare the worst: Under age 3, more than three-quarters of the blacks and Hispanics and nearly two-thirds of the whites in families headed by a woman are poor. Even as rates decline with age into the group 16 and 17, they remain high, and over half the blacks and Hispanics and a third of the whites in those ages are poor.

Thus, the familiar differences in poverty rates by race and Spanish origin persist for women and their children as persons, but the most crucial factor is whether the victims are part of a female-headed household or one with a male present. That factor is far more significant than race or ethnicity per se, for without controls by family type the poverty rates of males and females within each racial and ethnic group are not vastly different. With such controls the gender gap within each race invariably is wide and to the disadvantage of women and their dependent offspring. To the extent there is a group of persistently poor, these persons, along with vulnerable elderly women, are apt to be its members. In fact, about two-thirds of the nonelderly persistent poor live in female-headed families, and about three-quarters of those householders are black.[18] "Most of these heads have the double economic burden of children at home who increase needs and decrease a single parent's ability to work."[19] For these reasons, the poverty rates of women in various racial and ethnic groups can be understood best if they are seen not just as categories of persons, but as members of particular kinds of families—the analysis provided in chapters 2 and 3.

INFLUENCE OF EDUCATION

As suggested in chapter 2, when the level of education of female householders rises, the poverty rate generally falls, though with some exceptions. The same is true of persons, as shown in Table 4–5.

The plunge in poverty rates as educational levels rise is striking for women of all ages collectively. The poverty rates for those who completed 0–7 years of schooling are more than five times higher than for women who have a year or more of college. In addition, the declines are substantial in all of the specific age groups with sufficient cases (25,000 or more poor women) to make the data base acceptable. The poverty rates at each level of schooling completed also generally fall with age, though they rise a bit for elderly women who have 1–4 years of high school. These patterns also apply to

Table 4–5

Percent of Women below the Poverty Level, by Race, Age, and Years of Schooling Completed, 1985

Race and Age	Percent in Poverty				
	Elementary School		High School		College
	0-7	8	1-3	4	1 or More
All races					
Ages 15 and over	34.5	25.2	22.6	11.5	6.0
15–17	45.8	25.0	13.9	a	a
18–21	51.3	50.0	32.6	17.0	10.9
22–34	48.1	51.5	39.7	15.1	6.9
35–44	37.9	31.7	28.2	10.3	4.8
45–54	32.0	23.2	18.9	7.1	3.3
55–59	38.4	23.6	15.8	7.4	4.4
60–64	32.1	19.7	18.0	7.8	5.4
65 and over	29.9	20.7	17.5	10.0	5.5
White					
Ages 15 and over	32.3	22.3	18.2	9.4	5.2
15–17	43.5	19.3	10.4	a	a
18–21	43.9	49.3	29.1	13.7	10.2
22–34	47.3	48.3	33.0	11.5	5.9
35–44	38.8	27.3	22.2	8.3	4.1
45–54	27.9	20.4	12.8	6.1	2.8
55–59	37.0	20.4	12.6	6.6	3.9
60–64	27.4	17.1	15.7	7.6	5.2
65 and over	27.2	19.3	15.4	9.5	5.0
Black					
Ages 15 and over	45.3	45.3	44.0	28.4	13.2
15–17	53.2	51.5	31.2	a	a
18–21	a	a	49.6	33.9	16.5
22–34	61.0	69.1	65.1	35.9	14.4
35–44	40.0	54.0	46.2	23.9	11.2
45–54	50.1	33.3	42.5	16.2	8.4
55–59	45.7	38.8	32.3	20.5	a
60–64	49.3	a	31.3	a	a
65 and over	41.8	37.7	36.5	22.4	a

Source: U.S. Bureau of the Census, "Poverty in the United States: 1985," Current Population Reports, Series P-60, No. 158 (Washington, DC: Government Printing Office, 1987), Table 9.

aPoverty population less than 25,000.

black and white women separately. The average woman, black or white, who is not officially poor is a high-school graduate with a few months of college, whereas the average woman below the poverty level is a high-school dropout. In fact, 27 percent of the poor white women of all ages never got past the eighth grade and 52 percent failed to complete high school. For poor black women the proportions are 25 and 59 percent, respectively. Among white women above the poverty level, only 10 percent stopped their educations with the eighth grade and 34 percent did not complete high school. About 13 and 45 percent of the black women above the poverty level are in those respective educational situations.

The effect education has on poverty should not be misinterpreted. We know that poor people of both sexes often have low educational attainment, just as some have physical disabilities which keep them from working. We also know that women, children, elderly people, and minorities have poverty rates far above the national norm. But to a considerable degree, "these characteristics—age, gender, race, and education—do not cause poverty. Rather they are the characteristics used in the United States to *allocate* poverty."[20] In pervasive though often not fully intentional ways, persons in positions to hire, fire, dispense governmental benefits, write poverty definitions, and otherwise influence economic standing and how it is measured, use these characteristics to ascertain who should get what and how they should be classified.[21]

Even so, while it is easy to overemphasize the role of education and to neglect the part played by other structural factors in determining the level of poverty, educational standing certainly is among the crucial variables which affect a woman's life chances and poverty risks. It is also one which women, with help from the larger society, can improve in many cases. Therefore, the much-discussed welfare reform must encourage young women to remain in school as long as possible and provide dropouts with realistic opportunities to resume education. The content of education also needs to enhance their life chances, and the job market needs to be. rebuilt in ways which enable self-sufficiency at a decent income level after women have improved their educational attainment and skills. It then remains to compensate for the other conditions most associated with poverty: single motherhood; advanced age and low, relatively fixed income; minority affiliation; disability; migrant labor; and recent foreign origin.[22] Any or all of these conditions can affect the likelihood, type, and level of a woman's employment and influence her earning prospects and, therefore, her probability of falling below the poverty level.

POOREST OF THE POOR

So far the analysis has compared persons officially designated as poor with the nonpoor. But how poor is poor? How large a share of persons in poverty fall not just below a specified income threshold, but far below it? Specifically, what proportion of poor people receive 50 percent or less of the designated poverty-level income and how do females and males compare by this measure? Who, by gender, are the poorest of the poor?

To address these questions one can use data on persons living in families with a female householder and no husband present, comparing them with data on persons in other types of families, almost all married-couple units. Figure 4–2 shows the percentage of persons in the two types of families who had particular shares of poverty-level income in 1985. Each circle represents the entire poverty population of each race and family type. Within the circle the darkest shading shows the percentage of the poor population below 50 percent of the official poverty level, the medium shading shows the proportion between 50 and 75 percent, and the lightest shading shows the share between 75 and 100 percent. The last group is still officially poor, but not plagued by the desperate poverty which afflicts the first group and even the second.

In 1985 about 45 percent of the persons in female-headed families were in the poorest category, compared with 31 percent of those in other types of families. Conversely, only 22 percent of the persons residing with a female householder were in the least poor group, contrasted with 39 percent of those in married-couple and male-headed families. Similar patterns apply to blacks and whites, except that blacks are especially likely to occupy the poorest class. In 1985 well over half the poor persons in families with a black female householder ranked below 50 percent of the official poverty level, and only a sixth placed in the 75–100 percent group. The poor in families with a female householder, disproportionately locked in at rock bottom, are more likely to stay poor, whereas the larger percentages who stand just below the poverty level in families with a male present are more apt to move in and out of the poverty class as their fortunes improve or deteriorate.

NEAR-POOR PERSONS

The concerns expressed in this book go beyond the persons with survival-level income. Thus, any combination of private and public efforts to create a better level of living for Americans of both sexes needs to help not only the persons who fall below the official poverty level, but those who rank just above it. Statistically, they are the ones whose incomes are 0–25 percent above the official poverty threshold. Individually and as a group they are the near-poor, many of whom place above the poverty level in one year or season, below it the next, above it a few months later, and so on.

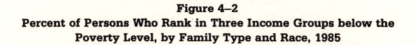

Figure 4–2
Percent of Persons Who Rank in Three Income Groups below the
Poverty Level, by Family Type and Race, 1985

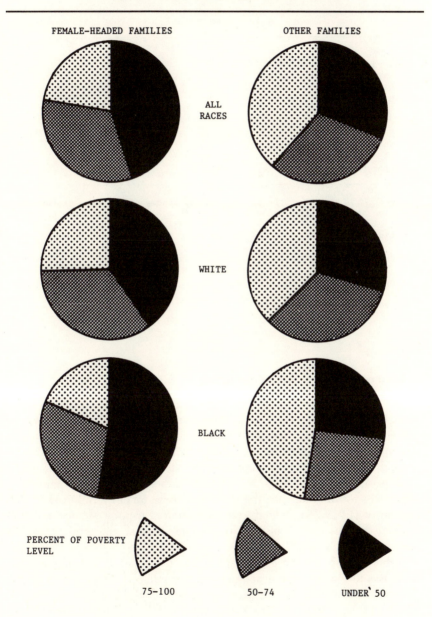

Table 4–6
**Percent of Poor and Near-Poor Persons in Two Types of Families, by
Race and Hispanic Origin, 1985**

Family Type and Race	Percent		
	Poor + Near-Poor	Poor	Near-Poor[a]
Female Householder[b]			
All races	44.5	37.6	6.9
White	36.2	29.8	6.4
Black	61.3	53.2	8.1
Hispanic[c]	63.7	55.7	8.0
Other families			
All races	11.9	8.2	3.2
White	10.8	7.3	3.5
Black	21.8	14.8	7.0
Hispanic[c]	28.3	20.6	7.7

Source: U.S. Bureau of the Census, "Money Income and Poverty Status of
Families and Persons in the United States: 1985," Advance Data, Current
Population Reports, Series P-60, No. 154 (Washington, DC: Government
Printing Office, 1986), Tables 16, 17.

[a]Income 0–25 percent above official poverty level.

[b]No husband present.

[c]May be of any race.

Size of the Near-Poor Population

In 1985 more than 20 million persons living in woman-headed households
were below 125 percent of the poverty level. Over 16 million of them were
under the poverty level, leaving 4 million in the marginal near-poor category.
Taking a family of three as an example, a near-poor unit would have had
a total cash income somewhere between the poverty threshold of $8,573
and the upper limit of $10,716. Even the higher figure scarcely amounts to
affluence, considering that the median income for all families with three
persons was $29,265. Added to the 4 million near-poor persons in female-
headed families were 7 million in other families, so the total (11 million
persons) is not small.[23]

Table 4–6 shows the percentage points by which the poor population
increases if one adds the near-poor—a manipulation illustrated in chapter
1. It also shows that for all races collectively and for whites, blacks, and
Hispanics separately, adding the near-poor increases the combined per-

centage of persons in and near poverty by a much larger increment for married-couple and male-headed families than for those with a female householder. When near-poor persons are added to the poverty population of all races, they raise the overall proportion among female-headed families by 18 percent, the proportion among other types of families by 45 percent. This further confirms that persons in female-headed families with significant economic disadvantages are especially likely to fall below the poverty line, whereas persons in disadvantaged families with a male present have a much better chance to hover above it.

Combining the proportions of near-poor and poor persons results in very high figures for children. In 1985 about 54 percent of all children under 18 living in female-headed families were poor; with the near-poor added the proportion rose to 61 percent. In other types of families, 12 percent of the children were poor and adding the near-poor brought the figure to 17 percent. The percentage of children who were near-poor and in female headed families did drop a little between 1970 and 1985, however, while the percentage of near-poor persons of all ages collectively in those families rose. In the same period the proportion of children in female-headed families and below the poverty level changed very little, while the poverty rate of persons of all ages in those families fell. Thus, although some children moved up out of the near-poor category, more left it by dropping below the poverty threshold.

The group of near-poor persons 65 and over is also quite sizable, and combining them with the poor elderly group raises the total significantly. In 1985 the poverty rate of the elderly living in female-headed families was 23 percent, and adding the near-poor brought the figure to 37 percent. In other families the proportion rose from 7 to 13 percent. These manipulations show that a relatively large number of elderly people who are not officially poor are not far from it, and if the incomes of the entire group were to decrease by even a modest amount or fail to rise at the same rate as inflation, 2.3 million persons could join the 3.5 million already in poverty. Those whose incomes are 125 percent or less of the poverty level (i.e., the poor and the near-poor), make up 21 percent of all elderly, so while the poverty rates of persons 65 and over fell significantly after 1959, more than a fifth still occupy economically deprived or precarious positions.

Variations by Race and Hispanic Origin

Black and Hispanic people are more likely than non-Hispanic whites to fall below the poverty line but less apt to be near-poor. In 1985 in female-headed families, the poor were 82 percent of the combined poor and near-poor category among whites, but 87 percent among blacks and Hispanics. This suggests further that when the fortunes of minority groups are low, they tend to be very low. This is less the case with a male present, for then the poor are only 68 percent of the combined poor-and near-poor category among both whites and blacks, though 73 percent among Hispanics. The figure for blacks is especially significant, because it reflects the relatively rapid socioeconomic progress black married-couple families have been making as compared with those headed by women and even with white married-couple families.

EFFECT OF NONCASH BENEFITS

Chapter 1 discusses how the treatment of noncash benefits can affect poverty rates. Those methods now can be applied to categories of persons to show how their poverty rates change when noncash benefits are counted as income.

The noncash benefits fall into three large categories: food, housing, and medical. Some are means-tested benefits and others are not. Whatever their form, the noncash benefits have a significant effect on poverty, because most "welfare payments" actually come in the form of noncash allocations. In fact, cash welfare payments are governmental assistance to needy persons who are part of specific programs, and those amounts go to a relatively small share of the poverty population.[24] Naturally, if the more widespread noncash benefits are taken into account as income, the poverty rate falls.

The result of doing this and including near-poor persons in the poverty population is illustrated in Table 4–7, which provides data separately for whites, blacks, and Hispanics. It is based on persons in female-headed and married-couple families. The analysis also uses the combined market value of the three large categories of noncash benefits as a way to compute the poverty rate, so worth "is equal to the private market value of the benefits received by the individual."[25] The data show the percentages of persons who are poor and near-poor according to the official poverty definition and how those figures are altered by including noncash benefits, though it is important to recognize that many poor people do not receive the benefits and many persons who do get them are not officially poor.[26] In 1986, for example, 48 million persons received welfare of some kind, whereas only 32 million were classified officially as poor.[27] This is because the various programs do not use official poverty-level income to determine eligibility, but some multiple of it (e.g., families whose incomes are less than 130 percent of the poverty level can receive food stamps).[28] So, the population receiving benefits is substantially larger than the one classified as poor.

Noncash benefits reduce poverty significantly for persons in all types of families, but more so in those with female heads than with married couples. In this sense, at least, the woman-headed units have an apparent advantage, though they also need the benefits most. For all races collectively, including noncash benefits drops the poverty rate 18 percent for persons in married-couple families, but 40 percent for those in female-headed families. In the

Table 4–7

Percent of Persons Who Are Poor and Near-Poor under the Official Poverty Definition and with the Value of Noncash Benefits Added to Income, by Family Type, Race, and Hispanic Origin, 1985

Family Type and Race	Percent					
	Official Poverty Definition			Noncash Benefits Added[a]		
	Total	Poor	Near-Poor[b]	Total	Poor	Near-Poor[b]
Female householder[c]						
All races	44.5	37.6	6.9	36.5	22.6	13.9
White	36.2	29.8	6.4	29.7	17.8	11.9
Black	61.3	53.2	8.1	50.1	32.6	17.5
Hispanic[d]	63.7	55.7	8.0	50.7	29.7	21.0
Married-couple families						
All races	11.6	7.9	3.7	9.5	5.7	3.8
White	10.6	7.1	3.5	8.7	5.2	3.5
Black	20.8	13.8	7.0	16.1	9.3	6.8
Hispanic[d]	28.4	20.6	7.8	24.4	15.2	9.2

Source: U.S. Bureau of the Census, Estimates of Poverty Including the Value of Noncash Benefits: 1985, Technical Paper 56 (Washington, DC: Government Printing Office, 1986), Table 2.

[a]Market value of food, housing, and all medical benefits.

[b]Income 0–25 percent above official poverty level.

[c]No husband present.

[d]May be of any race.

latter, poverty rates fall by about 40 percent among whites and blacks and 47 percent among Hispanics. In married-couple units they fall by about a quarter for whites and Hispanics and a third for blacks.

Noncash benefits also affect the proportions of persons who shift out of the poverty group into the near-poor category. In particular, the proportion of near-poor persons of all races in female-headed families increases substantially when noncash benefits are added to their income, whereas the figure for persons in married-couple units remains essentially unchanged. Among whites in female-headed families, adding noncash benefits raises the proportion of near-poor persons 60 percent; among blacks and Hispanics the increases are 116 and 162 percent, respectively. These changes suggest that noncash benefits help lift many persons in female-headed families out of their low depths of poverty to a point just above the poverty threshold, while poor persons in other families are more likely to be raised out of poverty and above the near-poor class as well. Their initial tendency to be up near the poverty line rather than far below it helps facilitate that movement. Thus, when noncash benefits increase income, the situation of women is still particularly punishing and the benefits elevate many only to near-poor status. While the present ways of allocating noncash benefits do help ameliorate the problem of poverty among women and children, much more must be done to solve it.

Noncash benefits are more instrumental in reducing poverty rates among the elderly than in other age groups, largely because of subsidized medical programs. In 1985, for instance, the poverty rate of all elderly persons (noncash benefits excluded) was 13 percent. (See Table 4–8.) It fell to 11 percent when the market value of food and housing was included, but to only 3 percent when medical benefits were added. Without the three benefits elderly persons have higher poverty rates than those aged 25–64, but with them the rates are lower among the elderly than in any other age group. This is true for whites, blacks, and Hispanics.

These changes show how two programs—Medicare and Medicaid—have changed poverty conditions, though the programs are expensive and individual access to them varies widely. The relative success of Medicare in particular should urge policy makers (i.e., those who control budgets) toward more innovative ways to protect younger adults and children from poverty. Those ways include better prevention and cure of health problems; widespread, reasonable or even free day care for the children of mothers who do or could work; programs to improve skills so persons' abilities match the available jobs; job-creation efforts to ensure that the available positions pay above the poverty level; and more affordable housing for the poor. The last need is especially misunderstood, because nearly a quarter of the homeless actually work full-time or part-time, but there is insufficient housing available at affordable prices. Many of the homeless also are families with children whose parents are involuntarily without work, and the homeless population is by no means confined to mentally-ill, alcoholic, or drug-abusing loners. Therefore, the poor who end up on the streets or in shelters, squatter settlements, or their cars are a diverse group which conforms poorly to prevailing stereotypes. The programs necessary to help more of the homeless and other categories of poor people will be costly, as are subsidized medical benefits for the elderly, but they will convert into producers that sizable share of the poor now unable to contribute much to the system. That change will help offset costs and achieve the goal of self-sufficiency. With other problems, too, the returns should more than justify the expense: The cost of good prenatal care is a fraction of the amount for hospitalizing an underweight infant; the price tag for child care which enables a mother

Table 4–8
Percent of Persons below the Poverty Level When Noncash Benefits Are Excluded or Included as Income, by Age, Race, and Hispanic Origin, 1985

Benefits and Age	Percent in Poverty			
	All Races	White	Black	Hispanic[a]
Benefits excluded				
Under 6	23.0	18.3	47.7	41.4
6–17	19.5	15.0	41.4	39.6
18–24	16.5	14.0	31.2	28.0
25–44	10.6	8.8	22.4	22.6
45–64	9.5	8.0	22.2	16.8
65 and over	12.6	11.0	31.5	23.9
Food and housing included[b]				
Under 6	20.8	16.6	43.5	37.1
6–17	16.9	13.1	35.8	34.4
18–24	15.3	13.2	28.1	25.9
25–44	9.4	8.0	19.4	20.2
45–64	8.7	7.4	19.6	14.4
65 and over	10.7	9.3	26.9	17.1
Food, housing, and medical included[b]				
Under 6	16.2	13.3	32.9	28.6
6–17	12.5	10.1	24.4	23.8
18–24	13.1	11.7	21.6	22.4
25–44	7.6	6.5	14.0	15.6
45–64	6.5	5.8	12.9	10.5
65 and over	2.9	2.5	6.8	5.3

Source: U.S. Bureau of the Census, Estimates of Poverty Including the Value of Noncash Benefits: 1985, Technical Paper 56 (Washington, DC: Government Printing Office, 1986), Table 2.

[a]May be of any race.

[b]Based on market value concept.

to work is less than AFDC payments; vocational training for a teenager costs a small part of the dollars spent processing and incarcerating a juvenile delinquent. With more investment in preventing problems, the rate of increase in the cost of some noncash benefits might even slow down, though they can never be eliminated without increasing the poor population significantly.

Nor does welfare of all kinds stand much chance of doing away with poverty, given the ways in which the programs are structured and funded and even considering some of the proposed changes in them. In recent years the amount of money necessary to lift the incomes of all persons above the poverty level has been about $50 billion. But in fiscal 1985 about $130 billion went into welfare and there were still 32 million people in poverty. Thus, one must conclude that even when the value of noncash benefits is added to cash transfers, the programs are designed partly to help the middle class and to provide only bare subsistence for most poor recipients, not to eliminate poverty.[29] Accomplishing that goal is the ultimate challenge for the welfare reformers.

TRENDS IN PERSONAL POVERTY

Changes in the Poverty Rate and the Number of Poor

Poverty rates for persons in all race and gender categories have fallen since 1959, but the rate of decline has been faster for those in married-couple and male-headed families than in units with a woman householder, regardless of race. Therefore, because women family heads, who had the initial disadvantage, are in a worse position relative to men now than they were in 1959, whether one lives in a female-headed or married-couple family is crucial in determining one's progress out of poverty. This relationship is reflected in Figure 4–3.

Between 1959 and 1986 the poverty rate of persons living in families with a female householder and no husband present went from 50 to 34— a 32–percent drop. But in families with a male present, the rate decreased from 19 to 8—a 58–percent reduction. The same pattern pertains separately for blacks and whites, though poverty rates for persons in black female-headed families fell the least (28 percent), while those for persons in other black families dropped the most, by an impressive 70 percent. Blacks of each sex still fare worse than whites, but while the poverty gap between black and white married-couple families has diminished significantly, the reverse is true for female-headed units. Relatively speaking, persons in black female-headed families have fallen behind those in all other types of families in the struggle to escape poverty. They are also among the people most likely to be persistently poor and with the least chance to improve.

Even so, and despite periodic reversals in the economy, changes in government programs, and revised methods for counting the poor, the poverty rates for persons of both races and in both types of families are significantly lower now than in 1959. That represents one kind of progress. The data on numbers of poor persons, however, illustrate quite a different situation. It appears in Figure 4–4 and Table 4–9, which show how the number of poor persons in the two types of families changed between 1959 and 1986.

The feminization of poverty is reflected in a substantial increase in the number of poor persons in female-headed families and a significant decrease in the number in other types of families. In 1959 about 10 million poor people resided in female-headed units, but by 1986 the number had jumped

Figure 4–3
Poverty Rate of Persons in Female-Headed and Other Types of Families,
by Race, 1959–1986

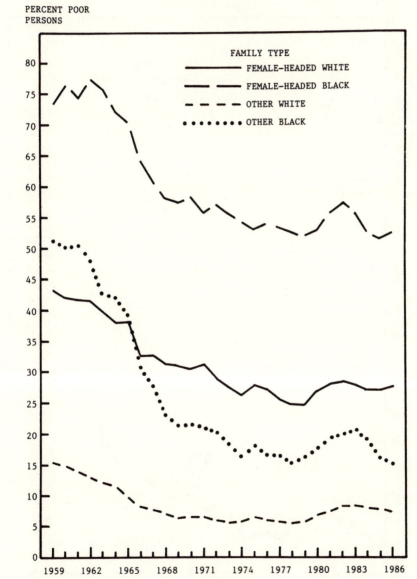

PERCENT POOR
PERSONS

FAMILY TYPE
——————— FEMALE-HEADED WHITE
—— —— —— FEMALE-HEADED BLACK
— — — — OTHER WHITE
• • • • • • • • OTHER BLACK

YEAR

Figure 4–4
Change in the Number of Persons below the Poverty Level, by Family Type, 1959–1986

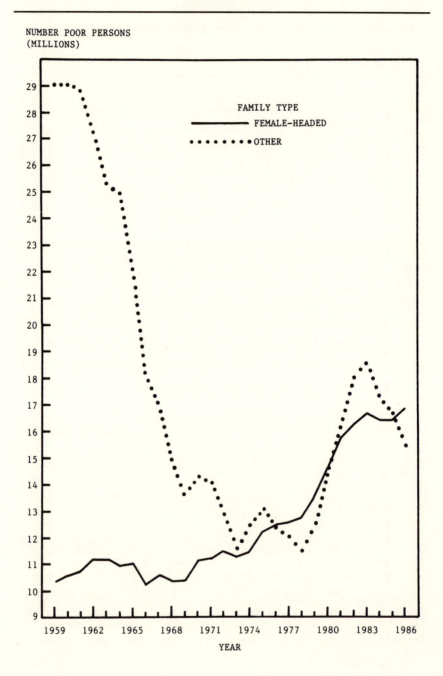

NUMBER POOR PERSONS
(MILLIONS)

FAMILY TYPE
——————— FEMALE–HEADED
• • • • • • • OTHER

YEAR

Table 4-9

Change in the Number of Persons below the Poverty Level, by Family Type and Race, 1959–1986

Family Type and Race	Number of Poor Persons (Thousands)		Percent Change, 1959-1986
	1959	1986	
Female householder[a]			
All races	10,390	16,926	+62.9
White	7,115	10,052	+41.3
Black[b]	3,275	6,454	+97.1
Other families			
All races	29,100	15,444	-46.9
White	21,369	12,131	-43.2
Black[b]	7,731	2,529	-67.3

Source: U.S. Bureau of the Census, Current Population Reports, Series P-60, annual issues (Washington, DC: Government Printing Office).

[a]No husband present.

[b]Includes other races in 1959, when blacks were about 95 percent of the total.

to 17 million—a 63 percent increase. This jump compares with a 36 percent increase in the nation's total population during the 1959–86 period and shows that the poverty population in woman-headed households grew disproportionately rapidly. On the other hand, in 1959 there were 29 million poor persons in married-couple and male-headed families, but by 1986 their number had fallen to 15 million—a 47 percent drop. Thus, in 1959 there were 19 million fewer poor people in female-headed than in other types of families, but in 1986 there were 1.5 million more in the female-headed units. Furthermore, in 1959 about 26 percent of the nation's total poverty population lived in female-headed families, compared with 52 percent in 1986. This change occurred because a 32 percent drop in poverty rates in female-headed families was more than offset by the 56 percent drop in other families, and because the units with a female householder increased greatly in number.

The size of the poor population in woman-headed families also grew in 20 of the 27 years between 1959 and 1986, but it increased in other types of families in only nine of the 27 years. Five of those nine years were 1979–83, inclusive, and the rest were all during other recessionary periods. The increases show that when the economy slumps many persons in married-couple families move into poverty because of temporary unemployment and/or decreases in median income, and then move out when the economy recovers. Persons in female-headed units are subject to the same forces, but they are much more likely to rank below the poverty level even in good years and to stay there whether or not the economy improves.

Trends in Children's Poverty

The analyses in this and earlier chapters show that children in female-headed families are seriously afflicted by persistent poverty. In absolute numbers, that situation has gotten markedly worse. Between 1959 and 1986 the number of children under 18 living in poor female-headed families increased from 4.1 million to 6.9 million, or 68 percent. In other types of families the number dropped from 13.1 million to 5.3 million, or 60 percent.

The change in the poverty rates of children—the rising generation of adults—is not encouraging either, because in both types of families the rates fell sharply until about 1970, after which either there was no progress or some prior improvements reversed. (See Figure 4–5). In female-headed families of all races collectively there was only one year (1979) between 1959 and 1986 in which the poverty rate of children under 18 was below 50 percent. Among blacks it was never below 63 percent and among whites it held at 39 percent or above. All are extremely high proportions by any standard of modest well-being in an affluent society. Furthermore, the poverty rate among children in female-headed families fell slightly in 1984 and 1985 and then inched back up. In other families the poverty rate was much lower, of course, but even there the lot of children improved only from 1959 to 1970, changed relatively little until 1980, and then got worse for a few years. The rate did fall again in 1985 and 1986, while that in woman-headed families rose in 1986. In white female-headed and married-couple families children's poverty rate in the 1980s was back up to the levels of the late 1960s, just as it was in black female-headed units. In other black families, however, children's poverty rate was lower in 1986 (17 percent) than at any prior time, having fallen from 61 percent in 1959 and 26 percent in 1970. The rate did increase after 1978, however, and did not fall significantly again until 1985. Part of that later drop resulted from changed methodology for reporting poverty, but part was the real consequence of improvements in the black intact family. In fact, it now differs in so many ways from the black female-headed family, that the 1986 poverty rate for persons in the latter was four times that in the former. For whites it was almost five times higher. Regardless of race, the poverty rate of children increases several times over if they live only with their mothers rather than with both parents.

Figure 4–5
Percent of Children under 18 below the Poverty Level, by Family Type and Race, 1970–1986

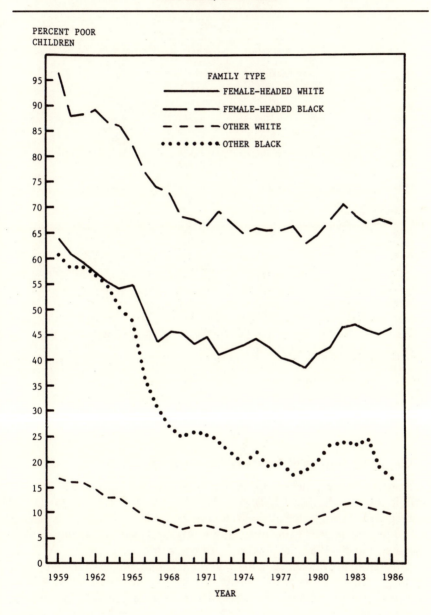

PERCENT POOR
CHILDREN

Table 4–10

**Reduction in the Number and Percent of Poor Persons Because of
Noncash Benefits, by Family Type, 1979–1985**

Family Type and Year	Number of Poor Persons (Thousands)		Reduction in Poor Persons	
	Noncash Benefits Excluded[a]	Noncash Benefits Included[a]	Number (Thousands)	Percent
Female householder[b]				
1979	9,400	4,741	4,659	49.6
1980	10,120	5,535	4,585	45.3
1981	11,051	6,716	4,335	39.2
1982	11,701	7,438	4,263	36.4
1983	12,101	7,615	4,486	37.1
1984	11,831	7,500	4,331	36.6
1985	11,600	6,977	4,623	39.9
Married-couple families				
1979	10,074	6,613	3,461	34.4
1980	11,861	7,946	3,915	33.0
1981	13,177	9,372	3,805	28.9
1982	14,839	10,762	4,077	27.5
1983	15,111	11,230	3,881	25.7
1984	13,717	10,032	3,685	26.9
1985	13,213	7,491	3,722	28.2

Source: U.S. Bureau of the Census, Estimates of Poverty Including the
Value of Noncash Benefits: 1985, Technical Paper 56 (Washington, DC:
Government Printing Office, 1986), Table 1.

[a]Market value of food, housing, and all medical benefits.

[b]No husband present.

Changing Impact of Noncash Benefits

Noncash benefits helped lower the numbers and percentages of poor
people more in the late 1970s than they do now. In 1979 the number of
poor people living in female-headed families could be reduced 50 percent
by adding the market value of food, housing, and medical benefits to their
incomes, but by 1982 the potential drop was only 37 percent. (See Table
4–10.) The figure fluctuated in the next three years and was up to 40 percent
in 1985, still far short of the impact of noncash benefits in 1979. Adding
noncash benefits reduced the size of the poverty population in married-
couple families by 34 percent in 1979, 26 percent in 1983, and 28 percent
in 1985. Thus, the benefits still reduce poverty in a larger share of female-

headed than other families, but the difference between the two has diminished. Furthermore, married-couple families are in a much better position initially and their average need for the benefits is considerably less.

Since most of the welfare benefits available to all types of poor and nonpoor families are noncash rather than cash forms, the impact and cost of programs such as Medicaid and food stamps is larger than that of cash benefits such as AFDC and SSI.[30] In fact, by 1988 the cost of the Medicaid program had grown to about $50 billion, but inequities in allocations among the poor, especially in the South, prevented large numbers from getting adequate care, partly because state and local governments do not administer the program uniformly. The people who are not adequately protected symbolize a variety of problems which pervade much of the present noncash-benefit system.

The poverty status of children also has been variously affected by the availability of noncash benefits. In 1979 the number of persons under 6 and in poverty was reduced 36 percent by such benefits, in 1983 it fell 26 percent, and in 1985 it dropped 29 percent. For children aged 6–17, the decrease was 44 percent in 1979, but 30 percent in 1983 and 35 percent in 1985.[31] Thus, children came to be less well covered by noncash benefits in the 1980s than they were earlier, partly because eligibility requirements were tightened and dollar increases allocated to the benefit categories did not keep up with inflation or the rate of growth in the number of children living in poor female-headed families.

Among the elderly the story is different, for while various program cutbacks in the 1980s diminished the poverty-reducing value of noncash benefits to children and other persons in families headed by a woman under 65, continued improvements in programs for the elderly enhanced their situation. In 1979 the size of the poverty population 65 and over could be reduced 68 percent by accounting for noncash benefits, especially medical assistance. That was a large drop compared with the ones among children and other nonelderly. The reductions among older people grew even larger, reaching a peak of 76 percent in 1984, though falling a bit to 75 percent in 1985, partly because of increases in Medicare premiums and subscriber deductibles. A far larger share of the nation's elderly than its children receives noncash benefits, and in the 1980s the poverty rates of older people continued to fall because of those benefits. Thus, progress by the oldest group contrasts with a loss of some previous gains by the youngest. The changes parallel growing activism by and for the elderly and continued concern for their well-being, along with greater dismay over rising illegitimacy rates and various misconceptions about the plight of children in one-parent families. This is not to begrudge the elderly their gains nor to minimize the poverty which still afflicts a sizable share of them, but it is to argue that equivalent improvements should be extended to other segments of the population, especially the dependent young.

NOTES

1. Greg J. Duncan, "The Volatility of Family Income Over the Life Course," paper presented at the Annual Meetings of the Population Association of America (Chicago: April 30–May 2, 1987), p. 13.

2. Joan Smith, "The Paradox of Women's Poverty: Wage-earning Women and Economic Transformation," in Barbara C. Gelpi, Nancy C. M. Hartsock, Clare C. Novak, and Myra H. Strober, eds., *Women and Poverty* (Chicago: University of Chicago Press, 1986), p. 121.

3. Greg J. Duncan, Richard D. Coe, and Martha S. Hill, "The Dynamics of Poverty," in Greg J. Duncan, Richard D. Coe, Mary E. Corcoran, Martha S. Hill, Saul D. Hoffman, and James N. Morgan, *Years of Poverty, Years of Plenty* (Ann Arbor, MI: Institute for Social Research, 1984), p. 34. See also pp. 40–52.

4. Greg J. Duncan and James N. Morgan, "An Overview of Family Economic Mobility," in Duncan and others, *Years of Poverty*, p. 26.

5. Ibid, pp. 21–22.

6. For the data, see U.S. Bureau of the Census, "Poverty in the United States: 1985," *Current Population Reports,* Series P–60, No. 158 (Washington, DC: Government Printing Office, 1987), Table 7.

7. For the method, see Henry S. Shryock and Jacob S. Siegel, *The Methods and Materials of Demography,* Vol. 1 (Washington, DC: Government Printing Office, 1973), pp. 236–240. See also Paul E. Zopf, Jr., *Population: An Introduction to Social Demography,* (Palo Alto, CA: Mayfield, 1984), p. 425.

8. For an explanation of this idea, see Ellen Greenberger and Laurence Steinberg, *When Teenagers Work: The Psychological and Social Costs of Adolescent Employment* (New York: Basic Books, 1986).

9. Thomas J. Espenshade, "Marriage Trends in America: Estimates, Implications, and Underlying Causes," *Population and Development Review* 11:2 (June 1985), pp. 213, 215.

10. Duncan, Coe, and Hill, "The Dynamics of Poverty," p. 62.

11. For a more comprehensive account, see U.S. National Center for Health Statistics, *The Feminization of Poverty and Older Women: An Update* (Washington, DC: Government Printing Office, 1985).

12. Richard A. Easterlin, "The New Age Structure of Poverty in America: Permanent or Transient?" *Population and Development Review* 13:2 (June 1987), pp. 195, 198, 206.

13. Rachel Floersheim Boaz, "Work as a Response to Low and Decreasing Real Income During Retirement," *Research on Aging* 9:3 (September 1987), pp. 437–438.

14. Duncan, Coe, and Hill, "The Dynamics of Poverty," p. 34.

15. U.S. Bureau of the Census, "Poverty in the United States: 1985," p. 164.

16. For the data, see ibid, Table 11.

17. For the data, see U.S. Bureau of the Census, "Marital Status and Living Arrangements: March 1985," *Current Population Reports,* Series P–20, No. 410 (Washington, DC: Government Printing Office, 1986), Table 1.

18. Duncan, Coe, and Hill, "The Dynamics of Poverty," p. 63.

19. Mary Corcoran, Greg J. Duncan, and Martha S. Hill, "The Economic Fortunes of Women and Children: Lessons from the Panel Study of Income Dynamics," in Gelpi and others, *Women and Poverty*, p. 19.

20. Donald Tomaskovic-Devey, "Labor Markets, Industrial Structure, and Poverty: A Theoretical Discussion and Empirical Example," *Rural Sociology* 52:1 (Spring 1987), p. 59.

21. Ibid.

22. Elaine Zimmerman, "California Hearings on the Feminization of Poverty," in Gelpi and others, *Women and Poverty*, p. 192.

23. For the data, see U.S. Bureau of the Census, "Money Income and Poverty Status of Families and Persons in the United States: 1985," Advance Data, *Current Population Reports*, Series P–60, No. 154 (Washington, DC: Government Printing Office, 1986), Tables 16, 17, A–1.

24. William P. O'Hare, *America's Welfare Population: Who Gets What?* occasional paper no. 13 in the series Population Trends and Public Policy (Washington, DC: Population Reference Bureau, 1987), p. 1.

25. U.S. Bureau of the Census, *Estimates of Poverty Including the Value of Noncash Benefits: 1985*, Technical Paper No. 56 (Washington, DC: Government Printing Office, 1986), p. 2. See pp. 2–4 for a detailed description of three valuation techniques: Market Value; Recipient or Cash Equivalent Value; Poverty Budget Share Value.

26. O'Hare, *America's Welfare Population*, p. 2.

27. Ibid, p. 1.

28. Ibid, p. 3.

29. Ibid, pp. 12–13.

30. Ibid, pp. 1, 4.

31. For the data, see U.S. Bureau of the Census, *Estimates of Poverty*, Table 1.

5

Personal Income and Poverty

The analysis of women's poverty would be incomplete without considering personal income. Therefore, this chapter looks at the notorious income gap between men and women, variations between blacks and whites, fluctuations by residence, and differences by educational attainment. It also deals with sources of income and how their importance differs by gender, including variations in the value of noncash benefits. The analysis focuses especially on income differences by work experience and within occupations which are predominantly "male" or "female," and it emphasizes the concept of comparable worth. The chapter concludes with income trends. The account does not deal with housework, because it pays no wages and there are no data on its money value. But, like a paid job, it is productive work carried out in a network of relationships which implies the existence of a contract, informal though it may be.[1] Thus, while housework is not analyzed here, it should not be underrated.

VARIATIONS BY GENDER AND AGE

The income discrepancy between men and women has complex causes and its actual extent is not precisely known, though it is clear that the jobs which occupy most women pay less than those which employ most men.[2] Job segregation by gender, differences in average years of work experience, discrimination, and other factors preserve this relationship.[3]

To illustrate the gender gap, Table 5–1 shows the median income of persons aged 15 and over by specific age groups and gender, and it gives women's income as a percentage of men's income at each age. This is the *female/male income ratio*. Both the dollar figures and the ratios emphasize women's serious relative income inferiority—the direct financial cause of

Table 5–1

Median Income of Persons, by Age and Gender, 1985

Age	Income (Dollars)		Female/Male Income Ratio[a]
	Female	Male	
All ages	7,217	16,311	44.2
15–19	1,796	1,893	94.9
20–24	6,155	8,629	71.3
25–29	9,763	16,647	58.6
30–34	10,012	20,984	47.7
35–39	10,150	24,692	41.1
40–44	10,416	26,291	39.6
45–49	10,159	26,563	38.2
50–54	8,875	25,062	35.4
55–59	7,680	22,693	33.4
60–64	6,833	17,835	38.3
65 and over	6,313	10,900	57.9
65–69	6,524	12,581	51.9
70 and over	6,225	10,023	62.1

Source: U.S. Bureau of the Census, "Money Income of Households, Families, and Persons in the United States: 1985," Current Population Reports, Series P-60, No. 156 (Washington, DC: Government Printing Office, 1987), Table 34.

[a]Median income of females as a percentage of median income of males.

their higher average poverty rate.[4] In the youngest ages, when less than 6 percent of the females and 7 percent of the males have income from year-round, full-time employment, the incomes of both sexes are very low and roughly similar. Most of these people are in school, living at home, or not full-time workers for other reasons which accompany youth. One reason is the scarcity of jobs above minimum wage for teenagers, although as their age cohorts shrink they are more in demand and their wage situations are improving somewhat. Even so, about 36 percent of the women and 32 percent of the men aged 15–19 have no income at all.

Median income jumps for both sexes aged 20–24 and rises to a peak in the ages 40–44 for women and 45–49 for men. It then declines gradually with age, until the median for persons 65 and over is not much greater than for people aged 20–24. But the peak income for women in 1985 was only $10,416, that for men $26,563. Thus, the female/male income ratio decreases steadily from the ages 15–19 to 55–59, though it does rise some after 59, when men's income begins to drop because of retirement, especially early retirement due to disability or a scarcity of jobs for which they have

Table 5–2
Median Income of Persons Aged 15 and Over, by Gender and Race, 1985

Race	Income (Dollars)		Female/Male Income Ratio[a]	Percent Without Income	
	Female	Male		Female	Male
All races	7,217	16,311	44.2	10.2	5.5
White	7,357	17,111	43.0	9.4	4.4
Black	6,277	10,768	58.3	14.7	12.7

Source: U.S. Bureau of the Census, "Money Income of Households, Families, and Persons in the United States: 1985," Current Population Reports, Series P-60, No. 156 (Washington, DC: Government Printing Office, 1987), Table 34.

[a]Median income of females as a percentage of median income of males.

skills. In all ages between 30 and 64, however, women's income is less than half that of men, and in late middle age it is only a third.

Elderly women are a bit better off in this respect, for while the incomes of both sexes drop in the older years, the relative situation of women improves because men's income drops more. For example, men aged 65 and over have 39 percent less income than men aged 60–64, while the difference for women is only 8 percent. The gender income ratio continues to rise past age 65, but despite this convergence the smaller median income of women at all ages and the decline in the gender income ratio with age from 15 to 59 is the primary direct cause of women's higher poverty rates. It stems from gender variations in work experience, unemployment patterns, disability, homemaking responsibilities, and other influences on income and poverty. Incomes do fluctuate over time, however, and the decade-long Panel Study of Income Dynamics (PSID) at the University of Michigan shows that only about two-thirds of the families with cash incomes below the poverty level one year were still below that line the next.[5]

DIFFERENCES BY RACE

The income difference between black and white females aged 15 and over is fairly small, because neither group fares very well, but also because black working women have made enough progress to narrow the racial gap.[6] Thus, in 1985 black women of all work statuses collectively received 85 percent of the amount received by white women, though blacks were much more likely to have no cash income at all. (See Table 5–2.) Due to the long-term advantages which set white men financially apart from black men and women of both races, black men received only 63 percent as much income as white men. Black men were nearly three times more likely to have no cash income at all. But the gender differences within each race are greater than the racial differences within each gender, though the gender gap is wider for whites than for blacks. In the worst case, black women have only 37 percent as much income as white men.

The black population has a lower median age than the white group, so age must be controlled in any examination of racial and gender income differences. In addition, women and men and blacks and whites have different work experience, so that factor needs to be held constant. Figure 5–1, which accounts for these variables, shows the median income of year-round, full-time workers in several age categories from 20–24 to 60–64, separately for blacks and whites and women and men. Younger and older age groups are omitted because they contain relatively few workers. With age and work experience taken into account, the income relationships among the several groups are promising in some respects, discouraging in others.

For females, the median income of blacks is 79 percent of that of whites in the ages 30–34, and in all other age groups the ratio is even higher, reaching 94 percent in the age group 35–39. Thus, black women who are year-round, full-time workers compare fairly well with working white women of the same ages, though the blacks do have lower incomes at every age.

For males, the black-white income discrepancy is greater than the one for females. Black men workers aged 50–54 have 65 percent as much income as whites, and while the ratio is higher at every other age, it never exceeds the 79 percent for men aged 20–24. Since the highest ratio appears in the youngest group of workers, however, one can infer with some caution that recent labor force entrants have a more equitable income situation than their elders did as young workers and often still do. Improvements in education account for some of the difference.[7] So does a decline in the virulence of racism in the workplace, partly because of earlier struggles by older blacks, though racism certainly has not disappeared.

The female-male comparisons within each race also represent improvement, though many discrepancies persist. White year-round, full-time female workers aged 20–24 have 84 percent of the median income of men with similar work experience, but the ratio declines steadily to 56 percent in the ages 45–49 and then climbs because white women's income rises somewhat while that of men falls. But a ratio of 56 among middle-aged working women is not exactly equity, and it calls for substantial improvement. At the same time, young workers are much closer to equity, which suggests that as they age and their successors enter the work force with a smaller relative disadvantage, the gender income gap will narrow even more, though the process is slow. In addition, with increasing age men tend to get larger raises and

Figure 5–1
Female/Male Income Ratio of Year-Round, Full-Time Workers, by Age and Race, 1985

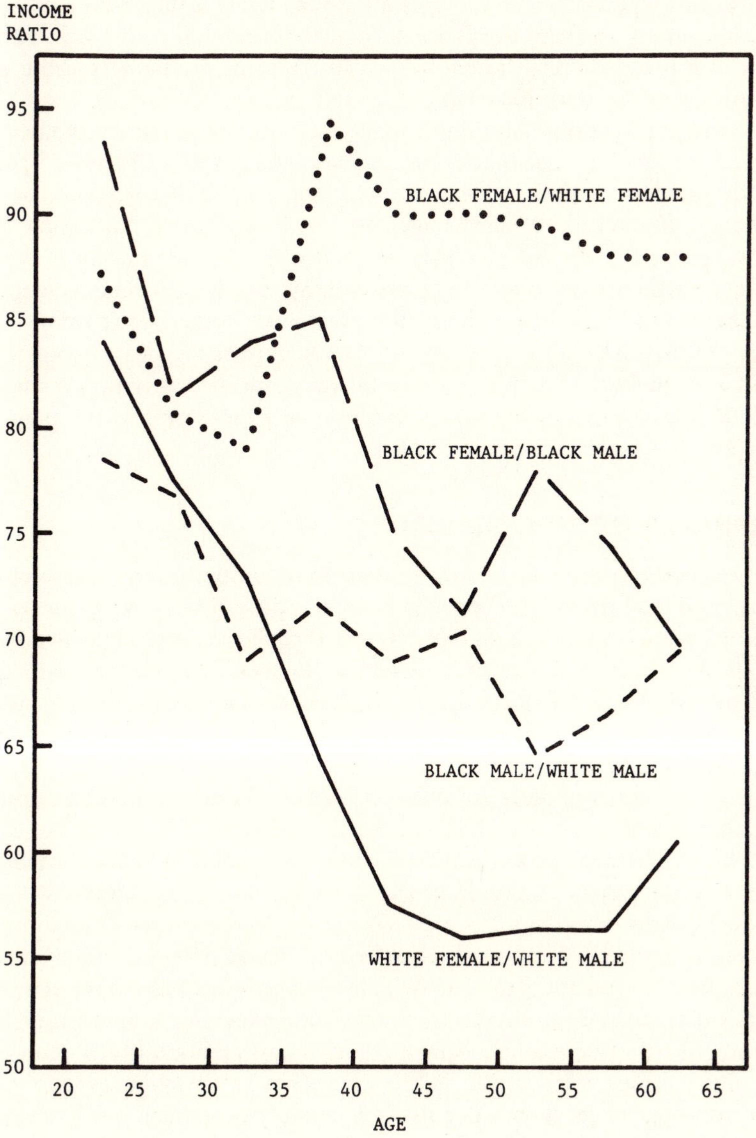

more promotions than women, and this accounts for part of the drop in the income ratio with age. That does not move toward equity either.

Among blacks, the female/male income ratio is higher at every age than it is for whites, because the income of black men still lags behind that of white men and is a lower base figure against which to measure women's income. Nevertheless, the highest female/male income ratio among black workers (94 percent) is in the ages 20–24, so while it falls with age, greater income equity seems in the making for year-round, full-time black workers, just as it is for whites, though subject to the same disclaimers about raises and promotions with increasing age.

These observations should not suggest a better situation for women than actually exists, because black working women aged 20–24 have 73 percent of the median income of working white men in those ages and the ratio falls steadily to only 49 in the ages 60–64. Furthermore, the people under consideration make up an "elite" group—year-round, full-time workers. Women who are not working or are employed only part time have median incomes drastically lower than fully employed women, let alone working men. Thus, controls for age, race, and work experience allow a look at men and women who are similar in certain ways, but the many persons who do not fit the work category are an exceptionally large part of the poor population.

DIFFERENCES BY RESIDENCE

Comparing personal income by metropolitan and nonmetropolitan and farm and nonfarm residence suggests where some of the poverty group lives, just as the discussion of family poverty did. The lowest cash incomes for both sexes are in the farm population, followed by the nonfarm group outside MSAs. (See Table 5–3.) The highest incomes are inside metropolitan areas with 1 million or more persons, followed by those in smaller MSAs. The population in large MSAs but in suburbs outside central cities fares the best in the metropolitan group—considerably better than suburbanites in smaller MSAs.

The female/male income ratio is 53 or less in all of the residence categories, but is most nearly equitable in the central cities of the largest MSAs. In suburbs, however, the ratio is exceptionally low, for even though median incomes for both sexes are highest there, men receive far larger amounts than women and the gap is wide. This is partly because many women in affluent suburbs do not work for wages and have no formal income of their own, and partly because women in two-earner households receive the smaller average wage by far. While the incomes of both sexes are lower in central cities of large MSAs than in suburbs, the gender gap is narrower. The cities also have unusually large numbers of poor persons, but poverty rates are higher in rural areas.

Table 5-3
Median Income of Persons Aged 15 and Over, by Residence, Race, and Gender, 1985

Residence	Income (Dollars)					
	All Races		White		Black	
	Female	Male	Female	Male	Female	Male
Inside MSAs						
All sizes	7,742	17,476	7,891	18,681	6,743	11,709
In central cities	7,747	15,419	8,187	16,833	6,461	10,987
Outside central cities	7,738	19,282	7,710	19,836	7,763	13,425
1,000,000 and over	8,355	18,662	8,612	20,213	7,193	12,435
In central cities	8,158	15,498	9,046	17,226	6,687	11,314
Outside central cities	8,519	21,183	8,408	21,762	10,048	15,570
Under 1,000,000	7,070	16,399	7,207	17,108	5,924	10,582
In central cities	7,282	15,321	7,556	16,421	6,002	10,393
Outside central cities	6,921	17,100	6,977	17,502	5,725	10,875
Outside MSAs						
All places	5,841	12,636	6,013	13,315	4,463	7,210
Nonfarm	5,929	12,941	6,123	13,679	4,477	7,255
Farm	4,430	10,002	4,455	10,117	a	a

Source: U.S. Bureau of the Census, "Money Income of Households, Families, and Persons in the United States: 1985," Current Population Reports, Series P-60, No. 156 (Washington, DC: Government Printing Office, 1987), Table 31.

[a]Base less than 75,000 persons.

MSAs with less than 1 million people have lower median incomes than larger MSAs. The female/male income ratio is also lower, both in central cities and suburbs. Men fare better in the suburbs than in the central cities, however, while the reverse is true for women. Many are householders living in relatively small cities and towns with serious poverty problems. In fact, women in the outlying areas of smaller MSAs have only 81 percent of the median income of women in the outlying parts of larger MSAs. The regional distribution of MSAs of various sizes affects this situation: In 1985 the median income of year-round, full-time female workers was $15,044 in the South, where many MSAs are relatively small, compared with significantly higher amounts in other regions where more of the large MSAs are located. The regional variations are less than they were, however, and differences among the regions in the purchasing power of income help moderate some of the remaining discrepancies.

Persons in nonmetropolitan places, both farm and nonfarm, have much lower median incomes than those in MSAs, at least the suburban parts. This gives nonmetropolitan populations their higher poverty rates, although that group is slightly better off than the one living in the central cities of MSAs, where most of the poverty population is concentrated.

Both sexes in the farm population have far higher poverty rates than the nonfarm group.[8] In 1985 about 20 percent of all farm persons in all types of families collectively were designated as poor, compared with 14 percent in the nonfarm segment. But for reasons discussed in chapter 3, while the poor are overrepresented in the whole rural-farm population, they are underrepresented in farm female-headed families; that is, the farm poor are more likely than the nonfarm poor to live in married-couple families. Persons in the farm population as a whole suffer unusually low incomes and high poverty rates; farm men have less than half the median income of men in suburbs of the largest MSAs, while farm women have just over half the income of their suburban counterparts. This does not prevent the female/male income ratios from being about the same and low in the two types of residence areas, however, and women are at a striking income disadvantage relative to men in all sorts of nonurban settings. Not only do persons in the rural population have the lowest incomes, but their prospects for improvement are minimal. Nearly all income must be consumed, so few rural poor can accumulate enough to escape poverty. Moreover, these problems are intergenerational despite outmigration, and the traditional ways of confronting them produce little change for the rural poor. For many rural people, low income, limited earning prospects, scarcity-oriented money management, and restricted job opportunities reinforce each other in a repeating cycle.[9]

The residential income patterns do differ significantly by race, beginning with the lower incomes and higher female/male income ratios among blacks than whites. In addition, the highest median income for black women is outside the central cities of large MSAs, whereas white women fare best inside those cities. For both races the lowest incomes are found in nonmetropolitan sections. The female/male income ratio for whites is highest in the central cities of MSAs, lowest in the areas just outside those cities. Conversely, the ratio for blacks is at its peak in the outlying places and lowest in the outlying parts of smaller MSAs. Many of the latter contain communities which are almost exclusively black and afflicted by high unemployment rates, poverty, and other consequences of local residential segregation. In contrast, most blacks who have made it to the suburbs of large MSAs are in the middle class, often because both members of the couple work. At the same time, single, separated, divorced, and widowed black women are more likely to live in central cities than in suburbs, and they

Table 5-4

Median Income of Persons Aged 25-34, by Educational Attainment, Work Experience, and Gender, 1985

Years of Schooling Completed	All Work Statuses			Year-Round, Full-Time Workers		
	Income (Dollars)		Female/Male Income Ratio[a]	Income (Dollars)		Female/Male Income Ratio[a]
	Female	Male		Female	Male	
Elementary school						
0-7 years	4,718	8,131	58.0	b	10,824	...
8 years	4,608	9,485	48.6	b	14,091	...
High school						
1-3 years	5,098	11,950	42.7	11,123	15,897	70.0
4 years	8,302	16,981	48.9	14,551	20,053	72.6
College						
1-3 years	10,897	19,994	54.5	16,694	22,828	73.1
4 years	15,733	25,561	61.6	20,430	27,371	74.6
5 or more years	18,737	27,812	67.4	23,441	31,964	73.3

Source: U.S. Bureau of the Census, "Money Income of Households, Families, and Persons in the United States: 1985," Current Population Reports, Series P-60, No. 156 (Washington, DC: Government Printing Office, 1987), Table 35.

[a]Median income of females as a percentage of median income of males.

[b]Base less than 75,000 persons.

have many more financial problems than married women. These conditions sort populations so that black women in the suburbs of major metropolises are relatively well off on the average.

DIFFERENCES BY LEVEL OF EDUCATION

The personal incomes of both sexes generally rise and the gender income gap narrows somewhat as the level of educational attainment increases.[10] There are exceptions, however, and the gender gap is actually smaller for persons who never finished the eighth grade than for those with 1-3 years of college. Since the data in Table 5-4 refer only to persons aged 25-34, age variations do not account for the tendency toward income parity at the lowest level of schooling. Instead, the jobs held by both women and men tend to pay poorly and other income sources are more equally deficient for both sexes. Moreover the median income of women who only completed the eighth grade is a little lower than the income of women who failed to attain even that level. Nor does women's income increase significantly as educational attainment rises until the level which separates high-school graduates from high-school dropouts. In fact, in 1985 the median incomes of women at all educational levels below high-school graduate were under the official poverty threshold for one person ($5,469). In contrast, the incomes of men at every educational level, including a mere 0–7 years of schooling, were above that threshold.

The largest difference in women's income by education (44 percent) is between those who completed 1–3 years of college and the ones who graduated, so a college degree is clearly a major asset. Post-graduate work, however, produces a smaller income increase (19 percent), though the category does range all the way from persons with a few weeks of graduate work and no degree to those with doctorates.

The female/male income gap is narrower for persons with the least amount of schooling than for any other eduational level below college graduate. Post-graduate training narrows it still further, but even at that plane women receive only a little more than two-thirds the income of men. On the whole, a woman college graduate receives a smaller median income than a man high-school graduate, and her median income is actually equivalent to that of a male high-school dropout.[11] In addition, a woman with a year or more of post-graduate study has a lower median income than a male college dropout, and even a female high-school graduate is no better off on the average than a man who never completed the eighth grade. These are serious inequities despite narrowing of the gender income gap and even though "educational attainment is relatively powerful in distinguishing individuals with different levels of earnings."[12] Educational achievement alone is far from enough to eradicate women's income disadvantage.

Combined Influence of Education and Work Experience

One can argue that women's incomes are lower than men's because women are more likely to work part year and part time. The argument has *some* merit, but much of the differential persists for other reasons.

If levels of education are held constant, as in Table 5–4, the incomes of female and male year-round, full-time workers are significantly closer than are the incomes of part-time employees and nonworkers. Moreover, college graduates working full time fare the best, and at that level women's median income is 75 percent of men's. Even for high-school dropouts the ratio is 70, and it is a bit higher for high-school graduates and college dropouts. Post-graduate work, however, still produces no increase in the female/male income ratio, and while post-graduate training raises men's median income 17 percent above those whose schooling ends with a bachelor's degree, for women the increase is only 15 percent.

This situation suggests that the highly educated working woman—often a professional or technical employee—is not rewarded commensurate with her training and is making relatively slow progress toward that goal. Part of the problem is a legacy of the past, when many highly skilled women (e.g., college professors) were hired at wages well below those of equally qualified men and since have found their incomes lagging, especially if both sexes received equal percentage raises. In addition, post-graduate education is more likely to produce a master's degree for a woman and a doctorate for a man, and the income discrepancy reflects that difference. Some women also delay childbearing until they complete advanced degrees, for "the more education a woman has the more likely she is to delay both marriage and childbearing."[13] But the delay can have costs, and the career interruptions which may follow late childbearing help account for the width of the income gap between highly educated men and women. Seniority, responsibility, promotion, and other avenues to higher income then become less available to women than to men. Thus, we need more flexible arrangements to accommodate delayed childbearing (or childbearing at any age) without penality, because a mother's job and income are often jeopardized as a result of bearing and nurturing the next generation.[14]

Net Assessment of Education

It would be foolish to infer from these conditions that education does not help women increase their incomes, lessen their chances of poverty, and improve their prospects for occupational and income parity with men. On the contrary, those who complete degrees leading to careers such as doctors and lawyers may earn at least five times as much as high-school dropouts and twice what holders of the bachelor's degree earn. Regardless of field and gender, the higher the level of education, the greater one's income is likely to be. This factor has been especially important for blacks, and it helped narrow the racial income gap among persons who entered the labor force in the 1970s and later.[15] Futhermore, while the gender income gap at the highest educational level has not closed, it is much smaller than at lower levels, though more because the best-educated women have good prospects for good positions than because they receive the same income as men once they are in them. Moreover, job mobility is somewhat limited because college women still tend to choose majors which are less likely than men's choices to ensure high-paying work.[16]

Nevertheless, education is one way up the status and wage scale and either out of or farther away from poverty. It also gives women more value as employees, makes them less expendable, improves their bargaining power as more of them fill strategic jobs, and tends to boost their incomes closer to those of men. For these reasons, two patterns are especially significant: (1) in 1985 only 16 percent of all women aged 25 and over but 23 percent of the men were college graduates; but (2) 21 percent of the women aged

25–29 and 23 percent of the men in those ages were graduates.[17] As the youthful group replaces older workers, women's progress in education should help them get better jobs and incomes. Well-educated women also have higher labor force participation rates than poorly educated women, and both the education and the participation have already helped raise working women's wages since 1980. They should narrow the gender gap even more in the 1990s.[18]

SOURCE OF PERSONAL INCOME

Among persons with cash income, wages and salaries provide the large bulk of income for women and men under age 65. Nonetheless, the relative importance of wages and other sources does differ by age, and the differences reflect socioeconomic variations between men and women and young and older adults.

Persons Aged 15–24

While young women derive far more of their income from wages and salaries than any other source, men are even more likely to do so. (See Table 5–5.) Women are also much less likely to have income from farm and nonfarm self-employment and from property, although interest accounts for the large bulk of property income which young adults of both sexes do receive. The proportion of young women with income from Social Security and SSI also is similar to that among young men—less than 5 percent. Public assistance, or welfare, however, provides income for five times as many women as men, while the latter are more likely to receive veterans benefits and workers' compensation. Finally, a much larger share of women receive alimony and child support, though the proportion is less than 2 percent of all those aged 15–24.

Persons Aged 25–64

Wages and salaries are the most likely income source for persons of both sexes aged 25–64, but property income rises to a fairly close second as a source, though not in dollars. A larger proportion of women than men receive property income, and interest remains the chief form for both. Income from Social Security rises in importance, more so for women than for men and often as survivors' benefits. Still, only 7 percent of the women and 5 percent of the men cite Social Security as a source, and a large share of them are people who retired at 62, 63, and 64. SSI for the aged, blind, and disabled remains a minor source for both sexes, but it is somewhat more important to women than to men. Welfare is a less important income source than it is for younger women, but still is cited four times more often by

Table 5–5
**Percent of Persons Who Have Income from Specified Sources, by Gender
and Age Group, 1985**

Income Source	Age Group		
	15–24	25–64	65 and over
Female			
Wages or salaries	84.1	71.4	8.9
Nonfarm self-employment	1.8	5.5	1.2
Farm self-employment	0.1	0.3	0.2
Property[a]	16.5	65.8	66.4
Social Security or railroad retirement	3.5	7.0	94.3
Supplemental Security Income (SSI)	1.0	1.6	8.2
Public assistance or welfare	7.2	4.7	0.6
Veterans, unemployment, or workers' compensation	3.6	6.1	3.2
Retirement pensions[b]	0.2	3.2	21.2
Alimony or child support	1.7	5.4	0.2
Other sources	13.0	4.4	1.5
Male			
Wages or salaries	88.8	83.5	16.7
Nonfarm self-employment	3.1	11.1	4.6
Farm self-employment	0.5	2.3	2.2
Property[a]	39.2	62.8	71.3
Social Security or railroad retirement	3.7	5.0	91.5
Supplemental Security Income (SSI)	0.8	1.1	4.0
Public assistance or welfare	1.4	1.3	0.3
Veterans, unemployment, or workers' compensation	5.7	11.2	6.9
Retirement pensions[b]	0.1	6.0	44.0
Alimony or child support	0.2	0.2	c
Other sources	12.1	4.0	1.5

Source: U.S. Bureau of the Census, "Money Income of Households, Families,
and Persons in the United States: 1985," Current Population Reports,
Series P-60, No. 156 (Washington, DC: Government Printing Office, 1987),
Table 38.

[a]Includes interest, dividends, rent, estates, and trusts.

[b]Includes private, military, federal, state, and local employee pensions.

[c]Less than 0.1 percent.

women than men. Veterans benefits and unemployment and workers' compensation grow in importance for both sexes in these ages, but mostly for men. This is because women have always received less than their fair share of most transfer payments, including unemployment compensation and disability benefits and governmental and private pensions, which they cite only half as often as men. The reasons include "earnings eligibility, regulations concerning 'domestic quits,' disqualification rules, pregnancy discrimination, sexual harassment, and requirements on availability, ability, and willingness to work."[19]

Many more women than men get alimony and child support, but still only 5 percent of the women claim that source. Both women and men aged 25–64 cite "other" sources at one-third the rate of those aged 15–24, because more of the younger people patch together incomes from families and other sources to supplement their frequently meager earnings.

Persons 65 and Over

The importance of various income sources is quite different for the elderly than for young and middle-aged people. Wages and salaries are a relatively minor source, though men are twice as likely as women to cite it. Self-employment income also declines in importance, though nearly five times as many elderly men as women receive it. Property income grows in significance for both sexes, but more for men than for women. Over 90 percent of both get Social Security income, though a larger share of women than men claim that source, partly because women are much less likely to have other pension income and must rely more heavily on Social Security. Usually a woman chooses a portion of her husband's benefit, because it is larger than what she could receive based on her own prior earnings, although this will change as more women with long work histories reach retirement. SSI, which helps the elderly poor far more than other age groups, is about twice as important a source for women as for men. So is welfare, but the proportion of elderly persons of either sex receiving it is a small fraction of the percentage in younger age groups, because Social Security replaces public assistance for most elderly poor. Veterans benefits and unemployment and workers' compensation decrease in importance as people leave the labor force, but men are still the principal beneficiaries.

Retirement income from private and government pensions grows significantly as a source, but only about 21 percent of the women and 44 percent of the men receive it. These proportions vividly underscore the need to extend private pensions to a far larger number of Americans, especially women, and to increase the average benefits, partly to meet the demands on Social Security when the baby boom retires.

Finally, alimony and child support and "other" income are minor sources for the elderly, and both sexes report them about equally.

These variations in sources of income by age and gender show that women are less likely than men to have income from wages and salaries; farm and nonfarm self-employment; veterans benefits and unemployment and workers' compensation; and private, military, and government pensions. Women are more likely to rely on Social Security, SSI, welfare, and alimony and child support. Very young and elderly women are less likely than men in those ages to have property income, whereas women aged 25–64 are more apt to cite that source. On balance, women have to depend more heavily than men on sources created in response to poverty, divorce, widowhood, and childbearing responsibilities, and they are less likely to rely on sources which reflect financial self-sufficiency and old-age security derived from their own work. Even so, wives who depend totally on their husbands' incomes have become a progressively smaller minority, and as married women age they become less dependent because more do have earnings as a base for Social Security benefits.[20] To some degree this applies to nonmarried women, though not enough to offset more than part of their average income deficiency. More women also participate in private pension plans and work long enough without interruption to be vested. In addition, the 1984 Retirement Equity Act requires that husbands get the consent of their wives before giving up any widow's benefits in their pensions, though many women whose husbands died before 1984 have no such protection. In a number of ways women's income situation is gradually growing more like that of men. The changes generate some optimism about prospects over the next few decades, though deliberate efforts rather than haphazard social evolution are necessary to speed the process and make it as rational as possible.

WORK EXPERIENCE AND INCOME

In the discussion of how income and education are related, work experience stood out clearly as a variable, showing that women's tendency to work fewer hours per day and fewer weeks per year than men is one important cause of their lower median income. In 1985, 54 percent of all male income recipients aged 15 and over but only 32 percent of the females were year-round, full-time workers, even though women surged into the labor force after 1970. Women always have been much more likely to be underemployed and unemployed and to receive less than their fair share of unemployment insurance, which was created largely for male householders and full-time workers.[21] This section accounts for the role work experience plays in producing age and gender income discrepancies.

Age of Workers

At every age, higher proportions of males than females work year round and full time, so different amounts of time invested in paid work do account for some of the gender income gap. Table 5–6 shows about how much. It gives 1985 median incomes, by age, of year-round, full-time workers. It also shows the female/male income ratios among these workers, and whenever the figure is below 100, other factors than the time worked must account for women's poorer position.

Table 5–6
Median Income of Year-Round, Full-Time Workers, by Age and Gender,
1985

Age	Income (Dollars)		Female/Male Income Ratio[a]
	Female	Male	
All ages	16,252	24,999	65.0
15–19	8,372	9,050	92.5
20–24	11,757	13,827	85.0
25–29	15,986	20,499	78.0
30–34	17,805	24,573	72.5
35–39	18,453	28,020	65.9
40–44	17,507	30,341	57.7
45–49	17,195	30,290	56.8
50–54	16,788	29,250	57.4
55–59	16,716	28,967	57.7
60–64	16,835	27,483	61.3
65–69	17,832	27,714	64.3
70 and over	19,178	23,694	80.9

Source: U.S. Bureau of the Census, "Money Income of Households, Families, and Persons in the United States: 1985," Current Population Reports, Series P-60, No. 156 (Washington, DC: Government Printing Office, 1987), Table 34.

[a]Median income of females as a percentage of median income of males.

"Equal pay for equal work," a goal articulated by Susan B. Anthony over a century ago, remains elusive. Women workers of all ages collectively still have a median income roughly two-thirds that for men—a figure which is rising slowly. But the ratios among women under 35 are much higher than the average for all ages, the ones for women over 40 significantly lower, at least up to age 65. Therefore, while the jobs held by women aged 35–64 still produce less than two-thirds the income of men, the situation of younger workers is better. At no age, however, do women workers have median incomes equal to those of men, and there is still substantial room to improve. Moreover, some of the favorable relative income situation in the younger ages is because men have not yet advanced into high-paying jobs, often leaving their female counterparts behind.

More young women are moving into positions with high wages, though most still enter jobs traditional for their sex. As noted earlier, sizable numbers of the jobs created during most of the 1980s carry relatively low status and pay, and they are disproportionately filled by women, which is one reason why 42 percent of the female poverty population aged 18–64 consists of women who work, many year round and full time. Thus, the nature of the local job structure, the forces which push more women than men toward the bottom of the occupational hierarchy, and lower pay for approximately the same work restrain women's job mobility and income and keep their poverty rates relatively high. So do the responsibilities faced by many women as sole parent or principal caregiver for aging relatives.

Weeks Worked

The major income discrepancy by gender is in full-time rather than part-time jobs, which pay both sexes poorly but which men are much less likely than women to accept.[22] Futhermore, many female part-time workers do choose that status, mainly because home responsibilities conflict with full-time work. However, "given that they have made the decision to work at all, most women now work full time, and nearly half also work all year."[23] A significant minority of part-time workers would prefer full-time jobs but lack them because employers curtail their hours during slack times or because they can find only part-time work.[24]

Table 5–7 shows the median incomes of full-time workers who are at their jobs year round or for shorter periods. It also gives the incomes of part-time employees who work year round or less. The largest income difference between the sexes is among people who work 50–52 weeks annually and on a full-time basis. Full-time workers who invest 13 weeks or less each year have the smallest differential, but the earnings for both sexes are very low—only about $1,100 in 1985. Such part-year jobs are subject to frequent layoff and rehiring, are inherently seasonal, or are otherwise relatively unstable and unpredictable.

Teachers with long summer vacations are among those who work 40–47 weeks each year. The income ratio in that group is higher than for people who work longer and shorter periods, largely because women incur somewhat less income discrimination in teaching than in many other fields, though this is more true in elementary and secondary schools than in colleges and universities. Women employed full time in other occupations also are more likely than men to work part year, to move in and out of the labor force, and to shift between full-time and part-time jobs.[25] Their incomes and poverty rates are affected accordingly, though partly by choice and partly by forces they cannot control.

People working in part-time jobs, even for 50–52 weeks per year, are poorly paid. Women are especially affected, because more than a quarter of all female workers are employed part time and the proportion rises during recessions when hours are cut back.[26] Consequently, part-time employment and the relatively high unemployment associated with it lead to higher poverty rates than other types of work commitment.[27] But even if poor women now working part time were to work full time at their present jobs, their hourly wages are so low that many would remain below the poverty

Table 5-7
**Median Income of Persons Aged 15 and Over with Various Types of
Work Experience, by Gender, 1985**

Work experience	Income (Dollars)		Female/Male Income Ratio[a]
	Female	Male	
Full-time workers			
Total	12,869	20,714	62.1
50-52 weeks	15,624	24,195	64.6
48 and 49 weeks	11,424	17,105	66.8
40-47 weeks	10,337	13,633	75.8
27-39 weeks	7,209	9,943	72.5
14-26 weeks	4,345	5,340	81.4
13 weeks or less	1,461	1,745	83.7
Part-time workers			
Total	2,906	2,735	106.3
50-52 weeks	5,552	5,386	103.1
40-49 weeks	4,264	4,785	89.1
27-39 weeks	3,130	3,342	93.7
14-26 weeks	1,711	1,843	92.8
13 weeks or less	1,074	1,117	96.2

Source: U.S. Bureau of the Census, "Money Income of Households, Families,
and Persons in the United States: 1985," Current Population Reports,
Series P-60, No. 156 (Washington, DC: Government Printing Office, 1987),
Table 41.

[a]Median income of females as a percentage of median income of males.

level. Thus, the relationship between limited work hours and poverty is a
fairly weak one, whether the hours worked result from the nature of the
job or periodic voluntary or involuntary unemployment.[28]

Among year-round, part-time workers, women have a slightly higher
median income than men. Even among those who work fewer than 50
weeks a year the earnings gap is fairly small. This greater equity results
partly from women's tendency to combine relatively stable part-time jobs
with childrearing and other responsibilities, whereas part-time male workers
are more apt to be elderly, disabled, or otherwise unemployable full time
and must settle for low earnings from unstable part-time sources. In addition, many women work longer hours at their part-time jobs, and while
their hourly wage may be only the legal minimum, their weekly earnings
may be slightly greater than those of men who work fewer hours. Even so,
in 1985 any person earning the minimum wage ($3.35) would have had to
work 50 weeks per year and somewhat over 33 hours per week just to earn
a poverty-level income for one person without dependents ($5,593). Add

Table 5–8
Median Income of Year-Round, Full-Time Workers, by Major
Occupational Category and Gender, 1985

Occupational category	Income (Dollars)		Female/Male Income Ratio[a]
	Female	Male	
Managerial and professional	21,322	32,787	65.0
Technical, sales, administrative support	15,117	24,957	60.6
Service	10,204	16,824	60.7
Farming, forestry, fishing	6,783	10,361	65.5
Precision production, craft, repair	15,093	23,269	64.9
Operators, fabricators, laborers	12,309	19,648	62.6

Source: U.S. Bureau of the Census, "Money Income of Households, Families, and Persons in the United States: 1985," Current Population Reports, Series P-60, No. 156 (Washington, DC: Government Printing Office, 1987), Table 39.

[a]Median income of females as a percentage of median income of males.

one dependent, and such an income would be far below the poverty threshold ($7,410), as is true for a person working year round and full time at the minimum wage. In fact, the median incomes of both male and female part-time workers were below the official poverty threshold, and persons who worked 13 weeks or less had a median income which was only 20 percent of the poverty level.

In sum, the greatest income gap persists between women and men who work year round and full time. Since differences in the amount of time worked cannot account for that gap, it leads to questions about how the jobs which women fill affect their incomes and how they and men are rewarded in the same occupational categories.

INCOME BY OCCUPATION

It is not feasible to compare men's and women's median incomes for an exhaustive list of occupations. But an abbreviated comparison suggests several things about how close the occupational structure comes to producing equitable earnings for roughly similar jobs. The comparison is confined to year-round, full-time workers and is based on two approaches. First, Table 5–8 lists all six major occupational categories used by the Bureau of the Census to organize the data on civilian occupations, each with median incomes for women and men and the female/male income ratio. Second,

Table 5–9 presents incomes and ratios for one group of specific occupations numerically dominated by women, another dominated by men.

Occupational Categories

Both women and men receive the highest median incomes in the managerial and professional occupations. For women those occupations as a whole pay about 41 percent more than the two nearest competitors: (1) technical, sales, and administrative support jobs; and (2) precision production, craft, and repair occupations. Men in the managerial and professional group receive 31 and 40 percent more, respectively, than men in the other two categories. The service occupations, where many new jobs for women have been created, have only half the median income of the managerial and professional group. In fact, the service industries (e.g., food service, cleaning and building service) generate an inordinate number of low-wage and intermittent jobs (e.g., fast-food cooks, janitors). Many workers in them are "contingent employees" who work part time on a temporary basis and who have significant periods of nonwork. Even the more stable positions provide low pay, few benefits, and no long-term security. Futhermore, the status and remuneration in these jobs are often affected by the assumption that women have income beyond their own earnings and are not fully committed to paid work.[29] The flood of women into the labor force after 1970 also increased competition and allowed employers to hold wages down, some to the point where the income did not keep even full-time workers and their dependents above the poverty level. Furthermore, women are not yet equal and full participants in the labor movement, and that limits the collective power they need to bargain for job and income equality.[30] Sexual harassment at work has similar effects, and since seven of every ten women face it at some time in their work lives, it can have significant effects on decisions about wages, job security, and other occupational conditions.[31]

The economy also has been losing jobs in many specific occupations in the category of precision production, craft, and repair workers or has been adding them slowly, and since women in that category receive a median income one-third larger than those in the service occupations, that loss of jobs is significant. Women who work as operators, fabricators, and laborers also receive a larger median income than service workers, but many manufacturing jobs in that category have been lost, especially in the automotive, consumer electronics, and textile industries. Consequently, the category which pays relatively low wages is adding jobs the fastest, whereas others which pay much better provide fewer opportunities. Even the process of creating new jobs in the service industries may slow down as more tasks are done without human labor and as employers seek ways to reduce their vulnerability to economic reversals, such as the October 1987 stock market drop and growth in foreign imports. The eventual loss of jobs in these areas

Table 5-9

Median Income of Year-Round, Full-Time Workers in Selected Occupations, by Gender Predominance, 1985

Gender and occupation	Income (Dollars)		Female/Male Income Ratio[a]
	Female	Male	
Women 70 percent or more of all employees			
Health assessing and treating workers	23,075	29,017	79.5
Teachers, except postsecondary	20,810	25,575	81.4
Health technicians	17,213	21,176	81.3
Licensed practical nurses	15,422	23,354	66.0
Cashiers	10,055	12,008	83.7
Computer operators	15,951	26,230	60.8
Secretaries, stenographers, typists	15,178	15,000	101.2
Financial records processors	14,861	19,294	77.0
Clerical and related workers	14,285	21,433	66.6
Health services workers	11,839	14,529	81.5
Personal services workers	8,842	15,645	56.5
Men 70 percent or more of all employees			
Manufacturing administrators	24,096	42,733	56.4
Engineers	31,361	36,615	85.7
Health diagnosing workers	30,755	58,557	52.5
Teachers, postsecondary	23,295	35,136	66.3
Lawyers and judges	30,703	48,679	63.1
Sales supervisors and proprietors	14,724	26,455	55.7
Farm operators and managers	1,724	6,979	24.7
Mechanics and repairers, except auto	25,204	25,111	100.4
Supervisors, precision production	18,032	28,506	63.3
Motor vehicle operators	11,783	19,494	60.4
Handlers, equipment cleaners, helpers, laborers	12,704	15,755	80.6

Source: U.S. Bureau of the Census, "Money Income of Households, Families, and Persons in the United States: 1985," Current Population Reports, Series P-60, No. 156 (Washington, DC: Government Printing Office, 1987), Table 39.

[a]Median income of females as a percentage of median income of males.

may come to parallel the loss of manufacturing jobs, and if more of the latter go abroad to low-wage countries, both men and women may find their prospects diminishing.[32] The job situation in manufacturing could improve, however, as the many older workers retire and the demand for entry-level, blue-collar skilled workers increases.[33] Moreover, as the value of the dollar began to fall in 1985 and American products were priced more attractively in overseas markets, manufacturing enjoyed some resurgence, especially in the late 1980s. This slowed the loss of some manufacturing jobs and escalated the creation of others, and by 1988 the net result was a fairly constant number of those positions, even while service jobs were increasing.

Technical, sales, and administrative support occupations also are creating more opportunities for women, and that category has a relatively high median income. It also employs a larger share of the female work force than any other category—47 percent in 1985. Within it, however, women are heavily represented as retail clerks; personal service employees; secretaries, stenographers, and typists; and financial records processors. Each of those specialities pays less than the median for female workers in all occupational categories collectively, so many of the prospects are none too bright in those fields either.

Despite the problems, more women are moving into occupations which do pay well, especially in the managerial and professional category. That group now employs about 29 percent of all year-round, full-time workers of both sexes. The sorting process still at work within it, however, tends to place women in the lower-paying specific occupations, but that segregation is decreasing slowly and should not obscure the progress underway. Progress or no, the median income of year-round, full-time women workers is still two-thirds or less that of men in all of the large occupational categories. (See Table 5–8.) To see whether this results from using the large categories or also applies to specific occupations, the analysis shifts to the latter.

Specific Occupations

The list of occupations in Table 5–9 consists of the two groups mentioned earlier: (1) those in which women are 70 percent or more of the work force; and (2) those in which men make up 70 percent or more of the total.[34] Each group happens to contain 11 occupations, listed in descending order of size of their work forces.

Except for farming, the typically "male" occupations generally pay members of both sexes more than the traditionally "female" jobs.[35] Consequently, as more women take nontraditional jobs, especially high-status ones, their incomes tend to improve. For example, women in six of the predominantly male occupations have higher median incomes than women earn in any of the predominantly female occupations. Futhermore, women in all of the male-dominated occupations collectively receive a median income 34 percent higher than women in the female-dominated group. Men in the male-dominated occupations, however, receive an income 54 percent higher than men in the female-dominated jobs. Therefore, even though women's average incomes are significantly higher in many of the nontraditional occupations, their incomes in the nontraditional ones are a smaller percentage of those received by men. For instance, while female health diagnosing workers (e.g., physicians) have a much higher income than women in any of the 11 female occupations, they still receive only 53 percent of the median income of male health diagnosing workers. This supports the contention that "women's work, whatever its content, is systematically devalued."[36]

In the 11 male-dominated occupations collectively, women receive only 65 percent of the income men get, whereas in the female-dominated occupations the figure is 75 percent. In two cases women even have slightly higher incomes than men. One is secretaries, stenographers, and typists, partly because it is a nontraditional field for men and they are less likely to have become executive secretaries or to have achieved seniority. Some also may be less authoritarian and assertive than men who seek more traditional jobs and, therefore, less inclined to demand higher wages.[37] They may also realize there are plenty of female workers to take their places should they become *too* assertive. The second instance is nonautomotive mechanics and repairers, where many of the female minority are employed in manufacturing at fairly high wages. In still other cases, mostly in the female-dominated occupations, the gender income ratio is 80 or more. That group includes elementary and secondary teachers, health workers, cashiers, and engineers. In the first three cases women are the large bulk of employees and many have acquired job security and its rewards, whereas men—in the minority— are more apt to be recent entrants with fewer of those perquisites.[38] Incomes in engineering, however, reflect the progress women have made recently by breaking into male occupations, and female engineers have a median income above those of women in any of the other 21 occupations listed in Table 5–9.

These comparisons reflect improvements in women's income in several occupations, but also the persistent gender income gap and the tendency for most working women to end up in jobs traditionally filled by women.[39] So progress is underway, but by many criteria it is not rapid and the road to income equity will be long. Moreover, about two-thirds of all women who work are either single, separated, divorced, widowed, or married to men who earn less than $10,000 a year. So most women still work because of economic necessity, often while they juggle child care, and many cannot spend the long training periods necessary to climb the status and income ladder. That problem, among others, forces many women to settle for the jobs they can get with the skills they have, and it contributes to low compensation and "burnout." Thus, "poverty and dependency are now the results not of women's relative exclusion from the wage labor force but of the very conditions under which women are actively incorporated into its ranks."[40]

Some women do attempt to improve their job and wage equity by various kinds of training. For instance, more have acquired the skills to move into automotive work, heating and air conditioning, woodworking, electrical installation, and other typical male preserves. Those fields, along with some of the professional service jobs, pay well. In the training programs for those fields, however, women are greatly outnumbered by men and often lack support for their efforts, including peer support. Many drop out of the programs and settle for traditional female work and its lower wages. Their childhood socialization also tends to push them toward female rather than male jobs, although less than it did in the past.[41] Even education, dispensed in part according to norms about "appropriate" male and female behavior and especially the home/mother role of women, is still partly differentiated by gender and helps perpetuate those differences in the occupational system.[42] In addition, entry into female occupations is often followed by differential on-the-job training and mobility opportunities which perpetuate gender segregation.[43]

On the bright side, employers are increasingly interested in women trained in the more lucrative trades, especially if those employers are women. The need to meet affirmative-action goals also prompts change. So there are opportunities, but if women are to use them fully they also need intangible supports such as assertiveness training and nurturing, along with tangible aids such as child care and transportation.

The preceding occupational comparisons do not account for differences in years worked, variable skill levels within an occupation, types of job responsibilities, absenteeism because of childbearing, and other factors which often work against women and help preserve the income gap. Nor do they account for women's role in the "informal economy," which involves work or other economic activity, whether or not for pay, outside the market economy and which is essentially unregulated and unmeasured by official agencies.[44] For these reasons and given the scope of this volume, the occupational comparisons are not a precise indicator of women's work roles or sexism, but they do show that women are still at a relative income disadvantage compared to men in nearly all occupations.[45]

COMPARABLE WORTH

The look at female and male incomes by occupations leads to a consideration of *comparable worth*. Basically, the concept implies that fewer women would be in poverty and their earnings would be closer to those of men if the jobs they hold and the work they do in those jobs were not undervalued. The need to correct that problem reflects the concomitant need to create a workable standard of comparable worth and techniques to make it operational.[46] The effort must deal with two kinds of occupational segregation.

First, women (and minorities) tend to be segregated into jobs demanding "less skill, effort, and responsibility than jobs filled by white males."[47] The lower median earnings of women follow from that segregation, although part of the income gap is due to the jobs women choose. That choice, in turn, is affected by their job skills and prior work experience, the constraints imposed by socialization, the length of time women plan to work, and the commitments they make to paid work and home responsibilities. If a woman's job skills and labor force commitment are lower than those of a man, she may be a less productive worker and paid accordingly. These factors actually do play some part in the gender income gap, but seem to explain no more than a third of it.[48]

Second, women suffer discrimination because disproportionate numbers who do have the same skills, exert the same effort, and exercise the same responsibility as white men are segregated into female jobs where the job itself is undervalued and the earnings are inadequate as a result.[49] This is a structural and attitudinal defect which few individual women can attack successfully. It may be useful to argue that an undereducated woman should acquire appropriate skills, but if a man does the same and then gets a traditionally male job which pays more than a comparably trained woman can earn in a traditionally female job, the solution does not get at the basic problem. Thus, efforts to implement comparable worth are necessary, but they also are threatening, partly because fair wage scales, unaffected by gender, would cost private and public employers more than they are willing to pay, and partly because comparable worth would undermine discrimination long accepted as "right." Yet as long as women are heavily segregated into female jobs, income equity is impossible without implementing comparable worth, because even when the demand for workers in predominantly female jobs rises, undervaluation of those jobs keeps incomes relatively low. Moreover, women's wages are rather weakly related to the skills they bring to the job; many of the skills they do have are not even seen as skills; and women often are felt not to need or be entitled to the same wages as men.[50] Comparable worth would address all of these anomalies, though alone it would neither dispel them nor eradicate women's poverty.[51] For women to be comparable to the 1.3 million men who work year round and full time but who are still poor, obviously would perpetuate a large residue of female poverty.

Comparable worth standards are affected by the market value of various jobs, the number of prospective employees available to fill them, and variable conditions from industry to industry and even firm to firm. Therefore, it is a fluid concept. But if wage discrimination and that portion of women's poverty related to it are to be reduced, the content of various jobs must be assessed to determine whether those jobs are compensated according to consistent standards of value or at artificially low standards which reflect (1) an abundance of women available to fill them, and (2) undervaluation of the things women do in their jobs. Such an analysis requires a description of what is performed in various jobs and a judgment about the value of that performance, excluding gender and using criteria which are as objective as possible to establish standards of worth.[52] With such information used to restructure the relationships between jobs, job holders, and earnings, women could receive the same wages as men for comparable yet different work.

It is difficult to conceputalize and implement comparable worth, but the alternatives are perpetual income inequity and exceptionally high poverty rates for a large group of women. Conversely, the benefits of comparable worth would accrue not only to working women, but to husbands in two-income families, to all males whose taxes now help support poor women and their children, and to children in female-headed families.[53] At base, "comparable worth is a concept that rejects the premise of a separate and lower wage hierarchy for women."[54] It reiterates the principle of equal opportunity which supposedly undergirds American workers' access to jobs and wages. If this is a goal, comparable worth cannot be accomplished by "free-market" dynamics, because they incorporate gender inequality. Instead, its implementation calls for deliberate change in those dynamics and in values and institutions.

TRENDS IN PERSONAL INCOME

Trends by Gender and Race

The median income of women has been increasing faster than that of men, though not dramatically so. Table 5–10 and Figure 5–2 show that overall income growth between 1959 and 1985 was greater for women than for men, both in current dollars and constant 1985 dollars. There was no individual year between those dates when women's income in current dollars failed to rise by at least 1.4 percent (1961) and as much as 13.1 percent (1980). Men's income also rose, though in 19 of the 26 years the pace of increase was slower for them than for women. As a result, the female/male income ratio, unadjusted for work experience, rose from 31 in 1959 to 44 in 1985.

Each year and for both sexes, however, the purchasing power of the income either increased more slowly than the current dollar amount or dropped, especially during periods of high inflation. The fluctuations in real income are reflected in Figure 5–2, which shows the percentage change in constant 1985 dollars, using the annual Consumer Price Index (CPI) to adjust for alterations in the purchasing power of persons' income.

For women the constant dollar amount of income rose as much as 7.6 percent (1968) and fell as much as 4.1 percent (1978). For men, however, the greatest increase was only 6.3 percent (1965), the largest drop 6.3 percent (1980). The constant dollar income of men also rose slower than that of women in 21 of the 26 years between 1959 and 1985. Therefore, women's somewhat greater increases gradually narrowed the gap in real income, and after 1974 the gap decreased steadily.

Table 5-10
Increase in Median Income of Persons, by Gender and Race, 1959-1985

Gender and Race	Income					
	Current Dollars			Constant 1985 Dollars		
	1959	1985	Percent Increase 1959-1985	1959	1985	Percent Increase 1959-1985
Female[a]						
All races	1,223	7,217	490.1	4,514	7,217	59.9
White	1,312	7,357	460.7	4,841	7,357	52.0
Black[b]	808	6,473	701.1	2,982	6,473	117.1
Male[a]						
All races	3,997	16,311	308.1	14,752	16,311	10.6
White	4,209	17,111	306.5	15,533	17,111	10.2
Black[b]	1,981	11,350	472.9	7,312	11,350	55.2

Source: U.S. Bureau of the Census, "Money Income of Households, Families, and Persons in the United States: 1985," Current Population Reports, Series P-60, No. 156 (Washington, DC: Government Printing Office, 1987), Tables 29, 30.

[a]Persons aged 14 and over in 1959 and 15 and over in 1985.

[b]Includes other races.

White women made slower progress than black women. Because black men still have only two-thirds the median income of white men, however, the female/male discrepancy remains less for blacks than for whites. In the 1959-85 period, white women's real income went from 31 to 43 percent of that of white men. For blacks the proportion rose from 41 to 57 percent. At the same time, the income of black men increased considerably faster than that of white men as blacks improved their labor market status, especially in the 1960s and 1970s.[55] The gender gap decreased 0.46 percent per year for whites and 0.62 percent for blacks. Both convergences represent progress for women, but not rapid progress.

Trends by Educational Attainment

The educational standing of both sexes has improved steadily and has helped increase women's income and narrow the gender gap. This section examines that relationship using only the 25-34 age group, because the analysis needs an age control, this group represents fairly recent educational

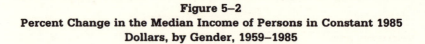

Figure 5–2
**Percent Change in the Median Income of Persons in Constant 1985
Dollars, by Gender, 1959–1985**

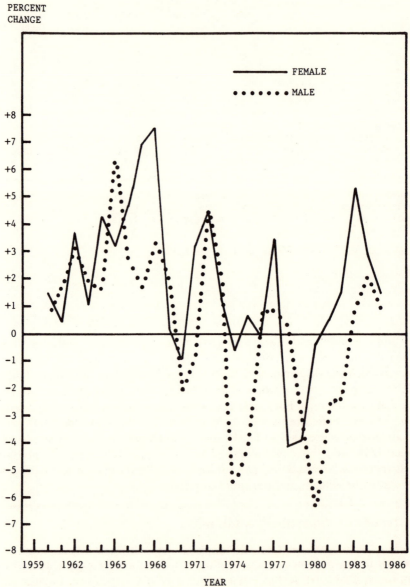

Table 5-11
Highest Level of Schooling Completed by Persons Aged 25–34, by Gender, 1980–1985

Years of Schooling Completed	Female			Male		
	Number (Thousands)		Percent Change 1980–1985	Number (Thousands)		Percent Change 1980–1985
	1980	1985		1980	1985	
Elementary school						
0-7 years	490	504	+2.9	535	581	+8.6
8 years	368	299	-18.7	372	361	-3.0
High school						
1-3 years	1,986	1,910	-3.8	1,679	1,887	+12.4
4 years	8,427	8,953	+6.2	6,991	8,359	+19.6
College						
1-3 years	4,013	4,616	+15.0	4,185	4,488	+7.2
4 years	2,548	3,329	+30.7	2,881	3,338	+15.9
5 or more years	1,371	1,485	+8.3	1,981	1,941	-2.1
Median years	12.8	12.9	...	13.0	12.9	...

Source: U.S. Bureau of the Census, "Money Income of Households, Families, and Persons in the United States: 1980," Current Population Reports, Series P-60, No. 132 (Washington, DC: Government Printing Office, 1982), Table 51; U.S. Bureau of the Census, "Money Income of Households, Families, and Persons in the United States: 1985," Current Population Reports, Series P-60, No. 156 (Washington, DC: Government Printing Office, 1987), Table 35.

changes, and it is making relatively rapid progress in closing the gender income gap. In addition, 1980–85 was chosen as the time period in order to examine changes when the Reagan administration refocused spending priorities and the 1982–83 recession hit.

Percentage changes in the numbers of persons at most of the seven levels of schooling reflect greater educational improvement for women than for men. (See Table 5–11.) That is, the number with a mere 0–7 years of schooling rose for both sexes, but faster for men; the number of women who had finished only the eighth grade dropped six times faster than the number of men at that level; the number of female high-school dropouts fell while that of men rose significantly. The number of male high-school graduates did rise three times faster than that of female graduates, but the number of women who had 1–3 years of college, who graduated, and who pursued post-graduate schooling all increased faster. The rate of increase among female college graduates was twice that among males. Thus, the greater reductions in numbers of women at the lower end of the educational scale and their larger increases at the upper end suggest the extent to which they are using higher education to enhance their economic circumstances, including career prospects and wage-earning potential. Significant discrepancies persist, however, for in 1985 women college graduates received a median income of only $15,733, while male high-school graduates received $16,981.

Trends by Education and Work Experience

Education is not the only factor which raises income, and since it and work experience are both influential, they need to be considered together. Table 5–12 provides data for year-round, full-time workers aged 25–34, and it compares 1980 with 1985. The trends are fairly encouraging. For several decades the median income of working women at all educational levels lodged at about 60 percent of that of men.[56] Between 1980 and 1985, however, the figure rose to 65 percent. In the latter year women who were high-school graduates and those who attended college and the ones who graduated all had median incomes closer to those of comparably educated men than they did in 1980. Among college graduates, in 1985 women received about three-quarters the income of men. But the picture clouds for working women with post-graduate degrees, for their income fell as a percentage of men's income, and the female/male income ratio ended up close to the one for college dropouts. For nonworking women at the post-graduate level the gap did narrow, but less than at any other educational plane.

These patterns show that even though education and work experience strongly affect the earnings gap between men and women, when both variables are held constant there is still a significant gap. Nor do work interruptions seem to play a major role, even though women are more likely than men to have them.[57] That leaves a substantial residue of structural and attitudinal flaws, such as sexism, racism, the "old-boy network," persistent job segregation and gender-typing, and socialization for certain careers over others.

Trends by Occupation

Women's incomes have risen faster than those of men in most of the major occupational categories. In presenting the changes this section compares 1982 with 1985, because descriptions of the occupational categories were altered sufficiently in 1982 to affect comparability. Table 5–13 shows the percentages by which the median incomes of male and female year-

Table 5-12
**Median Income of Women Aged 25-34 as a Percentage of Median
Income of Men Aged 25-34, by Educational Attainment and Work
Experience, 1980-1985**

Years of Schooling Completed	Female/Male Income Ratio[a]				
	All Work Statuses		Year-Round, Full-Time Workers		
	1980	1985		1980	1985
Elementary school					
0-7 years	46.5	58.0		b	b
8 years	47.3	48.6		b	b
High school					
1-3 years	36.8	42.7		63.8	70.0
4 years	41.4	48.9		66.9	72.6
College					
1-3 years	50.2	54.5		68.2	73.1
4 years	55.3	61.6		71.1	74.6
5 or more years	66.5	67.4		76.1	73.3

Source: U.S. Bureau of the Census, "Money Income of Households, Families, and Persons in the United States: 1980," Current Population Reports, Series P-60, No. 132 (Washington, DC: Government Printing Office, 1982), Table 51; U.S. Bureau of the Census, "Money Income of Households, Families, and Persons in the United States: 1985," Current Population Reports, Series P-60, No. 156 (Washington, DC: Government Printing Office, 1987), Table 35.

[a]Median income of females as a percentage of median income of males.

[b]Base less than 75,000 persons.

round, full-time workers rose and how the female/male income ratio changed in each of the six major occupational groups.

Women gained ground faster than men in the managerial and professional category, which is the fastest growing occupational group.[58] Their incomes also improved more rapidly in technical, sales, and administrative support positions, in service jobs, and even in farming. On the other hand, women's incomes grew slower than those of men in precision production, craft, and repair occupations, and in the group of operators, fabricators, and laborers, where the number of jobs has been decreasing.[59] The relative deterioration in those two categories reflects the loss of many well-paying jobs in manufacturing, the high overall unemployment rates in some of those industries,

Table 5–13

Change in Median Income of Year-Round, Full-Time Workers, by Occupational Category and Gender, 1982–1985

Occupational Category	Percent Change, 1982–1985 (Current Dollars)		Female/Male Income Ratio[a]	
	Female	Male	1982	1985
Managerial and professional	18.5	15.6	63.4	65.0
Technical, sales, administrative support	20.2	16.6	58.8	60.6
Service	19.1	16.4	59.2	60.7
Farming, forestry, fishing	26.8	13.9	58.8	65.5
Precision production, craft, repair	11.1	11.3	65.0	64.9
Operators, fabricators, laborers	11.6	14.1	64.0	62.6

Source: U.S. Bureau of the Census, "Money Income of Households, Families, and Persons in the United States: 1982," Current Population Reports, Series P-60, No. 142 (Washington, DC: Government Printing Office, 1984), Table 51; U.S. Bureau of the Census, "Money Income of Households, Families, and Persons in the United States: 1985," Curent Population Reports, Series P-60, No. 156 (Washington, DC: Government Printing Office, 1987), Table 39.

[a]Median income of females as a percentage of median income of males.

and the higher unemployment rates among women than men. The modest improvements for women relative to men in the other occupational categories reflect the movement of more women into former male strongholds, a gradual tendency toward more equitable pay at the same level of skill and responsibility, and some increases in women's job seniority. That factor is especially promising, because young women in traditionally male jobs now have no higher turnover rates than men, and that should contribute to women's lengthening job tenure and whatever benefits go with it.[60]

Within the major categories, women's income gained on that of men most rapidly in the following specific occupations, ranked in descending order of closure of the gender income gap: elementary and secondary teachers; nonautomotive mechanics and repairers; engineers; financial records processors; clerical and related workers; manufacturing administrators; health service workers; and handlers, equipment cleaners, and laborers. Thus, some of the largest relative improvements are in nontraditional fields, so opening male jobs to more women does raise their incomes. Other improvements occurred in jobs traditionally held by women, but where rewards for their skills and performance have improved.

In the other occupations discussed earlier and shown in Table 5–9, women's median incomes increased slower than those of men. Women lost the most ground relative to men as college and university teachers, cashiers, personal service workers, computer operators, lawyers and judges, health diagnosing workers, health assessing and treating workers, and salaried sales supervisors and proprietors. There was little change among health technicians and precision production supervisors. Some women in some of these fields are recent entrants and their incomes are comparatively low for that reason. Others were hired several years ago at lower wages than men, so identical percentage salary increases actually widen the female/male dollar gap. In still other occupations the number of jobs has decreased and women are more likely to be relegated to the poorer ones which remain.

Whatever the reasons, progress in closing the gender income gap in various occupations is mixed. In certain fields, including some in which women are scarce and others in which they are abundant, the gap has shrunk. In other fields, especially those which remain strong male bastions and where the few women are relative newcomers, there has been little or no progress. Overall, much of the work women do is still undervalued and many women are still in low-paying jobs. Past and present discrimination also keeps all but a few women out of the top levels of administration and management in virtually all occupations, so appropriate role models for women who aspire to those levels are scarce.[61] In addition, for several decades the jobs which are gender-typed as "female" have produced more demand for workers than "male" jobs, and employers have tended to seek women rather than men to fill them. This demand for women has helped increase their labor force participation, but it also has helped preserve gender-typing, which slows women's entry into male jobs.[62] Because the female jobs pay lower average wages, these dynamics have retarded closure of the gender income gap.

TRENDS IN UNEMPLOYMENT

Women are more likely than men to be unemployed, though the peaks and valleys from year to year follow the same pattern for both sexes. (See Figure 5–3.) This situation changed somewhat in 1982 and 1983, however, when unemployment rates for women were lower than those for men. When the economy slows, as it did in those years, women's unemployment does not rise as much as men's because the clerical and service jobs where women are concentrated are less affected than construction, heavy industry, and other fields where men predominate. But the male-dominated industries also recover faster in good times, and men's unemployment rates drop more dramatically. Furthermore, women in male-dominated fields are apt to be the first fired in bad times because they lack seniority, so the lower unemployment rates of women in at least two fairly recent years are due to their concentration in traditionally female jobs.[63] Even there, however, job tenure

Figure 5–3
Percent of Persons Unemployed, by Gender, 1970–1985

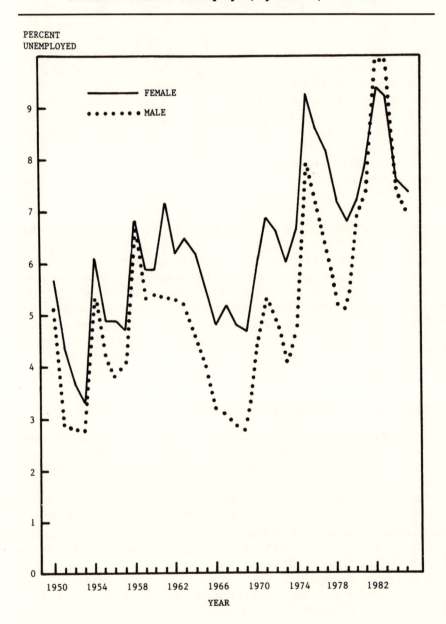

often is shorter for women than for men. In January 1987, for instance, 32 percent of all women workers but only 26 percent of the men had been with their current employer for a year or less, and only 5 percent of the women but 13 percent of the men had been with the same employer for 20 years or more.[64]

The unemployment pattern also changes when one considers it in a family context, and as in so many other ways, female-headed families are at a distinct disadvantage. In 1986, for example, 6 percent of the persons in married-couple families were unemployed, compared with 14 percent in those maintained by a woman. Conversely, while 78 percent of the married-couple units had at least one employed member, that was true in only 46 percent of the families headed by a woman.[65] On balance, unemployment patterns are especially unfavorable for women and their dependents—even more so than the official statistics suggest.

NOTES

1. Paula England and George Farkas, *Households, Employment, and Gender* (New York: Aldine, 1986), p. 121.

2. U.S. Bureau of the Census, Cynthia M. Taeuber and Victor Valdisera, "Women in the American Economy," *Current Population Reports*, Series P–3, No. 146 (Washington, DC: Government Printing Office, 1986), p. 31.

3. England and Farkas, *Households, Employment, and Gender*, p. 177.

4. For a history of low wages for American women, see Roslyn L. Feldberg, "Comparable Worth: Toward Theory and Practice in the United States," In Barbara C. Gelpi, Nancy C. M. Hartstock, Clare C. Novak, and Myra H. Strober, eds., *Women and Poverty* (Chicago: University of Chicago Press, 1986), pp. 165–170.

5. Greg J. Duncan, Richard D. Coe, and Martha S. Hill, "The Dynamics of Poverty," in Greg J. Duncan, Richard D. Coe, Mary E. Corcoran, Martha S. Hill, Saul D. Hoffman, and James N. Morgan, *Years of Poverty, Years of Plenty* (Ann Arbor, MI: Institute for Social Research, 1984), p. 60.

6. James P. Smith and Finis R. Welch, *Closing the Gap: Forty Years of Economic Progress for Blacks* (Santa Monica, CA: Rand Corporation, 1986), p. 103.

7. Greg J. Duncan and Saul D. Hoffman, "Recent Trends in the Relative Earnings of Black Men," in Duncan and others, *Years of Poverty*, pp. 138–139.

8. Donald Tomaskovic-Devey, "Labor Markets, Industrial Structure, and Poverty: A Theoretical Discussion and Empirical Example," *Rural Sociology* 52:1 (Spring 1987), p. 69.

9. Janet M. Fitchen, *Poverty in Rural America* (Boulder, CO: Westview Press, 1981), p. 100. See also Rachel Ann Rosenfeld, *Farm Women: Work, Farm, and Family in the United States* (Chapel Hill, NC: University of North Carolina Press, 1986).

10. James P. Smith and Michael P. Ward, *Women's Wages and Work in the Twentieth Century* (Santa Monica, CA: Rand Corporation, 1984), p. 68.

11. U.S. Bureau of the Census, "Women in the American Economy," p. 30. See also Congressional Caucus for Women's Issues, Sara E. Rix, ed., *The American Woman 1987–88* (New York: W. W. Norton, 1987).

12. Greg J. Duncan and Saul D. Hoffman, "The Dynamics of Work Hours, Unemployment, and Earnings," in Duncan and others, *Years of Poverty*, p. 123.

13. Wendy H. Baldwin and Christine Winquist Nord, "Delayed Childbearing in the U.S.," *Population Bulletin* 39:4 (Washington, DC: Population Reference Bureau, 1984), p. 2. See also David E. Bloom and James Trussell, "What Are the Determinants of Delayed Childbearing and Permanent Childlessness in the United States?" *Demography* 21:4 (November 1984), p. 607.

14. Baldwin and Nord, "Delayed Childbearing," p. 21.

15. Smith and Welch, *Closing the Gap*, pp. 40–41.

16. U.S. Bureau of the Census, "Women in the American Economy," p. 15.

17. U.S. Bureau of the Census, "Educational Attainment in the United States: March 1982 to 1985," *Current Population Reports*, Series P–20, No. 415 (Washington, DC: Government Printing Office, 1987), p. 2.

18. Smith and Ward, *Women's Wages and Work*, pp. 77–78. See also U.S. Bureau of the Census, "What's It Worth? Educational Background and Economic Status: Spring 1984," *Current Population Reports*, Series P–70, No. 11 (Washington, DC: Government Printing Office, 1987).

19. Diana M. Pearce, "Toil and Trouble: Women Workers and Unemployment Compensation," in Gelpi and others, *Women and Poverty*, p. 152.

20. Annemette Sørensen and Sara McLanahan, "Married Women's Economic Dependency, 1940–1980," *American Journal of Sociology* 93:3 (November 1987), p. 659.

21. Pearce, "Toil and Trouble," p. 141.

22. Joan Smith, "The Paradox of Women's Poverty: Wage-earning Women and Economic Transformation," in Gelpi and others, *Women and Poverty*, p. 135.

23. Linda J. Waite, "U.S. Women at Work," *Population Bulletin* 36:2 (Washington, DC: Population Reference Bureau, 1981), p. 24.

24. U.S. Bureau of the Census, "Population Profile of the United States: 1984–85," *Current Population Reports*, Series P–23, No. 150 (Washington, DC: Government Printing Office, 1987), p. 31.

25. Duncan and Hoffman, "The Dynamics of Work Hours," p. 95.

26. Pearce, "Toil and Trouble," p. 146.

27. Ibid, p. 149.

28. Duncan, Coe, and Hill, "The Dynamics of Poverty," pp. 53–54. See also Mary Corcoran and Martha S. Hill, "Unemployment and Poverty," *Social Science Review* 54:3 (September 1980), pp. 407–413.

29. Smith, "The Paradox of Women's Poverty," p. 122.

30. Margaret Beattie, "The Representation of Women in Unions," *Signs: Journal of Women in Culture and Society* 12:1 (Autumn 1986), p. 129.

31. Catherine MacKinnon, *Sexual Harassment of Working Women* (New Haven, CT: Yale University Press, 1979), p. 3.

32. Leon F. Bouvier, "Planet Earth 1984–2034: A Demographic Vision," *Population Bulletin* 39:1 (Washington, DC: Population Reference Bureau, 1984), p. 6.

33. Jane Newitt, "Will the Baby Bust Work?" *American Demographics* 9:9 (September 1987), p. 35.

34. A rationale for this classification is in the U.S. Bureau of Labor Statistics, Nancy F. Rytina and Suzanne M. Bianchi, "Occupational Reclassification and Changes in Distribution by Gender," *Monthly Labor Review* 107:3 (March 1984),

pp. 11–17. See also the related approach in Marta Tienda and Shelley A. Smith, "Industrial Restructuring, Gender Segregation, and Sex Differences in Earnings," *American Sociological Review* 52:2 (April 1987), p. 207.

35. Amy S. Wharton and James N. Baron, "So Happy Together? The Impact of Gender on Men at Work," *American Sociological Review* 52:5 (October 1987), p. 575.

36. Feldberg, "Comparable Worth," p. 171.

37. Wharton and Baron, "So Happy Together?" p. 585.

38. For a study of this and related phenomena, see Carol Tropp Schreiber, *Changing Places: Men and Women in Transitional Occupations* (Cambridge, MA: MIT Press, 1981).

39. Pearce, "Toil and Trouble," p. 147. See also U.S. Bureau of the Census, "Women in the American Economy," p. 18.

40. Smith, "The Paradox of Women's Poverty," p. 140.

41. England and Farkas, *Households, Employment, and Gender*, p. 154.

42. Sally Schwager, "Educating Women in America," *Signs: Journal of Women in Culture and Society* 12:2 (Winter, 1987), p. 336.

43. England and Farkas, *Households, Employment, and Gender*, p. 163.

44. Michele Hoyman, "Female Participation in the Informal Economy: A Neglected Issue," in Louis A. Ferman, Stuart Henry, and Michele Hoyman, eds., "The Informal Economy," *Annals of the American Academy of Political and Social Science* 493 (September 1987), p. 65.

45. For an evaluation of several factors which affect income, see Smith and Ward, *Women's Wages and Work*.

46. Ronnie J. Steinberg, "A Want of Harmony: Perspectives on Wage Discrimination and Comparable Worth," in Helen Remick, ed., *Comparable Worth and Wage Discrimination* (Philadelphia, PA: Temple University Press, 1984), p. 17. See also England and Farkas, *Households, Employment, and Gender*, pp. 166–172; and Steven L. Willborn, *A Comparable Worth Primer* (Lexington, MA: Lexington Books, 1986).

47. Steinberg, "A Want of Harmony," p. 17.

48. Greg J. Duncan and Mary E. Corcoran, "Do Women 'Deserve' to Earn Less than Men?" in Duncan and others, *Years of Poverty*, pp. 153–154, 163, 168.

49. Steinberg, "A Want of Harmony," p. 17. See also Feldberg, "Comparable Worth," pp. 163–164.

50. Tienda and Smith, "Industrial Restructuring," p. 197.

51. Feldberg, "Comparable Worth," pp. 172–174, 180. See also Duncan and Corcoran, "Do Women 'Deserve' to Earn Less than Men?" pp. 168–170.

52. Steinberg, "A Want of Harmony," pp. 18–19.

53. Kim M. Blankenship, review of *The Economics of Comparable Worth*, by Mark Aldrich and Robert Buchele (Cambridge, MA: Ballinger, 1986), in *Contemporary Sociology* 16:5 (September 1987), p. 627.

54. Feldberg, "Comparable Worth," p. 164.

55. Duncan and Hoffman, "Recent Trends in the Relative Earnings of Black Men," p. 129. See also Smith and Welch, *Closing the Gap*, p. vii.

56. England and Farkas, *Households, Employment, and Gender*, p. 163. See also Smith and Ward, *Women's Wages and Work*, p. 23.

57. U.S. Bureau of the Census, "Lifetime Work Experience and Its Effect on

Earnings: Retrospective Data from the 1979 Income Survey and Development Program," *Current Population Reports*, Series P–23, No. 136 (Washington, DC: Government Printing Office, 1984), p. 5. See also Larry E. Suter and Herman P. Miller, "Income Differences Between Men and Women," *American Journal of Sociology* 78:4 (January 1973), pp. 962–974.

58. U.S. Bureau of the Census, "Population Profile of the United States: 1984–85," p. 31.

59. Ibid.

60. Linda J. Waite and Sue E. Berryman, "Job Stability among Young Women: A Comparison of Traditional and Nontraditional Occupations," *American Journal of Sociology* 92:3 (November 1986), p. 593.

61. Alexander W. Astin, "Data Pertaining to the Education of Women: A Challenge to the Federal Government," in U.S. Bureau of the Census, Barbara B. Reagan, ed., "Issues in Federal Statistics Needs Relating to Women," *Current Population Reports*, Series P–23, No. 83 (Washington, DC: Government Printing Office, 1979), p. 81.

62. England and Farkas, *Households, Employment, and Gender*, pp. 148–149.

63. Waite, "U.S. Women at Work," p. 24.

64. U.S. Bureau of Labor Statistics, "Most Occupational Changes Are Voluntary," *News* (October 22, 1987), Table 4.

65. U.S. Bureau of Labor Statistics, "Employment and Earnings Characteristics of Families: Third Quarter 1987," *News* (October 26, 1987), Table 5.

6

Some Suggestions for Action

Chapters 2–5 present the nature and magnitude of some problems faced by women. Those discussions also show how unfavorably women compare with men on many measures of economic well-being, especially poverty rates and income. It is argued that women's relative disadvantage stems largely from the structure and dynamics of the American social system, including its family institution, socialization patterns, job market, and attitudes about women's work and worth. After recounting these things, the book would be incomplete without proposing some ways to change the basic flaws responsible for the problems, though some suggestions do appear in the context of each chapter.

In part, the abbreviated agenda for action which follows is an adaptation of numerous conclusions reached during the United Nations Decade for Women (1975–85), which culminated at the U.N. Decade for Women World Conference in Nairobi, Kenya, in 1985.[1] Naturally, not all problems of the world's women are of major significance in the United States: Few American women are landless agricultural laborers, for example, nor are many starving, though sizable numbers are hungry. But women are the world's largest minority group, if "minority" means a category of people who are treated as inferiors and who lack power because they share a particular characteristic, such as race, ethnicity, religion, or, in this case, gender.[2] In that sense American women do share sisterhood with women in all countries, and at least some problems are universal, often varying only in degree. Those problems relate in one way or another to subordination, so efforts to purge women's status of various forms of inequality also should help lessen and finally even solve the problems. Thus, the Nairobi document, *Forward Looking Strategies for the Advancement of Women to the Year 2000*, combined with other sources, identifies many steps necessary to improve the status of America's poor women and their children.[3]

The forms of action presented in the following pages are organized according to eight categories of needs:

1. Equality
2. Economic development
3. Political power
4. Education
5. Family strength
6. Health care
7. Welfare reform
8. Other needs

EQUALITY

Women's greatest need is for equality, not just legal equality which prohibits discrimination in jobs, credit, and other aspects of daily life, but also equal rights with men to have responsibilities and opportunities and to participate in decision-making processes at all levels.[4] With equality in place, women could help more fully to create hiring policies, reform government programs designed to help women, reassess other programs whose costs divert funds from the needs of women and children, shape the content of education, and propose and implement other changes. These long have been conceptualized and implemented primarily according to male perspectives about who should do and get what in the social system. Thus, equality means the full participation of women in deciding what the American system will become and what it will offer both females and males as dependent children, working adults, and elders.

Attitudes

Inequality is due largely to the attitude that women's productive and reproductive potential deserves a second-rate place in the social system. Thus, many norms—the basic expectations which constrain some behaviors and encourage others—subordinate women because men believe an inferior role is appropriate and because women are socialized to accept the belief or to accommodate even if they reject it. Any domination-subordination relationship requires a group willing to dominate and another willing or forced to submit, and attitudes which preserve that submission also generate persistent inequality. In fact, given the nature of gender-related attitudes in virtually all societies, it is remarkable that the women's movement has helped decrease inequality as much as it has. Women (and many men) will not let the process reverse, and as attitudes improve further, so will women's employment prospects, wages, and freedom from poverty.

Efforts to Achieve Equality

Positive change will continue only as long as women and men press actively for it. Otherwise, traditional beliefs and practices will persist, the forces for change will dissipate, and the attitudinal rationalizations for inequality will prevail. In particular, without continuing growth of an insistent, many-faceted women's movement, American society will tend to preserve sexism—belief in the inherent inferiority of women—and the discrimination it generates. In turn, discrimination gets rationalized by various sterotypes which *seem* a logical defense of it. The original belief even becomes a self-fulfilling prophecy if women yield to the constraints placed on them, because then "confident error generates its own spurious confirmation."[5] One of the most persistent sexist beliefs is that only women are "naturally" suited to household tasks, which also have little economic value attached to them because they produce no wage. Even now, household duties are inequitably shared by most working couples because of the intransigent belief that those duties are "women's work," though one should not underrate the many exceptions among couples and the progress which has been made.

The foregoing suggests that economic underdevelopment and attitudes which favor gender stereotyping are reciprocals: The existence of each flaw helps preserve the other. Both flaws are rooted in the differential socialization of girls and boys as the society impresses its expectations on them and helps form personality and self-concept.[6] To the extent the process is carried out in a sexist setting, it helps perpetuate sexism as a mindset, so proponents of a comprehensive action agenda can help change the attitudes by modifying any learning which preserves stereotyped behavior and the belief the stereotypes are true. Thus, movement toward overall equality and economic equity calls for resocialization of adult men and women whose role definitions were formed in a sexist context, and for child socialization free of sexist baggage.

Efforts to eliminate gender stereotyping in education by exerting pressure on local school boards, state and national education agencies, and publishers of classroom materials can help change the content of socialization. The Women's Educational Equity Act, the Education for Economic Security Act, and the Vocational Education Act all exist in part to eliminate sexist content and procedures from education. But these legislative attempts are underfunded and poorly enforced (or lack enforcement procedures), so pressure is necessary to see that they fulfill their potential. So are efforts to make parents more conscious of the education they impose through socialization. The mass media, with strong educational potential, also can do more to eliminate stereotypes and reshape attitudes, but without creating reverse stereotyping at the same time: We should no more expect to see women dominating most relationships than to see men in that role.

The goal of these several approaches is full participation of women in decision making about the content of education and other forms of learning, and power and persuasion are the ways to incorporate women's perspectives on equality. With attitudinal change leading the way, institutional change will follow and structural flaws in the labor market and other parts of the system will diminish. The process also can work in reverse, however, and if institutional changes can be effected through the use of political power, some alterations in attitudes should follow, just as they did because of civil-rights laws. No matter what the sequence, if these processes can be made to work better, the female/male income gap will decrease, and if poverty does not disappear, at least it will not discriminate disproportionately against women.

ECONOMIC DEVELOPMENT

This book is principally about the economic underdevelopment of American women, reflected in high poverty rates and inequitable income. It also is a call to restructure the economy and public programs for greater self-sufficiency as an antidote to these problems; it emphasizes the need to use women's talents more efficiently for the larger society. The process of developing a new national economic order to accomplish these things, basically by a more equitable distribution of opportunities, is in its early stages and its accomplishments are fragmentary. But they are real accomplishments, achieved in part through the political process in such forms as affirmative action. New economic relationships must address "protection and maintenance of family unity, employment, equal pay, equal conditions of work, health care, social security, racial discrimination, education and training," and other elements which affect fundamental socioeconomic justice.[7] But even conceived this broadly, economic development is only part of the total development necessary in women's lives, though it is the fundamental basis for many other forms, especially among poor women. Without economic justice, other accomplishments often are no more than meaningless abstractions, which is one reason why many poor people are indifferent to elections and other political participation.

Work and Wages

Women's present contributions to work need to be equitably rewarded in the formal labor market and in household tasks by providing fair financial compensation and recognition for what women do.[8] In addition, job segregation, gender-typing, and other forms of discrimination in the workplace must be eliminated. Women need equal access with men to the entire range of jobs in the United States and to equal pay for equal work—the comparable worth discussed earlier. This means, in part, eliminating the exploitation which is possible because such a large share of the female work force is concentrated in jobs at the low end of the wage scale. It also means reducing the concentration of women in part-time and part-year jobs, some of which are temporary on a day-to-day basis. The effort demands particular attention to the employment needs of inner-city and rural women, whose opportunities are poorest and whose poverty rates are highest.

Women are a growing proportion of the labor force, from 33 percent in 1960 to 44 percent in 1985 to a projected 54 percent in 1995.[9] This change has many positive features, but on the negative side the relative abundance of women workers often leads to their exploitation. In part, that is possible because job progress is limited for many by childrearing responsibilities, in which men should share more equitably and to which governments at various levels, along with private companies, should contribute more fully. Adequate subsidized child-care facilities are a major key to the full use of women's talents in the work force and to their advancement and fair remuneration. This includes women in married-couple families in which both spouses work and female householders caring for children alone. In addition, women and men need flexible work hours so they can share child care more easily. This flexibility is now encouraged by more and more firms, as is direct child care, with payoffs in higher productivity and worker morale.

Since women appear disproportionately in those service jobs which pay poorly, the private and public sectors also need more imaginative training programs to prepare large numbers for more rewarding positions in the 1990s and beyond. Even though many of those jobs may not pay handsomely, they will provide a better level of living than many of the occupations in which women are now concentrated. Furthermore, the number of jobs in several typically female occupations is expected to decrease rapidly, including stenographers, private household workers, sewing machine operators, and textile machine operators. Therefore, as the female work force grows, the competition in these fields will become more intense and the wages depressed, leading to even higher poverty rates. Conversely, many of the reasonably rewarding jobs which will increase the fastest are not so traditionally male or female, partly because some are in new fields where gender-typing is not deeply entrenched, although certain traditional fields will grow too. The rapidly increasing jobs are for computer programmers, computer systems analysts, medical assistants, electrical and electronics engineers and technicians, computer operators, lawyers, correction officers and jailers, accountants and auditors, mechanical engineers, and registered nurses.[10] Along with them comes the expanding number of low-paying service jobs, such as food service workers, janitors, and switchboard operators. Consequently, if women are to compete for the better jobs among those being created, they must have adequate training. Some of it is available now, but more programs and funding are needed to match prospective workers with the emerging jobs.

These steps would help not just women, but racial and ethnic minorities, so they are especially necessary in cities. Underemployment has been increasing there, particularly for black young adults with limited education, and a poorly educated, unemployed and underemployed, youthful and minority-group underclass appears to be growing at a rapid rate.[11]

Economic Security Programs

Certain priorities of the federal government work against programs to enhance women's economic role, productivity, and rewards. The most serious, because of its magnitude, is the huge expenditure on defense, which, in a time of mandated budget cuts, makes vulnerable the social programs which benefit the poor. In the 1980s they have suffered more than their fair share of reductions and limitations in food stamps, AFDC, Medicaid, and certain forms of Social Security for the nonelderly. The large majority of beneficiaries of these programs are women and children, and the cuts, both past and proposed, make it more difficult for women to stay out of poverty, let alone to prosper. This is particularly true of nonworking female householders, but it also applies to women who work for wages and need public assistance to resist poverty. Therefore, governmental priorities must be reexamined to ascertain how best to reconcile deficit and debt reduction with the need to empower the powerless. The latter need better mechanisms to influence spending priorities, while the Pentagon, the defense contractors, their lobbyists, the "pork-barrel" spenders who insist on maintaining unnecessary military bases, and other powerful military advocates should be less free to affect them.

Thus women—poor and nonpoor—have a strong vested interest in global disarmament so resources can be redirected to their development, and if peace includes genuine justice for all groups, women are more likely than men to be denied that justice in the absence of peace. The peace process also calls for changes in the content of socialization to minimize violent aggression, which often victimizes women and children. Therefore, gender equality as a part of peace efforts achieved by political and other means is inseparable from other forms of tolerance, egalitarianism, and mutual respect. In sum, peace is partly an economic issue and partly a matter of overcoming domination-subordination relationships, and since women and children have suffered especially from the negative results of violence and military preparation for it, they have a particularly important stake in peace.[12]

The proposed Federal Council on Women could help ensure economic security by assessing information on American women and poverty and making recommendations for new legislation. So could concerted federal efforts to develop a formula which makes comparable worth operational, because its implementation would shift more of the burden for income equity to the private sector and obviate the need for *some* expansion in governmental programs. Comparable worth in practice would help implement the often-repeated federal goal of self-sufficiency among the poor, at least those able to be trained and to work. That goal, however, must not become an excuse to reduce further those public programs which have been the main bulwark against poverty and which already have suffered significant funding losses. Nor should comparable worth be considered a panacea, because it would not alter gender segregation in jobs and would put women and men who occupy the same class level in competition, not necessarily to the economic advantage of either.[13] Work force reductions also might follow the implementation of comparable worth to offset its cost, unless the process were carefully regulated.

Some efforts are underway in the federal system to address the issue of wage and salary equity by gender, but too little improvement has materialized so far. It remains for women's organizations, sympathetic labor unions, and other groups to step up pressure to elevate comparable worth on the priority lists of governments and employers. Some of this has been happening in a quiet revolution; that is, the substantial increase of women in labor unions. In 1985 about 41 percent of the members of unions and labor associations consisted of women, up from only 25 percent ten years earlier.[14] Many individual unions are still overwhelmingly male, and women are poorly represented in union leadership (though not absent from it). Other unions, however, have large female membership, and the power to force change is there and women are becoming better organized to use it.[15] Comparable worth is only one of the ends to which that power can be directed, and now that women see more hope in collective activity, they are proving less difficult to organize than in the past. Some major inequities should change further as a result.

Finally, the Equal Rights Amendment (ERA) cannot be considered a dead issue. Its brief, straightforward provisions need to be put before the Congress and the states again, supported by clear information which tells what the ERA is and counters irrational fears. The ERA, after all, calls for the equal rights and equal access to responsibility which presumably undergird the entire society. Its passage would facilitate subsequent court interpretations to eliminate many kinds of economic underdevelopment among women. Much the same is true of the United Nations Convention on the Elimination of All Forms of Discrimination Against Women, which emerged from the U.N. Women's Decade and which the United States signed, but which the Senate has failed to ratify.

POLITICAL POWER

Basic changes in the status of women will not occur mainly because of a sense of fairness, any more than civil-rights legislation for minorities would have been written only for that reason, though many men certainly are sensitive to women's needs and want to see improvements. The most strategic changes depend on the use of power, and the political arena is where that power is best gotten and used to propose new legislation, guide its passage, and enforce existing laws to protect women's interests. These efforts apply from the federal to the local levels and involve protections which range from the fair treatment of rape victims in the legal system to enforcement of equal job opportunities and working conditions.

Potential and Real Power

Power also calls for organization, since the potential power of any large population segment becomes real power only when it is exercised through groups which the prevailing elites recognize, however grudgingly, as legitimate and with rightful claims to be heard.[16] In some cases that recognition comes only from confrontation; in all cases it requires collective strength. Women's power groups are likely to be admitted to full participation in the system only if "the risk of suppression appears to be as great as the risk of recognition," and if the new groups demand a fair share rather than all of the existing groups' perquisites.[17] Thus, the most promising role for women's organizations is fuller integration into the political structure, where the prospects are best to wield power and to improve that structure. Caution is necessary, however, in order to avoid co-optation. The political system is still strongly male dominated (e.g., women make up only 5 percent of the Congress), and while women do gain strength to the degree they can penetrate that system and make their claims heard, they suffer weakness if they simply get swallowed up in it. Such co-optation diminishes the challenge of women's power while it gives the appearance of accommodations to that power. More than one dominant group has strengthened itself further by absorbing, placating, and thereby weakening the opposition. Genuine readjustment of the power structure and disappearance into it are both forms of accommodation, but while the first should lead to greater gender equality, the second will not.

Political Organization

One power group notably lacking in the United States is a National Commission on the Status of Women—a deficiency not shared by the other industrialized countries. The United States does have many such organi-

zations at the state and local levels, though their effectiveness varies widely
and many are poorly funded. At the national level, even the Women's
Bureau, created in the U.S. Department of Labor in 1920, has proven itself
an inadequate substitute for a commission. The United States needs an
official group whose officers oversee women's interests within the federal
government, especially to draft legislation and promote enforcement of present laws. Such a commission would help elevate the difficulties of individuals
and small groups of women to the level of public problems, provide official
recognition of those problems by government and the society at large, and,
one hopes, generate even more effective mechanisms to solve them.[18] The
existence of an issue and a case for its consideration are insufficient for
action unless there is some structured way to consolidate and focus the
power necessary to accomplish the action and derive a discernible payoff
from it. The operations of existing women's organizations have shown
clearly that much potential for meeting women's needs inheres in a National
Commission on the Status of Women. Moreover, the commission would
place more women at higher levels in the decision-making process; these
women could help thwart actions which simply placate the discontented
but do not change power relationships, and they could promote actions
which do cause basic changes. The most functional goal is power sharing,
not monopoly by men or women, though very basic and pervasive changes
would have to occur before there was much prospect of women monopo-
lizing the national power structure! For the present and the foreseeable
future, therefore, preferential empowerment of women as a group would
simply help redress the traditional imbalance. This process calls not only
for a national commission, but for more women at other important places
in local, state, and national government, including elected and appointed
offices, and at upper levels in corporations, universities, and other major
systems. The content of socialization also needs to be reoriented at the
family and peer levels to encourage more women to seek those positions of
power.

One of the most fundamental uses of political power by women is to
achieve full economic rights. They include better access to all job categories,
fair unemployment benefits, more equitable wages, antipoverty safeguards,
and other advantages now enjoyed by much larger proportions of men,
though a sizable male minority also suffers serious economic problems. The
economic rights are antithetical to practices which still discriminate against
women directly or indirectly, such as the lower retirement benefits generally
paid to women under the Social Security system, particularly if their lifetime
work was in the home. Consequently, political power must be used to
eradicate these inequities and to cause the agencies charged with protecting
civil rights to direct more of their efforts to women.

Numerous groups and individuals in the women's movement are outspo-
ken on these matters, of course, and do focus on a wide range of economic
and other issues through the application of political power. They have had

numerous successes in the legislative, administrative, and judicial processes. At the same time, many women's groups do not have mass membership; spokespersons are sometimes thought to represent only small minorities and may get dismissed too easily as feminist malcontents. Yet the groups have created more cooperative relationships within and outside the women's movement, and that cooperation helps consolidate power to attack practical problems and sexist attitudes. Power consolidation is also a consciousness-raising dynamic for women and men, including policy makers who can effect change in areas of perceived injustice and abuse. The needs of poor women have become especially apparent, if unmet, in the 1980s, and the feminization of poverty has increased awareness and prompted tactics to correct that serious violation of economic justice. It and other issues are no longer ignored by policy makers, although the Reagan administration paid them less heed than they deserve, and changes in the 1980s did not fulfill the potential to reduce economic inequality for women.[19]

EDUCATION

Earlier chapters cite education as one way to deal with women's poverty and job problems, though they caution against assuming education is a cure-all. There are three reasons for the caution: (1) Using median years of schooling completed as a criterion, women are as well educated as men and that fact has not prevented women's poverty rates from being higher, their median incomes lower. (2) Any single-factor "solution" to a complex con-stellation of problems is likely to fail if applied in isolation from numerous other efforts. (3) If one assumes that education will solve women's economic problems, then those problems must result basically from a personal at-tribute; that is, inadequate schooling and/or job training. By implication, poverty and low wages must be largely the consequence of individual in-adequacy and somehow deserved—a view which neglects the fact that pov-erty and low wages stem fundamentally from "normal" social structures and dynamics.[20]

Illiteracy and Functional Illiteracy

Cautions accounted for, one cannot ignore education as a major part of any action agenda to fight poverty among women and children. Poorly educated people cannot contribute up to their potential, for even most low-level jobs require workers to read and write. For this reason, the nation's illiteracy problem is a major barrier to progress out of poverty.

The size of the illiteracy problem remains in question, but the National Commission on Excellence in Education estimated in 1983 that about 23 million Americans were illiterate—they could not perform simple reading, writing, and comprehension tests.[21] Jonathan Kozol estimates that as many as 30 million are illiterate and from 35 to 54 million more are *semi-literate*; that is, they lack reading, writing, and other skills adequate "to cope with the responsibilities of everyday life."[22] These figures are far higher than those compiled by the Census Bureau on *functional illiteracy*, which refers to people with less than five years of formal schooling and which is based on the assumption they lack the basic educational skills to operate successfully in a complex society.[23] In 1985 functional illiterates aged 15 and over officially numbered only about 3 million.[24] Since the Census Bureau also estimates there are about 19 million illiterates, the discrepancies in these several figures suggest that large numbers of people who do attend school for 0–4 years or even longer remain illiterate or semi-literate. The discrepancies also suggest that the concept of "functional illiteracy," formulated in the 1930s, needs revising to reflect the amount of education people require in order to handle the written and spoken language and the basic mathematical prerequisites for reasonable success in today's society.

Whatever the precise magnitude of educational inadequacy, efforts to deal with it are fundamental in any action agenda to reduce the poverty rates and enhance the self-sufficiency of adults of both sexes. Present efforts are far from enough, for even though the illiteracy problem became more apparent to policy makers in the 1980s, new funding largely bypassed the inner-city schools where the problem is most severe and where the content of education sorely needs revision. These schools, more than suburban institutions, are in the worst poverty areas; they have major discipline problems and high dropout rates; they graduate high proportions of illiterate students. Thus, while state and federal funding needs to be increased, the content of education has to be streamlined locally to respond to student needs, though not to the point of violating certain minimum standards or creating administrative chaos. The criteria for hiring, retaining, and paying teachers also need to be reworked so that teacher recruiting is easier and all who conduct classes actually do educate their clientele in ways which help provide an avenue out of poverty. Schools must not promote students unless they have mastered the material where they are, because the practice of promoting to get rid of problem children is partly responsible for illiterate graduates. Other agencies also need to cooperate with the schools to contend with drug and alcohol problems, gang conflicts, and other conditions which make education virtually impossible.

At the upper end of the educational spectrum, college costs have skyrocketed, federal grants to college students have decreased, the greater emphasis on loans than grants has left more students in debt, and the enrollment of blacks and Hispanics has declined sharply. In addition, more women than men attend college part time and so are not eligible for student loans. These and other constraints on college attendance are likely to hit nontraditional-age female students particularly hard, because two-thirds of all students 35 and over are women.[25] Many are single parents and some need child care while they attend classes, and though some colleges and universities provide it, the costs do not figure into computations of need for loans and other assistance.

Since many of these older women are seeking to improve their earning potential, it is imperative that the education be directly linked to job prospects and advancement and that governments help subsidize it more fully as an investment in better employment. In this way, more education for women who did not complete their schooling earlier also is an investment in their productivity, sophistication as socializing agents, and freedom from dependence on public assistance. The education also must be geared to preparation for the whole range of occupations, not just those which have been traditional for women. The Vocational Education Act was meant to accomplish this goal, but it is not adequately enforced. Nor is the Education for Economic Security Act, which is supposed to improve the teaching of science, mathematics, and computer science and provide more access to these fields for women and other relatively neglected groups in the job market.

Education might well include assertiveness training to help overcome women's subordination in the workplace. The training can be tied to the quest for equitable political power by emphasizing public affairs and administration and women's prospective roles in those areas, though the process actually needs to begin by teaching boys and girls similarly. The Women's Educational Equity Act, mentioned earlier, was designed to meet that goal, but an increasing loss of funds has subverted the effort. In short, education, whether for children, traditional-age high-school and college students, or older persons, can convey marketable skills in nontraditional fields, and it can do much more. The educational system also can act as a resocializing agency to help males and females overcome domination-subordination, both as a set of attitudes and a collection of discriminatory practices which follow from the attitudes. The schools can train *and* educate according to the best models of both undertakings.

Other Educational Needs

Some 129 of the 373 paragraphs in the *Forward Looking Strategies* which capped the Women's Decade concern education, thereby emphasizing the need to improve it, even in developed countries.[26] For American women certain needs identified in the document stand out.

1. Education needs more adequate financing, especially for poor rural and inner-city people, many of whom are minorities. Financing also is needed for women to return to school or to enter job-training and retraining programs.

2. Changes in the content of education are necessary to reflect women as full social participants and men as full partners in childrearing, socialization, and other family responsibilities. Some changes have been made in

textbooks, for example, to portray nonstereotyped images of women, but in order to offend as few people and groups as possible, many publishers fail to address fully the basic issues.

3.   In the spirit of affirmative action, education should be a consciousness-raising experience about discrimination and gender inequality, including information on women's rights and entitlements. This component is needed by boys and men and girls and women to prevent and overcome the attitudes which perpetuate domination-subordination and its negative results for both sexes.

4.   Education should allow women as much access as men to all of its levels and prepare them for equal occupational opportunities after they graduate. But perhaps women also should be provided certain kinds of preferential advantages to compensate for earlier deprivation. These include child care for parents in school; priority admission to education programs which lead to high-status careers where men predominate and from which women long were excluded; and women's studies which identify and help redress prior inequities. Some of these things are in place to some degree, but more are justified.

5.   Education should encourage women to expand their political role and prepare them for more leadership and involvement in decision making. This effort should pointedly include poor women, not just middle-class activists, because poverty stems partly from political powerlessness and its accompanying weak access to economic advantages.

6.   Children will continue to be the major consumers of schooling, so educational efforts to prevent gender stereotyping and abort boy-girl domination-subordination should be directed to them. The efforts include gender neutrality in teaching about careers, domestic responsibilities, parenting, and other roles.

7.   Education should help eliminate the double standard of responsibility for conception. It should deal candidly with all aspects of human sexuality, especially pregnancy and contraception, free of the assumption that ignorance equates with morality. This needs to be started as sexual awareness begins, not when people are already sexually active.

8.   Health education is imperative, not just to deal with such things as the hysteria over AIDS and how to slow the spread of it and other diseases, but to help make individuals responsible for their own general physical well-being. This includes attention to disease prevention, drug and alcohol problems, smoking, ways to live productively with one's own disabilities, care for those elderly who are ill or disabled, and information about available health facilities and personnel. These are needed at all class levels, but especially among the poor.

9.   Adult education should provide not only marketable skills, but information about the myriad social programs available, how to gain access to those programs, and some techniques for dealing with the personnel who run them. People also can be taught how to budget their incomes and

otherwise improve their money-management skills and chances to escape poverty. Adult programs which demonstrate that education is valuable for individuals make them more likely to demand and use it, but for this to work, education must have direct applications in relieving poverty.[27]

FAMILY STRENGTH

Family Changes

The questions posed early in chapter 2 imply that the family structure and dynamics which many poor children encounter set them up to fail in their own search for a way out of poverty. At the same time, poverty is a primary cause of family stress and breakup and failures in initial family formation. The point was made that high rates of divorce, separation, and births out of wedlock have helped feminize poverty, at the same time that conditions associated with poverty increase the rates of divorce, separation, and births out of wedlock. As a result of these reciprocal conditions, the number of women solely responsible for families has increased dramatically, and they are disproportionately represented in the informal economy, the ranks of the unemployed, the welfare population, and the group of workers whose low wages keep them under the poverty level.[28]

Groups which create policies and programs to deal with poverty need to abandon the myth that all families either can be married-couple units or have a functioning husband/father figure in the picture. Then, the female-headed family can be recognized as an operating unit rather than an aberration, and various job-training, child-care, and public-assistance programs can be restructured and funded so those families have a better chance to escape poverty. AFDC, for example, needs to be made more uniform from state to state, though with *some* variations in benefits according to the local cost of living. AFDC payments should continue for many women who find jobs, so a job and public assistance together will enable them to live above the poverty level. Governments and industries also need to help with child care, flexible work hours, and other measures which allow more effective parenting and wage earning. At present, the choice for many single parents is child care *or* income-producing work, and either alternative has financial and other costs for the parent and the society.

Sexuality and Fertility

Part of the feminization of poverty is the unwanted or mistimed birth and the one which is wanted for unrealistic reasons, particularly by very young women. As a consequence of these births, "childbearing by unmarried women increased substantially between 1984 and 1985, to levels never before observed in the 45–year period for which national statistics are available.[29] Teenagers account for a minority of births to unmarried women (33 percent in 1985), but most of those young women are ill-equipped to fulfill a child's physical and psychosocial needs and their own at the same time. Early childbearing also often means the end of a young women's formal education, a relatively large total number of children per woman, a comparatively high risk of illness and death among young mothers and their children, a high probability of single parenthood, and an abnormal risk of poverty.[30]

As a step toward strengthening the family, comprehensive sex education about pregnancy and contraception, mentioned earlier, needs to replace the timid, partial, and even naive approaches often used now. Such programs should involve all children before they become sexually active and should accomplish at least three things: (1) make sexual activity as rational and informed a choice as possible, (2) portray the realities of childbearing and childrearing, and (3) make adolescents aware of effective contraception. Rhetoric about sexual abstinence will not do the job, for even in the throes of the AIDS scare many adolescents see it as an adult disease and engage in unprotected sex based on that and other faulty assumptions.

Instruction about the realities of pregnancy is important for poor adolescents, since they are particularly likely to misperceive an infant as a substitute for other things lacking in their lives, especially love. Many also see childbearing as a way to raise a low level of self-esteem and to gain peer approval; they are apt to have only a mother as a parental role model. More affluent girls often have to contend with similar problems, but poor girls are inordinately affected by them. In addition, very young women of any class need assistance in making sensible decisions about their own sexual activity, much of which still depends on the persuasiveness of young men and on peer-group fictions.

Abortion is and will remain a major reality, no matter how strongly various groups oppose it. Therefore, the basic question is whether government can help make abortion safe, which it can under the *Roe v. Wade* decision, not whether it can prevent abortion. The latter would not be possible even if the decision were reversed, and criminalizing abortion again would make it more dangerous, particularly for poor women likely to use amateurish ways to destroy an unwanted fetus. That danger would be especially serious for unmarried women, who now account for the majority of abortions.[31] Government can reduce the incidence of abortion, however, by channeling adequate funding to groups which promote sex education and effective contraception, because to the extent those groups prevent unwanted or mistimed pregnancies, they also reduce the rate at which pregnancies are aborted. Witholding funds from family planning agencies because abortion is part of their programs merely reduces their ability to promote effective contraception and increases the incidence of abortion.

This happens because American women clearly wish to control their own fertility, and no denial of birth-control service is likely to nullify that wish. There also is still much room to improve the safety and effectiveness of birth control, so government and private groups need to fund additional research in this area to enlarge the arsenal of contraceptive techniques, especially for males.

Working women who bear children face problems which have been solved in other industrialized countries. That is, the United States has no national provision for maternity leave with a guarantee of some income and the right to return to a job. Some companies do provide these protections, but only voluntarily. Therefore, the United States needs to institute mandatory job and income protections for women who must take time off for childbearing, though the Family and Medical Leave Act, if passed, will provide such protection, as well as leave for persons who become temporarily disabled. The bill allows 18 weeks of job protection for *both* parents when a child is born, adopted, or seriously ill, and 26 weeks for the disabled.

Child Care

Decent preschool child-care facilities at affordable cost are scarce in the United States, and those which do exist are in jeopardy because of reductions in funding through Title XX of the Social Services Block Grant Act. As a result, many women in poverty and/or on welfare who want to work cannot do so because of child-care responsibilities. In the winter of 1984–85, for example, there were 8.2 million preschool children of working women, but only 23 percent could be found in day-care centers or preschools during the time their mothers worked. An additional 31 percent had supervised care in their own homes (by father, grandparent, other relative, or nonrelative), and 8 percent received care by the mother at work.[32] The children all have to be some place, of course, but many arrangements are inadequate because caregivers are not trained for the task, have other simultaneous responsibilities, suffer alcoholism or other problems, are merely somewhat older siblings, or are not available on a predictable basis. The last situation often forces parents to leave work unexpectedly. Day care is least available to black children and to those of all races in female-headed families. It is also poorly available to children with parents at the low end of the educational and occupational status scales where the need is greatest.[33]

In addition to the group of preschoolers, there are about 1.4 million "latchkey" children aged 5–13 whose mothers work and leave them unsupervised by any adult after school hours.[34]

These data reflect substantial neglect and semi-neglect of physical and emotional needs. One reason is cost, another is the scarcity of high-quality care. In both cases, even though federal laws allow tax credits for child care and there is federal funding for about half the day-care centers, the aid is far from enough. Consequently, any agenda for action to help relieve the poverty of women and children should transfer more costs for child care to the society as a whole, basically as an investment in the greater productivity of women and in the adequate socialization of the rising generation. As with most suggestions in this chapter, such a shift in costs calls for a basic reordering of national priorities. Some of the proposals before the Congress to improve the amount and quality of child care and to focus it better on poor mothers who work may help reorder those priorities. In particular, the proposed Act for Better Child Care, introduced in November 1987, would provide $2.5 billion to the states annually for three years, and it calls for 20 percent state matching funds to improve child-care facilities and reduce the cost to families with low and modest incomes. This assistance would help improve state programs, some of which already are good, and would help start others. The bill also would set standards for personnel qualifications, health and safety, group size, and other basic features of child care. Perhaps this bill and/or some others being proposed will help Americans see that a Strategic Socialization Initiative is as much in the interest of national protection as a Strategic Defense Initiative.

HEALTH CARE

Health care and wellness constitute a large category of study essentially beyond the scope of this book. It is possible here only to identify a few needs, basically in two categories: (1) the health needs of women themselves; and (2) women as providers of health care to others, especially children and the elderly.

Health Needs of Women

Certain of women's health needs are reflected in the fact that while they had greater increases than men in life expectancy for several decades, after the mid–1970s the trend reversed.[35] Thus, in 1973 the difference between males and females in life expectancy at birth was 7.8 years for whites and 8.9 years for blacks, but by 1985 it was 6.9 years for whites and 8.4 years for blacks. During that period the number of poor persons and the poverty rate increased somewhat faster among males than among females, so the diminishing differentials in life expectancy do not seem attributable to these poverty changes per se. In 1973, however, poor females were much more likely to be the wives of poor men than they were in 1985, when they were more apt to be family heads without a male present. In turn, poor women are much more likely than poor men to fall below 50 percent of the poverty threshold (i.e., to be the poorest of the poor), and the greater depth of poverty and its accompanying health and nutrition problems do help explain the shrinking differential in life expectancy. In fact, bad health is one reason why many women who receive welfare do not work, whether they or their children have the health problems.

In addition, the immigrations to the United States consist heavily of Hispanics and some other groups whose overall life expectancies are lower than the national average. The immigrations also contain majorities of women, so their lower life expectancy helps decrease the overall female/male differential.

One principal factor is the pattern of deaths from lung cancer. The death rates from this cause have risen for both sexes since 1950, because the cohorts with high proportions of smokers are aging into the years when death rates from most causes escalate rapidly. The rate of increase in lung cancer mortality has been slowing for men but accelerating for women, however, and among those aged 55–74 it has passed breast cancer as the leading cause of malignancy deaths.[36] After 1965 the proportion of smokers among males fell from 50 percent of those aged 20 and over to about 35 percent, but among females the decrease was only from 33 to 30 percent.[37] Thus, the narrowing gender variation in smoking also helped reduce the difference between the sexes in life expectancy. So did a recent, surprising rise in the death rate from breast cancer and the slightly slower pace of reduction in white women's age-adjusted death rates from heart disease and stroke.

The higher rate of births to unmarried women, especially very young women, also means that more children and mothers incur health risks, basically because of an immature reproductive system and the inadequate prenatal and postnatal care which poor teenagers are likely to receive. Drug and alcohol abuse are often complicating factors as well.

These are only a few of several conditions which call for concerted efforts to educate poor women about smoking, prenatal and postnatal care, substance abuse, and other influences on health. They also necessitate continuing increases in funds for such programs as Medicaid, because to the degree poverty is becoming feminized, the effects of excessive frugality are borne increasingly by women. The Congress has been making such increases, however, especially for better Medicaid coverage of children, pregnant women, and the elderly. Rises in health-care costs also need to be contained to no more than the overall Consumer Price Index, for they are growing half again as rapidly, while hospital costs are increasing about twice as fast. Part of the increase, however, is because many indigent persons cannot pay, and this raises the cost for persons who can. Many of the poor also are simply turned away.

As lifesaving technology, such as organ transplants, becomes more sophisticated and as overall medical care grows more expensive because of that technology and its underlying experimentation, the question of who lives and who dies is answered increasingly in financial terms. The poor are at a massive disadvantage in that decision-making process. For example, the Reagan administration contributed $240 million to develop the artificial heart, which is not likely to help many poor people, but at the same time health-care programs for the poor were cut. If equitable access to treatment is even a tangential consideration in health care, the present system needs different priorities and methods to allocate expertise, funds, and other resources. About 37 million Americans have no health insurance and are, therefore, likely to end up in overworked public-health facilities. In 1987 and 1988 private health insurance costs soared, and poor people, already with little coverage, were even less able to afford it and more likely to turn to public-health establishments or to receive no care at all. Poor children are especially apt to suffer because their parents cannot afford preventive care or treatment in the early stages of an illness. But poor children are a statistical mass rather than an identifiable individual who needs a heart transplant, so they are more easily ignored. Treating them is also much less challenging and profitable than are more exotic uses of medicine.

Overall, basic health services for poor women and children need to be improved and costs either held to a reasonable rate of increase or subsidized more than they are now. New federal legislation to help with the costs of catastrophic illness among the elderly is a step in that direction, but only one of many new ones needed. Even it does not protect against a physician's charges in excess of Medicare allowances for given treatments; nor does it provide for an extended nursing home stay, which can be catastrophically expensive too.[38] To deal with these problems the United States needs a comprehensive national health-care system such as those found in every other industrialized country.

Women as Caregivers

The role of women as chief caregivers for others who are ill, frail, or disabled also needs more support. This is especially true for middle-aged and young-old women who are looking after even older relatives, usually mothers and mothers-in-law, but many male family members as well. Women are now 70 percent of those who provide unpaid care for the frail elderly, and this role will grow in importance as the baby-boom cohorts reach 65, beginning about 2010, and especially as the entire baby boom becomes 75, 80, and older. Americans already care for all except the most seriously disabled elderly at home, and both the elderly and the society will be best served if the latter provides adequate financial assistance to middle-aged and young-old caregivers. It is simply cheaper and more humane than placing people in nursing homes, which house less than 5 percent of the elderly population anyway. Most disabled elderly also are maintained without agency help, and their care costs the public much less per person than does any form of institutionalization. Therefore, government at various levels can contribute more funds to the home-care effort and still keep it cost-effective. Otherwise, more families will have to look to public caregivers, and the costs to taxpayers will rise. The Older Americans Act provides the basis for necessary federal funding, though more needs to be done at that and lower levels.[39]

If most care for the elderly continues to be in the home, it is certain the great bulk of this burden still will fall on women, so it is they who will need most of the financial and other assistance, though the minority of male caregivers should receive similar help. The support should come in the form of more day–care arrangements for elderly dependents of persons who work, temporary assistance so caregivers can have periodic respite from their duties, and publicly provided home health services for the elderly at all income levels, though with a sliding scale which requires people to pay according to their ability and which keeps the system financially self-sustaining. At the same time, destitution should not be a requirement for Medicaid eligibility. More foster homes are needed for those elderly who have no relatives to care for them, largely to avoid institutionalization; so are centers which provide health testing, nutritional programs, recreation, and other services. They also can help acquaint the elderly and their families with available services and link clients with agencies.

Women also are likely to continue as principal caregivers for the nonelderly, although socialization and resocialization should help draw more men into that role. If the female-headed family continues to grow as a proportion of all families, however, women will provide more of that care alone, especially for children. In 1985 about one-fifth of the nation's children under 18 lived in female-headed households, and the figure has risen since then. Some of the care women provide relates to health, but the functions of family caregiver are much more numerous, complex, time-consuming, and expensive. Since these functions are partly in the public interest, they require more public assistance in the form of comprehensive medical programs and a drastically revised and revitalized welfare system. If the poor are to become nonpoor, better health care is one of the many things they need to make that transition.

WELFARE REFORM

Few issues involving the poor evoke more emotional responses and confusion than welfare reform, largely because of misunderstandings about the current magnitude and cost of welfare, the motivations and characteristics of its recipients, and the unresolved conflict between emphasis on individual achievement on the one hand and the charitable impulse to help those in need on the other.

The welfare population is large in the sense that at least one in four Americans needs welfare of some kind occasionally. But it is much smaller if one focuses on persons who are consistently dependent over long periods.

During the longitudinal study of poverty carried out at the Institute for Social Research, for example, only 2 percent of the nation's people depended heavily on welfare for eight or more years.[40] Moreover, recipients often shift between receiving welfare and working, and many who are temporarily eligible for benefits do not use them. Perhaps most significantly, welfare benefits do not create large-scale welfare dependence either for adult recipients or for their offspring when they become adults.[41] Thus, there is not a huge group of individuals with particular character flaws which cause them to rely on welfare, any more than receiving welfare creates such flaws in most recipients.[42] Nor does welfare seem to deter large numbers of people from working (if they can get jobs), break up significant numbers of families, or encourage many unmarried women to conceive in order to receive welfare.[43] This being so, there is little justification for keeping benefits punitively low and eligibility excessively tight, which is done partly to prevent large numbers of people from leaving the work force and seeking welfare. It does appear, however, that welfare in states with high benefits encourages many young single mothers to set up their own households rather than to remain in parental homes. There is also the risk that sufficiently high benefits would increase work disincentives, and those are to be avoided.

Welfare does have real and perceived problems: Its benefits are widely different from state to state, as are reform efforts; the question of whether work ought to be a requirement for benefits remains unresolved; welfare goes to many people above the poverty line and misses many below it. Welfare systems also contain no provisions for counseling to build confidence and self-esteem so people can compete in the job market; they have no allowances for day care so welfare parents can leave their children in order to work. In addition, the bureaucratic structure has grown large and unwieldy and sometimes is not responsive to real needs; it is not very successful in getting absent fathers to help support their children. Partly for that reason and partly because of growth in the number of female-headed families, the AFDC program has come to service a much larger clientele whose average stay on welfare has increased, although tighter eligibility rules did cause a small decline in the number of AFDC families after 1981, to just under 4 million.

AFDC is the principal focus of welfare reform efforts, though the Medicaid program is about three times as costly. AFDC, which began in 1935 under the Social Security Act, gives money to people with children they cannot support, and that feature draws more criticism than programs for the ill and disabled. The increase in births to unmarried teenagers also has brought mounting criticism to AFDC. Actually, however, AFDC benefits have increased so slowly that the real dollar value of federal and state funds has fallen by a third since 1970, and the system has not stopped the rise in poverty rates nor halted the growth of a relatively permanent underclass.[44] In addition, AFDC does not have a nationwide work requirement and, therefore, does discourage some recipients from entering the labor market, though other factors also keep many poor young women who left school prematurely from holding jobs. AFDC may not break up many families, but its existence does persuade some young men who father children irresponsibly not to form families or provide child support, although many of them have poor job prospects and no funds to offer.[45]

Given these difficulties with the welfare system, reform is needed. But how should that reform be made and what should it accomplish?

First, late in its tenure the Reagan administration proposed to consolidate various federal poverty programs into one, to make block grants to the states, and to let them spend the money according to local needs. This has some merit, but it would worsen the present patchwork of amounts and forms of aid and tend to create even more eligibility and disbursement inequities. It would risk missing even more people than the present system, partly because controls would be even less uniform.

Second, welfare reforms proposed by people across the political spectrum emphasize work as a condition for receiving benefits. This is necessary, but so are other incentives, including an adequate supply of jobs at decent wages, training programs which equip people to perform the available jobs, and day care and after-school care for the children of working welfare parents. In addition, work should not mean a loss of benefits which, coupled with wages, could provide a decent level of living. It makes little sense for a person to work to earn only the amount AFDC, Medicaid, and other benefits would provide if she/he did not work. Therefore, work *plus* welfare benefits should be parts of a package rather than mutually exclusive for many people, especially female householders with children and in low-paying jobs, but also some additional married-couple families. This approach still leaves room to require that able-bodied recipients of both sexes take work or enter job-training programs, but it does not create work disincentives owing to the loss of welfare. There need to be ceilings, of course, but at the very least a family should not lose welfare at any point where its income is below 125 percent of the poverty level.

This will be an expensive system, but so is the present one, and its record of success in obviating poverty is much poorer than the potential success of a revised system. Furthermore, it is important not to abandon welfare in the effort to encourage self-sufficiency, because direct assistance, such as AFDC and food stamps, have proven more successful so far in reducing poverty than have job training, adult education, and other programs aimed exclusively at decreasing dependency.[46] For this reason the recent cuts in spending for the poor are especially threatening. About $6 billion was lost for 1986, $11 billion for 1987, and $14 billion for 1988, principally in legal services, Head Start, housing and health, and food programs. Women and children were particularly hard hit. These cuts may have been meant to force greater self-sufficiency, but they also show that government partially defaults on its responsibility to help provide a decent level of living while it tries to foster self-sufficiency. The cuts also make government appear indifferent to the needs of those who cannot be self-sufficient (e.g., children, the disabled, and the elderly poor). In the end, if there are to be no far-reaching economic reforms which lead to full employment for the poor in well-paying jobs—the major key to reducing poverty rates—welfare is the next best alternative and it should be streamlined and expanded.[47]

Third, those who suffer the worst poverty are children, not adults. In 1985 about 13 million children under 18 were poor; they were 39 percent of all poor people (children under 18 were only 27 percent of all nonpoor people). Moreover, real-dollar benefits for poor children have dropped since 1970. The AFDC program, therefore, needs to be reformed drastically or even replaced. Senator Daniel Patrick Moynihan (D-NY) recommends the latter and calls instead for a "social contract" under which parents would take responsibility for adequate child support. Fathers would work to provide that support, as would able-bodied mothers of children over 3 years of age. In return the federal government would guarantee a minimally decent level of living, including health-care benefits to ensure that the family would not drop below the minimum level because of illness. The program essentially would be a federal one and not carried by the states alone, for unless the federal government makes a more massive commitment to attack poverty, it will continue getting worse. The social contract also would have to guarantee paid work, if not in private industry, then in various kinds of public-sector jobs. A sizable federally funded job corps would be very expensive, but it would enhance productivity, in part because it would convert from dependents to producers those persons who agree to child support and the other provisions but who could not find work in the private sector. Creating more good jobs would help both sexes and would counter a situation which developed after the early 1970s: growth in the percentage of working men at the lower end of the wage scale where real earnings have failed to rise at the same pace as those in the male work force as a whole.[48]

Fourth, more vigorous efforts are necessary to pursue absent fathers and to deduct child support from their incomes. Since 1984 federal law has allowed states to do this for AFDC families, but more states need to get involved more actively in enforcing fathers' responsibilities, provided they are able to meet them. Coupled with this effort should be reform in welfare allocation which allows two-parent families in all states to receive AFDC, thereby encouraging a father to remain with his family.[49] Many poor men are willing but unable to support families. Some also are single parents with significant poverty problems of their own.

None of these proposals nor a package of all of them will solve the problems in welfare or eliminate poverty. But they are steps in that direction. In turn, they will help ensure that the 13 million poor children do not become poor adults with deficient work skills, weak incentives, and shaky self-confidence, all of which are barriers to self-sufficiency. These are individual characteristics, and any reforms also need to account for the structural flaws in the whole social system which help create the characteristics. Reforms which are essentially individualist, such as efforts to prepare people for jobs which do not exist in sufficient numbers because of overall economic conditions, will fail.[50] But constructed humanely, welfare reform policies can work, because governmental decisions about programs do have a direct bearing on poverty and its attendant problems. "In a nation as smart, inventive, and rich as America, the continuation of poverty is a choice, not a necessity."[51]

OTHER NEEDS

The needs for action discussed in the preceding sections are only a sample of what should be done to improve the position of poor women, men, and children. Three others can be added briefly.

Housing

There is an acute shortage of housing for the poor, and the price of what is available has escalated so rapidly that many people, including numerous married-couple families, have become homeless for the first time in their lives. Moreover, while the problem affects people across the age spectrum, as with so many other aspects of poverty, it is especially widespread among young families and the elderly.

Many in the youthful group are workers but at or near the minimum wage, which provides too little money to pay rents which range upwards from $500, $600, or even more per month for meager accommodations, especially in those metropolitan areas with a high cost of living. Add to these costs the requirement for at least a month's rent and a security deposit in advance, and even the combined incomes of many two-earner couples are not enough to pay for what housing there is, let alone other necessities. Many of these people have become the new homeless, living in cars or other makeshift quarters or in charity shelters. Families sometimes must disperse in order to be housed, particularly in states which deny AFDC to those with a father present.

Part of the problem is that much low-cost housing has disappeared. Cheap hotels, rooming houses, and other one-room arrangements were often the first to go, and solitary individuals suffered from that loss. But now relatively low-cost housing for families is being lost at a rapid rate, because some apartment buildings are being converted into high-priced condominiums, others are being torn down in the name of central city rejuvenation, and still others become prohibitively expensive just because they are scarce and for other reasons. The loss of housing is proving especially difficult for female-headed families, because their average resources are so meager.

In July 1987, the federal government authorized $1 billion to provide some permanent housing and some temporary shelter for homeless people and to be used for other emergency assistance. But that funding did not prevent the growth of homelessness. Moreover, since 1981 funding for subsidized housing programs was reduced from $32 billion to less than $8 billion, and the $1 billion in emergency aid makes up only a small fraction of that 75 percent loss, which occurred largely because attacks on the national debt precipitate reductions in all sorts of assistance to the most vulnerable citizens—poor women, children, and married-couple families who have little power to influence national spending priorities. Consequently, growing numbers are on waiting lists for the insufficient subsidized housing still available. Some homeless people also are being housed at government expense in costly hotels and motels, but those taxpayer expenditures are an inefficient way to use money which could help build additional low-cost housing or renovate existing units.

At this writing, proposals are pending to improve the housing situation, but even the best ones provide far less for housing than was cut from existing programs in the 1980s. Therefore, whatever is approved seems unlikely to do more than ameliorate the problem in relatively minor ways and for limited numbers of people. Meanwhile, the crisis in housing for the poor is moving higher and higher on the list of problems requiring action. The 1986 Tax Reform Act does encourage the private sector to build some low-cost housing, because one can still claim losses and tax credits for such undertakings, but that alone will not do the job.

"Invisible" Homemaker

Many elderly women need better protection against the financial and emotional costs of becoming widows, particularly if they lack adequate pension coverage and work prospects. Most women in this situation spent their lives in the homemaker role, which still offers no wages or retirement benefits as an activity itself, and often only limited benefits as an ancillary activity to that of an income-producing male. In fact, in the midst of efforts to improve the status of women, the homemaker has received little positive attention and her contributions have been systematically undervalued and certainly underpaid, even though she remains largely responsible for home and family care.[52]

An action agenda calls for changes in the status of homemaker, whether she is in the 15 percent of families where only the father works and she remains at home to care for him and the children; is a wage earner in a married-couple family; heads a one-parent family; is a solitary widow; has remarried into a new family setting after divorce; or possesses any other combination of characteristics.[53] The common denominator among all these women is primary responsibility for the domestic tasks in the household, whatever its composition. The status of homemaker cannot be ignored as it has. The homemaker should not have to do the domestic chores essentially by herself, and the role should carry more financial security than the mere expectation a wage-earning male will stay on the scene and the hope there will be some residue of a pension in old age. The displaced homemaker—divorced, deserted, or widowed—is a product of the old assumption that men would care financially for their wives and children.[54] There are now so many departures from that idealized stereotype that society needs innovative ways to reward the homemaker role economically and psychically and for men and women to share it more fully.

Violence

Another area for action is violence against women, whether it takes the form of domestic abuse, street violence, rape, or some other. Poor women are the most susceptible to many forms of violence, especially wife abuse, although no class level is immune and there are many cases of husband abuse as well.

Education in a broad sense must convince submissive women that violence against them and their children is a basic affront to physical and emotional well-being and need not be tolerated. Other women require alternatives to living in violent homes, empathetic and protective treatment by law enforcement agencies, and compensation by offenders. Victims need assistance from agencies which can stop the violence, commit the offender to treatment or punishment, and help reduce the financial vulnerability and other forms of dependency which cause some victims to tolerate violence or which grow worse if they flee. Other agencies need to help heal the psychological wounds, especially shame and misplaced guilt, perhaps in an expanded network of shelters for battered women. Moreover, since the abusers themselves are a kind of victim, often because they were abused as children, they, too, require help to modify their behavior. These are all expensive and difficult undertakings, and most efforts to solve the problem falter because of cost, understaffing, and other limitations. But attempted solutions also are investments in the quality of the human resource of both genders.

PROSPECTS

The future of poverty among American women depends heavily on decisions to be made about welfare reform, especially about whether the poor are entitled to wholehearted, adequate assistance to free them from poverty. Future poverty rates also will depend on inflation, recession, and other economic forces which affect employment, types of jobs, and wages. Projections about those are difficult to make. Even so, it seems likely that the number and proportion of families headed by women will increase and that the percentage of children who live in them also will grow. Those continuing trends will cause the poverty rate to rise until at least 2000.[55] There may be periodic fluctuations, however, as the economy goes through better or worse times and as governmental programs wax and wane. The population also will continue to age, and if working Americans reject increasingly high taxes to support a growing number and percentage of elderly, the poverty rates of people 65 and over may rise. The elderly collectively are much more powerful than are poor young people, however, so the wishes of the aged population are likely to yield more protections.

Economic growth alone is unlikely to counterbalance these trends well enough to reduce poverty rates or even to hold them at current levels. Nor will women pour into the labor force at the rates which prevailed in the 1960s and 1970s, and the economic growth produced by that past influx is unlikely to be repeated in the future.[56] Various of the reforms suggested earlier in this chapter could lower poverty rates significantly, but the type and magnitude of the changes which actually will occur remain in doubt. Thus, whether poverty rates increase or decrease for female-headed families and their children depends on the governmental spending priorities which emerge from the contest between budgetary and human concerns. Given the priorities which have prevailed in the past two decades, poverty rates seem more likely to increase than decrease and the gap between the poor and affluent appears likely to widen.

NOTES

1. Arvonne Fraser and Kim Moutoux, *Forward Looking Strategies for the Advancement of Women to the Year 2000* (Minneapolis, MN: Hubert H. Humphrey Institute of Public Affairs, University of Minnesota, 1986), p. i.

2. Preston Valien, "Minority: Minority Group," in Julius Gould and William L. Kolb, eds., *Dictionary of the Social Sciences* (New York: Free Press for UNESCO, 1964), pp. 432–433.

3. *Forward Looking Strategies* is the last of four major documents created during the U.N. Decade for Women. The others are *World Plan of Action* (Mexico City, 1975), *Elimination of All Forms of Discrimination Against Women* (New York, 1979), and *Programme of Action* (Copenhagen, 1980). The 1975 *Plan of Action* was followed by an American adaptation, entitled *U.S. National Plan of Action* and created in 1977 at the National Women's Conference in Houston.

4. Fraser and Moutoux, *Forward Looking Strategies*, p. 4.

5. Robert K. Merton, *Social Theory and Social Structure*, 2nd ed. (New York: Free Press, 1968), p. 182. See also chapter 13.

6. Ian Robertson, *Sociology*, 3rd ed. (New York: Worth, 1987), p. 115.

7. Fraser and Moutoux, *Forward Looking Strategies*, p. 16.

8. For a comprehensive account of the matter, see Anne Statham, Eleanor M.

Miller, and Hans O. Mauksch, eds., *The Worth of Women's Work: A Qualitative Synthesis* (Albany, NY: State University of New York Press, 1987).

9. For the data, see U.S. Bureau of the Census, *Statistical Abstract of the United States: 1987* (Washington, DC: Government Printing Office, 1986), Tables 639, 640.

10. Ibid, Table 656.

11. Daniel T. Lichter, "Racial Differences in Underemployment in American Cities," *American Journal of Sociology,* 93:4 (January 1988), p. 771.

12. Fraser and Moutoux, *Forward Looking Strategies,* p. 12.

13. Linda M. Blum, "Possibilities and Limits of the Comparable Worth Movement," *Gender and Society* 1:4 (December 1987), p. 380.

14. Anne Nelson, "Women in Unions," in Congressional Caucus for Women's Issues, Sara E. Rix, ed., *The American Woman 1987–88* (New York: W.W. Norton, 1987), p. 232.

15. Ibid, pp. 232–234.

16. James E. Ennis and Richard Schreuer, "Mobilizing Weak Support for Social Movements: The Role of Grievance, Efficacy, and Cost," *Social Forces* 66:2 (December 1987), pp. 390, 392.

17. Jan Knippers Black, "Participation and Political Progress: The Collapsible Pyramid," in Jan Knippers Black, ed., *Latin America: Its Problems and Its Promise* (Boulder, CO: Westview Press, 1984), p. 169.

18. Paul B. Horton, Gerald R. Leslie, and Richard F. Larson, *The Sociology of Social Problems,* 9th ed. (Englewood Cliffs, NJ: Prentice-Hall, 1988), p. 30. See the original version of these steps in Richard C. Fuller and Richard R. Myers, "The Natural History of a Social Problem," *American Sociological Review* 6:3 (June 1941), pp. 320–328.

19. For some of these points, see Marian Lief Palley, "The Women's Movement in Recent American Politics," in Congressional Caucus for Women's Issues, *The American Woman,* pp. 150–153.

20. Robert K. Merton, "Introduction: The Sociology of Social Problems," in Robert K. Merton and Robert Nisbet, eds., *Contemporary Social Problems,* 4th ed. (New York: Harcourt Brace Jovanovich, 1976), p. 9.

21. National Commission on Excellence in Education, *A Nation at Risk* (Washington, DC: Government Printing Office, 1983), p. 9.

22. Jonathan Kozol, *Illiterate America* (Garden City, NY: Anchor Books, 1985), pp. 8–9.

23. John K. Folger and Charles B. Nam, *Education of the American Population* (Washington, DC: Government Printing Office, 1967), p. 126.

24. U.S. Bureau of the Census, "Educational Attainment in the United States: March 1982 to 1985," *Current Population Reports,* Series P–20, No. 415 (Washington, DC: Government Printing Office, 1987), p. 7.

25. U.S. Bureau of the Census, "School Enrollment—Social and Economic Characteristics of Students: October 1983," *Current Population Reports,* Series P–20, No. 413 (Washington, DC: Government Printing Office, 1987), p. 4.

26. Fraser and Moutoux, *Forward Looking Strategies,* p. 21.

27. Several of these needs are adapted from ibid, pp. 21–24.

28. Ibid, p. 15.

29. U.S. National Center for Health Statistics, "Advance Report of Final Natality

Statistics, 1985," *Monthly Vital Statistics Report* 36:4 (Washington, DC: Government Printing Office, July 17, 1987), p. 7.

30. Judith Senderowitz and John M. Paxman, "Adolescent Fertility: Worldwide Concerns," *Population Bulletin* 40:2 (Washington, DC: Population Reference Bureau, 1985), p. 3.

31. Ibid, p. 17.

32. U.S. Bureau of the Census, "Who's Minding the Kids? Child Care Arrangements: Winter 1984–85," *Current Population Reports,* Series P–70, No. 9 (Washington, DC: Government Printing Office, 1987), pp. 1–2.

33. Ibid, p. 8.

34. U.S. Bureau of the Census, Rosalind R. Bruno, "After-School Care of School-Age Children: December 1984," *Current Population Reports,* Series P–23, No. 149 (Washington, DC: Government Printing Office, 1987), p. 1.

35. U.S. National Center for Health Statistics, *Health, United States, 1985* (Washington, DC: Government Printing Office, 1985), p. 1.

36. Ibid.

37. Ibid.

38. American Association of Retired Persons, *AARP News Bulletin* 28:11 (December 1987), pp. 1, 12.

39. Paul E. Zopf, Jr., *America's Older Population* (Houston, TX: Cap and Gown Press, 1986), pp. 102–103.

40. Greg J. Duncan, "Welfare Use in America," *ISR Newsletter* (Winter 1986–87), p. 5.

41. Ibid.

42. Ibid.

43. For a widely known argument to the contrary, see Charles Murray, *Losing Ground: American Social Policy, 1950–1980* (New York: Basic Books, 1984).

44. George J. Church, "Fixing Welfare," *Time* (February 16, 1987), p. 19.

45. Ibid, p. 20.

46. An elaboration of this point is in Michael Morris and John B. Williamson, *Poverty and Public Policy: An Analysis of Federal Intervention Efforts* (Westport, CT: Greenwood Press, 1986).

47. Frances Fox Pixen and Richard A. Cloward, "The Relief of Welfare," in Jerome H. Skolnick and Elliott Currie, eds., *Crisis in American Institutions,* 7th ed. (Glenview, IL: Scott, Foresman, 1988), p. 470.

48. Martin Dooley and Peter Gottschalk, "The Increasing Proportion of Men with Low Earnings in the United States," *Demography* 22:1 (February 1985), p. 25.

49. Church, "Fixing Welfare," p. 20.

50. For a treatment of several aspects of welfare in a broad context, see Yeheskel Hasenfeld and Mayer N. Zald, eds., "The Welfare State in America: Trends and Prospects," *Annals of the American Academy of Political and Social Science* 479 (May 1985).

51. Robert B. Reich, "What We Can Do," in Skolnick and Currie, *Crisis in American Institutions,* p. 608.

52. Annegret S. Ogden, *The Great American Housewife: From Helpmate to Wage Earner, 1776–1986* (Westport, CT: Greenwood Press, 1986), p. 221.

53. Ibid, pp. 221–222.

54. Ibid, p. 225.

55. Martha S. Hill, "The Changing Nature of Poverty," in Hasenfeld and Zald, "The Welfare State in America," p. 46.

56. Ibid.

7

Summary and Conclusions

THE CONCEPT OF POVERTY

Poverty in the United States is disproportionately an affliction of women and children, partly because the economy is not structured to provide women with jobs and wage opportunities equal to those of men, and partly because governmental transfer payments are insufficient to make up for the disadvantage. This book is basically an exploration of these several realities and their ramifications.

The effort to measure poverty is difficult because of sampling problems and because the official poverty index has been changed several times. The poverty index also is based on cash income, so excluding noncash benefits of various kinds tends to overstate the extent of poverty. On the other hand, the poverty income thresholds are quite parsimonious, and their use understates the degree of hardship many people actually suffer. Despite their limitations, however, the official data compiled by the U.S. Bureau of the Census are the best ones available on poverty and are the empirical basis of the book.

Much of the poverty in the United States is relative rather than absolute. That is, no large percentages of people lack food and shelter and, therefore, suffer death by starvation or exposure, although many are hungry and the size of the homeless population is increasing rapidly. That group also has come to include a larger share of families, who join the ranks of solitary individuals living on the streets and in makeshift shelters. Much larger numbers of people do lack the income necessary to provide a level of living which is decent according to the standards which prevail in American society, and they are poor relative to those standards and by comparison with the average level of living. Furthermore, standards of adequacy change over time, so people who are classified as poor and who feel poor today might not have been in either situation a few decades ago. An assessment of poverty also involves the extent to which people have equitable access to the society's advantages. Since the poor generally lack such access, the causes of poverty are not primarily individual, but structural to the degree the social system does not provide enough good jobs, suitable health care, adequate education, and other amenities largely beyond a poor person's control.

The feminization of poverty would seem to refer to higher rates of poverty among women than men of the same age and marital status and with other similar characteristics. If these characteristics are controlled statistically, women do have somewhat higher poverty rates, but the difference is not great and it has not changed much over time. The change which is responsible for the feminization of poverty is the large increase in the number and percentage of families headed by a woman with no husband present. Those families are the product of a high divorce rate, increased numbers of separations, a greater incidence of births to unmarried women, and a relatively large number of widows because the population is aging. Female-headed families produced by these conditions have a median income far below that of married-couple and male-headed families and a poverty rate far above. In addition, since more than nine-tenths of all children in one-parent homes live with their mothers, the feminization of poverty also victimizes an unusually large share of dependent children of both sexes.

FAMILIES IN POVERTY: REALITIES AND VARIATIONS

The idealized and mythologized American family, in which childrearing was carried out by a nonworking mother and financial support was provided by a wage-earning father, now typifies a very small minority of all families. Instead, there is a great variety of family forms, and the one which has grown most rapidly in the past two decades is the female-headed family with no husband present—a family type which provokes many questions. Some of them deal with how well socialization is carried out; whether its content creates alienation and negative perceptions of education, work, self, and society; and how badly various racial and ethnic groups suffer from poverty. Much of the book is an effort to confront these matters. It also cautions against stereotyping, however, for most female-headed families are not poor and the married-couple unit is no guarantee against poverty, inadequate socialization, or other problems.

Female-headed families do have a much higher poverty rate than other types; they are a disproportionately large share of all persistently poor families; and their progress out of poverty has been relatively slow, because they are especially affected by flaws in the socioeconomic system. At base, the presence or absence of a husband and father is the most crucial determinant of whether or not a family is likely to be poor, because men's median income is significantly higher than that of women and in the majority of married-couple families both spouses work for wages. The female-headed family almost always lacks both of those financial advantages and runs a high risk of poverty as a result. Therefore, the data on family income and poverty show that many women are victims of the ways in which economic and other relations between the sexes are organized and conducted, and that those relations mirror broader definitions and practices which are deeply embedded in the whole society.

Poverty rates are particularly high for very young householders, somewhat lower for elderly ones, and lowest for the 25–64 age group. Moreover, at no age is the poverty rate of white female householders nearly as high as those of blacks and Hispanics, both of whom have roughly similar rates. Black women are more likely than whites to have births out of wedlock, to be divorced or separated, and never to have been married at all, partly because young black men also have high poverty rates and many of them cannot provide adequate financial futures as spouses. Behind these conditions lie racism, isolation from economic opportunities because of ghetto life, separation from black middle-class role models, and other realities which hinder progress out of poverty among poor blacks, especially female householders.

The presence of dependent children, particularly those under 6, also contributes to high poverty rates in female-headed families, not only because children cost money to rear, but because they limit a woman's prospects for year-round, full-time employment, particularly in the absence of affordable child care. Therefore, the poverty rate in woman-headed households with even one child is substantially higher than in those with none, and the poverty rate increases with each successive child. This problem worsened as the large increase in female-headed families expanded the percentage of poor children who live in them. Since the mother has responsibility for the children in 90 percent of all one-parent families, the presence of children has a powerful effect on women's poverty. Even in married-couple families, however, the poverty rate is higher for those with children than for those without, and it also is highest when the householder is very young.

These conditions lend scant support to the idea that women bear children so as to collect and live comfortably on welfare (AFDC) payments without having to work. If that were so, poverty rates would not rise so dramatically with each successive child. Moreover, even in the most generous states, AFDC provides an income below the poverty level, and in the least generous states the amount provides only a fraction of the poverty threshold. AFDC is an infrequent incentive to reproduce.

The level of education of the female householder is inversely correlated with the poverty rate, although at every educational level young women have higher poverty rates than older ones and black women are the most likely to be poor. The data are convincing evidence that a woman who drops out of school before finishing high school or college is more likely than a woman who completes those levels to become a householder and to be poor. Poverty among female householders is a very complex phenomenon, however, and its causes and cures cannot be reduced only to the education variable, although raising the level of education does help lower poverty rates. It will be even more instrumental in the future, given the level of sophistication necessary for the good jobs in the making.

When couples divorce or separate, the average man's economic status is not much affected or may even improve, for while the wife's earnings are lost, in most cases so are child-care responsibilities; the children become the wife's problem. Conversely, the average woman's economic well-being usually deteriorates dramatically. Thus, poor women suffer disproportionately from punitive economic conditions over which they have little control; they are chiefly responsible for the care of dependent children who are poor because their mothers are poor; and they average far too little support from the men who fathered the children. This reflects a stubborn double standard of responsibility for childbearing and childrearing, manifested particularly in those absent fathers who deliberately shun associations with their children and the children's mothers and who default on their support obligations.

Poor female-headed families are getting poorer relative to other types because the dollar gap between their median income and the official poverty threshold is widening. Not only has the number of poor people in female-headed families grown, but these people are falling deeper into poverty because of their increasing income deficits. This family householder situation contrasts with the one for women as individuals, because the income gap between them and men is narrowing gradually.

The relative importance of particular sources of income in poor female-headed families both reflects and contributes to their poverty status. For example, the percentage with earnings is only about half the percentage in nonpoor female-headed families, while the poor ones rely on public assistance much more heavily, especially if the householder is young, has children, and receives the assistance in the form of AFDC. Nevertheless, a sizable share of poor women do work, though often part time or part year and invariably at low wages, because work under such conditions is all they can get and still look after their children. Most poor families patch together meager incomes from many sources, both cash and noncash, but they are less likely than the nonpoor to have earnings, private pensions, Social Security benefits, and dividends and interest. Female-headed families with a householder under 65 are more likely to have income from public assistance than from any other source, and it makes the difference between survival-level poverty and complete destitution. Thus, not only must we keep the welfare system, but it must be reformed to help get more people out of the poverty class and off welfare at the same time.

The more humane and subjective parts of this look at family poverty reveal the need for society-wide action to provide female family heads access to the job skills, employment opportunities, child-care facilities, housing, medical care, and other necessities which enhance self-sufficiency and economic well-being. Moreover, the welfare reforms not only must reduce stigmatized reliance on public assistance, but must create an income floor under those women for whom there are no decent jobs, who are unable to work, or who still risk being poor for other reasons. A female householder without a husband present should not have an unusually high chance of falling below the poverty level and be forced to choose between tending to the emotional needs of her children and earning a living for them and herself. Therefore, additional federal, state, and local investment in programs to enhance self-sufficiency, while expensive in the short run, will be relatively inexpensive in the long run, as they enable more women to become productive taxpayers and rescue them and their children from the pernicious effects of poverty, including welfare dependency for some. Even though new approaches could help reduce reliance on transfer payments, a legitimate need for an improved welfare system will never disappear. Perhaps the most important step society can take, however, is to make structural changes in the occupational-industrial complex so as to provide good private-sector and public-service jobs at decent wages and to eliminate gender discrimination in filling them. Then the life chances of poor women and their dependent children will be on a par with those of nonpoor families. Anything less reduces the opportunity to achieve according to ability and incentive, both of which can be enhanced by basic socioeconomic reform.

FAMILIES IN POVERTY: DISTRIBUTION AND TRENDS

Female-headed families below the poverty threshold are quite unevenly distributed throughout the nation, although when other strategic variables are accounted for, in virtually every section of the country the rates in those families are far above the ones in married-couple and male-headed units. The racial and ethnic composition of families plays an especially significant role in the geographic variations which do exist.

Poverty rates are highest among female-headed families in the South, lowest in the West, though on the average and no matter where they live, black women fare worse than whites. The geographic patterns also show native Americans and Hispanics to be at a significant disadvantage in most places. Asians as a whole have only slightly higher poverty rates than whites, although national origin within the Asian group and present location do make a considerable difference. The states show substantially more variation than the census regions and divisions, though the racial and ethnic discrepancies and the disadvantages of female-headed families persist in all of them.

The worst poverty pockets, identified by the percentages of poor female-headed families in the counties, are rather heavily, but by no means exclusively, concentrated in the South. Most tellingly, perhaps, the average poverty rates of female-headed families are lower than those of other families in only 26 of the nation's nearly 3,100 counties. The counties with large proportions of black people, native Americans, and recent Hispanic arrivals have especially high rates. Some of them are in the old plantation areas and other rural sections which suffer chronically high poverty rates regardless of family structure. Many other high-poverty counties either contain the central cities of MSAs or are linked to the cities in ways which both create deprivation and segregate and concentrate its victims. The poorest places also make a relatively unfavorable showing on other social indicators besides the poverty rates of female householders, including poverty rates among all types of families and children, the percentage of high-school graduates, and per capita family income. Still other counties, generally containing affluent suburbs near large cities, have very low poverty rates and score favorably on the other social indicators.

Female-headed families in the rural population have somewhat higher poverty rates than those in the urban group, basically because of the problems women face in the hamlets, villages, small towns, and other population clusters which make up the heterogeneous rural-nonfarm contingent, which accounts for about 90 percent of the total rural population. The rural-nonfarm group has higher rates than the rural-farm segment, because the female-headed family is relatively uncommon in the latter, and because those which do exist have certain stronger protections against poverty than families in the rural-nonfarm group. In addition, very few blacks and Hispanics remain in the farm population, so their higher average poverty rates have little statistical impact on it.

Poverty rates are lower in the metropolitan than the nonmetropolitan population. This is partly because the rates among rural female-headed families are higher than those among urban families and especially suburban ones inside MSAs but outside central cities. Those central cities, on the other hand, contain relatively large numbers and percentages of poor female-headed families.

Woman-headed families have both the highest and the lowest poverty rates in cities with 25,000–85,000 inhabitants, mostly because of the cities' functions, location relative to large metropolitan centers, and racial and ethnic composition. At the same time, most cities with a half million or more people have poverty rates above the national average, and many are troubled by a constellation of other disadvantages reflected in the social indicators.

The trends in poverty rates among female-headed families show significant reductions since 1959, which is also the pattern for other types of families. The major reductions took place prior to about 1968, however, followed by slow declines until 1978 or 1979, increases from then into the early 1980s, and some slight decreases after 1983. Moreover, female-headed families, with a much greater initial disadvantage than other types, experienced a slower pace of improvement. Thus, in certain relative terms they are worse off now than they were when the first data on poverty were collected: In 1959 female-headed families were 2.4 times more likely than other families to be poor, whereas by 1986 the ratio had risen to 4.2. Black married-couple families made the fastest progress out of poverty, followed by white married-couple units, trailed by black female-headed families and finally by white female-headed units. This adds up to relative deterioration in the situation of women householders, who now head a larger share of all families and look after a greater percentage of the nation's children than ever before.

These conditions are related to the increase in divorce rates until 1980 or so, the advent of no-fault divorce, the poor record of alimony and child-support payments by absent husbands and fathers, the difficulties poor women face in finding suitable employment for themselves and day care for their children, growth in the proportion of births to unmarried women, and other factors. Behind many of these conditions lie adverse changes in the labor-market situation. Those changes include increased unemployment rates among young workers, a decline in their real income, and greater strains on domestic relationships, often resulting in divorce, nonmarriage despite pregnancy, and the formation of female-headed families. In turn, labor-market conditions deteriorated in the late 1960s because of decreased aggregate demand for goods and services and, thus, for young workers, who increased in number at the same time. The only alternatives for many were low-wage jobs, no jobs, and/or poverty.

Some of these conditions will be self-correcting as smaller cohorts enter the labor market. Other conditions will not, and they call for the reactivation or creation of whatever programs are necessary to help as many poor householders as possible toward the goal of self-sufficiency, largely by opening channels to well-paying work, but also by other means which protect those who are unemployable and vulnerable to poverty, such as very young women and elderly widows. The governmental cutbacks during the 1980s need to be followed by more innovative attacks on this set of problems in the 1990s.

PERSONS IN POVERTY

The study of persons in poverty is a companion to the analysis of families below the poverty level. Individual women fare worse on the average than individual men no matter what their age or race, but the gap is much narrower than the one between female-headed and other types of families. Those female family heads also have higher poverty rates than individual women of comparable age, because many of the latter are part of married-couple families and enjoy the greater financial protection they generally provide.

Young women are especially likely to be poor, particularly those who have left parental families and have dependent children but who have not been able to find satisfactory jobs with adequate pay. A considerable share of them dropped out of school and are either unemployable, holding poor-paying jobs, or dependent on public assistance. Most important, however, are the structural and attitudinal problems, such as sex discrimination and gender-typing in jobs—problems which overshadow personal attributes as causes of poverty, though personal characteristics need to be improved in many cases as well.

Elderly women also have relatively high poverty rates, and in the ages 65 and over the rate among women is more than 70 percent higher than that among men. Nevertheless, the poverty population has a significantly lower median age than the nonpoor group, so the problem afflicts young women and children of both sexes more than any other groups. People under 15 years of age are particularly hard hit, and the ones under 6 suffer the highest poverty rates of all. Again, the most crucial factor is whether a child is part of a female-headed or married-couple family.

No matter what their age, therefore, women's prospects of avoiding poverty are worse when they are independent of a man, because he is either a second wage earner, in most cases has the higher of the two incomes, or both. That dependency also points to major flaws in the system, because many women find that both independence and reasonable financial security for them and their children are not possible. To the degree there is a relatively permanent poverty population in the United States, young women and their offspring are heavily represented in it, though it contains many elderly women as well. This core problem must be solved if the poverty differential between the sexes is to be eliminated.

As in the case of female householders, individual black and Hispanic women have far higher poverty rates than white women at all ages, with blacks generally in the worst situation. Still, the male-female differential within each racial and ethnic group tends to be a greater problem. In addition, children in all of the groups suffer the highest rates of poverty, and it afflicts three-quarters of the black and Hispanic youngsters under 3 in female-headed families and almost two-thirds of the white children in that age group.

Education has a crucial effect on the poverty rates of persons. While those rates do not fall consistently as educational attainment rises grade by grade, over the entire educational spectrum the drop is dramatic. For instance, women of all ages collectively with less than eight years of schooling are more than five times as likely to be poor as are those who had at least one year of college. The average poor woman is a high-school dropout, whereas the average nonpoor woman has completed at least some college work.

Clearly, efforts to raise educational levels and improve the content and usefulness of schooling must be part—but only part—of any effort to lift more women above the poverty level. The job market, too, must be rebuilt so that women who do improve their educational status can find good jobs with good earnings, not merely minimum-wage, service-sector positions which still keep them in poverty.

The poorest of the poor are of particular concern. They are persons who have only 50 percent or less of the official poverty-level income and who not only are in desperate straits, but often are locked into persistent poverty as well. Persons in woman-headed families are far more likely than those in other families to be the poorest of the poor, whereas poor persons in married-couple families are more apt to rank just slightly below the official poverty level. Their situation also is more likely to be temporary as their employment, wages, and other conditions fluctuate. Blacks are at the greatest disadvantage in this process, because over half of all persons in poor black female-headed families rank at less than 50 percent of the poverty level. Whites fare better, but not a great deal. Thus, for a sizable share of both races, poverty represents a depth of financial deprivation from which a significant rise is difficult if not impossible. These persistently poor are usually very young or elderly and black.

The near-poor population consists of persons with incomes 0–25 percent above the official poverty level. If individuals in this group and living in female-headed families are added to the poverty population, it increases by about a quarter. The near-poor are a marginal group, and for many of them cutbacks in assistance programs, loss of a job, a significant increase in inflation, or other reversals could cause a quick plunge into poverty. Including these people as part of the poverty population is probably more realistic than using the current poverty thresholds, for their situations are scarcely worthy of an affluent society which could provide additional safeguards against the threat of a slide below the poverty level.

Trends in personal poverty show that poverty rates have fallen for persons in both major types of families, but more slowly in those headed by a woman. Thus, the group which had the greatest initial disadvantage finds its present relative disadvantage to be worse. Yet the drop in poverty rates is significant, because they fell for persons in female-headed families from 50 percent in 1959 to 34 percent in 1986. But the *number* of poor persons in those families rose by over 6 million, whereas the number in other types of families fell by 14 million. The same thing happened for children, whose number in poor woman-headed families rose by two-thirds during the same period that the number in other types of families fell by three-fifths. These variable changes in the numbers of poor persons are a vivid illustration of the feminization of poverty.

Finally, noncash benefits helped lower the number of poor persons and the poverty rates more in the 1970s than they do now, although the benefits are more a boon to persons in female-headed than married-couple families. Moreover, the advantages elderly women receive from noncash benefits have been improving faster than those available to young women and their children. Thus, progress by the oldest group contrasts with the loss of some earlier gains by the youngest. The growing number and proportion of children in mother-only families contributes to this trend, as does the focus of income-maintenance programs on the elderly.

PERSONAL INCOME AND POVERTY

The most striking feature of women's income situation is a median which still falls a third or so below that of men, even among year-round, full-time workers in the same occupational categories. This is the direct financial cause of women's significantly higher poverty rates. Moreover, the income discrepancy persists across the age spectrum, though it is least in the very young and the elderly ages, where men's incomes also are relatively low. The narrower gap in the ages 20–24 than in all older ages, however, suggests that many recent female entrants to the labor force do not face the same income discrimination as their elders, and that is hopeful. But it also suggests that among people aged 25–64 men's income rose faster and men were promoted more rapidly, thus leaving women farther behind as they aged out of the entry-level years.

The female/male income gap is smaller among blacks than whites, because black men still have median incomes significantly below those of white men, not because black women fare especially well. On the contrary, their incomes are the poorest of the race and gender groups, though they are closing the gender gap faster than whites, especially in the ages 20–24. Furthermore, the income discrepancy between white and black women is less than the one between white and black men. The income chasm between black women and white men, however, is still wide. Nor do the median incomes of non-working women, regardless of race, come close to those of year-round, full-time workers, and the nonworkers are likely to be either very poor or the wives of relatively affluent men.

Women's incomes are especially low in the places outside metropolitan areas, particularly on farms but also in relatively isolated villages and small towns. The female/male income ratio is lowest for white women in MSAs, but in the suburbs outside central cities rather than within the cities. That is true for blacks in MSAs with over 1 million people, but the reverse holds in smaller ones; the nation's largest central cities are the repository of disproportionate numbers of poor black women. In addition, median incomes of men in central cities are significantly lower than in the suburbs, and that helps raise the central-city female/male income ratio, even if not for the right reasons.

Levels of education have an especially crucial effect on personal income, which rises for both sexes as the level of schooling attained rises. Among year-round, full-time workers, however, while the gender gap is smaller at each educational level than it is for nonworkers, it narrows only a little at each successive level. Thus, while women do have a lower median income than men because they are less likely to work full time, that factor, along with educational differentials, accounts for only part of the discrepancy. Between 25 and 30 percent of it is due to other causes, especially the persistent tendency to segregate women into poorer jobs and to undervalue the work they do no matter what the job. Both factors slow reduction of the gender income gap. Education does help women increase their incomes, lessen their chances of poverty, and improve their prospects of reaching income and occupational parity with men. But as that improvement occurs, changes in attitudes and institutionalized job structures also are necessary to achieve equality.

Sources of personal income vary significantly by gender and age, but among people under 65 wages produce the bulk of income for the large majority of men and women. Young women rely more heavily on wages than do middle-aged and elderly women, and they are much less likely to have income from property, self-employment, and any form of pension or compensation benefits. They are more likely to receive welfare than are middle-aged or elderly women, but, strikingly, only 7 percent of those aged 15–24 list it as an income source; the proportion is even smaller for older age groups. Still, women at any age are several times more likely than men to receive public assistance.

Few elderly women receive wages and over nine-tenths have income from Social Security, as do nine-tenths of the men. Only a fifth of the women have other pension income, however, which is less than half the proportion of men with that source. In fact, Social Security and property income account for the great bulk of the income of elderly women, followed by other retirement, wages, and Supplemental Security Income. Elderly men are more than twice as likely to have wages, but only half as likely to receive SSI. Thus, the income of elderly women comes from fewer sources and more frequently from public funds because of the legacy of their work histories, unusually low wages and pensions, and heavy concentration in unpaid housework.

Women at all ages are less likely than men to work on a year-round, full-time basis, and the lesser amount of time they invest in work accounts for some of the gender income gap. But women who do work year round and full time still have only about two-thirds the median income of men workers, and while the gap is much narrower below age 35, even it is significant. But so is the fact that working women aged 20–24 have 85 percent of the income of working men in those ages, showing that some improvement is underway.

Despite the improvement, women in all of the broad occupational categories and most of the specific occupations receive lower median incomes than men. In a few occupations women are above parity, but these are rare cases and the advantage in each one is slight. In the occupations in which males are 70 percent or more of the work force, the income gap is generally wider than in those in which women are 70 percent or more. Women's incomes are comparatively high in some of the most prestigious occupations, but men's are so much higher that the gender gap remains wide. This applies to manufacturing administrators, physicians, college and university teachers, lawyers and judges, and salaried sales supervisors and proprietors. More women are entering those fields, however, and part of the discrepancy exists because they are relatively new workers competing with men who have seniority. The gap should narrow further as women's job tenure lengthens and if gender-typing and the undervaluation of women's work decrease.

The occupational comparisons prompt a consideration of comparable worth. If it is to be conceptualized and implemented adequately, two kinds of occupational segregation must be overcome: (1) diverting women into jobs which call for less skill, effort, and responsibility than jobs filled by males, especially whites; and (2) segregating women into "female" jobs where the work they do, no matter how comparable to that performed by men, is undervalued because it is done by women. Industry resistance to paying higher initial costs to implement comparable worth also needs to be overcome by showing that those costs will be balanced by greater productivity and lower public outlays to help support poor women and their children.

Income trends are somewhat encouraging, because women are improving faster than men and the gender gap is narrowing, though the process is slow. Nevertheless, in most years between 1959 and 1985 the income of women (in constant 1985 dollars) rose faster than that of men, and the female/male ratio slowly increased. Black women also are making somewhat faster progress than white women, but the blacks are still more likely to be poor whether or not they work.

SOME SUGGESTIONS FOR ACTION

The unfavorable economic position of women relative to men and the problems they face call for action. Many specific actions were suggested at the U.N. Decade for Women World Conference in Nairobi in 1985, when the decade ended. Some of the recommendations apply to American women, particularly but not exclusively those in poverty.

Equality is the basic need to which others are related. It translates into equal rights with men in jobs, remuneration, decision making, responsibility, access to credit, protection against poverty, and other specifics. Equality cannot be achieved without basic changes in attitudes about the worth of women and what they do, ranging from reproduction to salaried work.

Fundamentally, equality can thrive only if we eradicate sexism—the belief that women are inferior because they are women—and only if it is confronted directly, for no unguided, unprodded evolutionary process will eliminate sexism automatically. So, a continuing women's movement is indispensable to raise consciousness about sexist attitudes and their tangible manifestations and to influence legislation. Since the attitudes and economic underdevelopment are reciprocals, both must be attacked together, partly by revising the content of socialization.

Economic development means rebuilding the American economy to enhance women's self-sufficiency, which depends on more jobs, better jobs, improved training for and access to jobs, and higher wages. It also depends on using women's productive talents more effectively than is allowed by gender-typing, segregation, and poverty. Without economic justice many other gains women might make are impossible or meaningless, but with it women no longer would be exploited as a source of cheap labor, relegated to part-time jobs, or otherwise constrained because of discrimination and its problems. The constraints can be overcome through union organization, other collective efforts to achieve empowerment and better wages, and governmental expenditures which enhance women's economic interests. We need to look especially critically at massive military spending and the concomitant neglect of job training and other ways to improve skills and employment prospects. We also need to pass the Equal Rights Amendment so women will have clearer constitutional guarantees.

Political power is indispensable in achieving other goals, including economic justice. Equitable empowerment of women is unlikely, however, if it depends only on male benevolence, because cherished practices and inertia rarely yield except in the face of pressure and confrontation. Thus, more women need to enter higher offices in order to influence the processes which affect their rights. Potential power generally becomes real power only within organizations, and government at various levels is the most strategic organization in which to further women's interests. Moreover, if government is not a mechanism for poor women to make their needs heard, their problems will continue to be handled in a middle-class context or ignored. Another important organization to help meet women's goals is a National Commission on the Status of Women, yet to be created. It could become the locus of women's concerns and provide additional access to the governmental decision-making process so as to ensure that women's political and economic rights are fully protected.

Education can help deal with women's poverty and job problems, but alone it cannot solve them. Yet we do need to eliminate illiteracy and functional illiteracy so their victims can escape poverty and become more self-sufficient contributors. We need more adequate funding for inner-city schools, revised curricula and teaching methods so fewer children abandon education, workable discipline, resocialization out of poverty and gender domination-subordination, and vocational education to fill local jobs. The last is especially crucial for young women who left school prematurely and those middle-aged women who have been displaced from their homemaker role and must earn a decent wage. Education also should encourage more male involvement in domestic responsibilities, raise consciousness about gender issues, assist women into the political process, provide better knowledge about health, and otherwise act as a vehicle for social change.

Family strength and family forms changed dramatically in the last few decades because of increases in the divorce rate, more births to unmarried women, and larger numbers and proportions of female-headed families. Poverty became a more significant cause of family breakup, while many families helped perpetuate poverty through the socialization process. To overcome some of these conditions which have helped feminize poverty, welfare and other programs need to enhance family solidarity. Absent fathers also need to be made more accountable for the support of their children. Families (and schools and other institutions) need better instruction in ways to reduce unwanted and mistimed pregnancies, partly to keep young women in school and to minimize the risk of poverty. Families need help to deal better with information about sex and contraception, abortion, and sex-related diseases. Families in general, but especially poor ones, need a national program of maternity leave to protect jobs and income. They also desperately need a comprehensive day-care system, perhaps as provided for under the Act for Better Child Care, which allows mothers to work and still protects preschoolers and "latchkey" children. The present inadequate arrangements only perpetuate neglect and semi-neglect of the physical and emotional needs of many poor children. Nor are present arrangements good enough to enable enough poor women to take jobs.

Health care is inadequate for women and children in poverty, though also for women and children at other income levels. Women's life expectancy is no longer rising faster than men's, partly because more women are on their own financially and cannot afford rapidly escalating health-care costs. Thus, public programs need to help more, not less, with those costs; to modify behavior, such as smoking, which has become increasingly dangerous among women; and to provide good prenatal and postnatal care for mothers and infants. In particular, funding for Medicaid needs to be increased and a national health system created to help poor women deal with these specific problems and to emphasize preventive care. About 37 million Americans, a large share of them poor, have no health insurance, and government programs are their only protection against having to neglect both chronic and acute health problems.

Women also are the chief caregivers for ill and disabled children, elders, and other family members, and they need more financial and other support in this role—a role which more women will play as the baby boom ages. It is much cheaper to provide home care for the disabled than to put them in nursing homes, but while some families do have some outside assistance in providing home care, most have little or none.

Welfare reform is tangled in divergent political ideologies and beliefs about whether society should help the poor out of poverty or they should accomplish that alone. Some argue that welfare causes family disintegration, destroys incentives to work, and creates a permanent underclass. Others insist that welfare is the principal reason there are not many more poor people, that it is only temporary for most recipients, and that most prefer work when it is available. Welfare reform has to be accomplished in this atmosphere of disagreement, though virtually everyone is clear that something significant must be done. Probably the best steps one can hope for are (1) ways to encourage and provide work for able-bodied recipients; (2) welfare benefits which continue until wages alone provide a decent level of living; (3) adequate protection for children, the disabled, and others who cannot work; and (4) mechanisms which encourage people to regard welfare as a temporary buffer rather than a way of life. In addition, since children are the poorest of the poor, AFDC must be improved so the status of many children will not deteriorate further. Moreover, because welfare is temporary for most recipients, improving it probably will not diminish work incentives for more than a small minority. Benefits also need to be more uniform from state to state, though they still can account for local variations in the cost of living. AFDC also should be available to poor two-parent families in every state (they are in some) so the program does not discourage family formation and solidarity. Perhaps most important, if we make work a nationwide requirement to receive benefits, the social system needs to provide adequate jobs at decent wages and the training necessary to do those jobs, whether private or public.

Most of the actions proposed will be expensive, but they also are investments in society's future. Whether we can rescue a large share of people in poverty and make women's status equal to that of men will determine the nature of that future. The prospects for fundamental improvements depend on the priorities we attach to our use of money, time, and energy. Present priorities have given us the problems discussed in this book. Different priorities can help solve them.

Bibliography

Aldrich, Mark, and Robert Buchele. *The Economics of Comparable Worth.* Cambridge, MA: Ballinger, 1986.

American Association of Retired Persons. *AARP News Bulletin* 28:11 (December 1987): 1, 12.

Astin, Alexander W. "Data Pertaining to the Education of Women: A Challenge to the Federal Government." In U.S. Bureau of the Census. Barbara B. Reagan, ed. "Issues in Federal Statistical Needs Relating to Women." *Current Population Reports.* Series P–23, No. 83. Washington, DC: Government Printing Office, 1979.

Baldwin, Wendy H., and Christine Winquist Nord. "Delayed Childbearing in the U.S.: Facts and Fictions." *Population Bulletin* 39:4. Washington, DC: Population Reference Bureau, 1984.

Barnes, Leroy W., ed. *Social Problems 87/88.* Guilford, CT: Dushkin, 1987.

Barrett, Nancy Smith. "Data Needs for Evaluating the Labor Market Status of Women." In U.S. Bureau of the Census. Barbara B. Reagan, ed. "Issues in Federal Statistical Needs Relating to Women." *Current Population Reports.* Series P–23, No. 83. Washington, DC: Government Printing Office, 1979.

Beattie, Margaret. "The Representation of Women in Unions." *Signs: Journal of Women in Culture and Society* 12:1 (Autumn 1986): 118–129.

Belbin, R. Meredith. "Retirement Strategy in an Evolving Society." In *Retirement,* edited by Frances M. Carp. New York: Behavioral Publications, 1972.

Beller, Andrea H., and John W. Graham. "Child Support Awards: Differentials and Trends by Race and Marital Status." *Demography* 23:2 (May 1986): 231–245.

Berman, Phyllis W., and Estelle R. Ramey, eds. *Women: A Developmental Perspective.* Washington, DC: National Institutes of Health, 1982.

Billy, John O. G., Nancy S. Lansdale, and Steven D. McLaughlin. "The Effect of Marital Status at First Birth on Marital Dissolution among Adolescent Mothers." *Demography* 23:3 (August 1986): 329–349.

Black, Jan Knippers, ed. *Latin America: Its Problems and Its Promise*. Boulder, CO: Westview Press, 1984.

Blankenship, Kim M. Review of *The Economics of Comparable Worth*, by Mark Aldrich and Robert Buchele. Cambridge, MA: Ballinger, 1986. In *Contemporary Sociology* 16:5 (September 1987): 627–628.

Bloom, David E., and James Trussell. "What Are the Determinants of Delayed Childbearing and Permanent Childlessness in the United States?" *Demography* 21:4 (November 1984): 591–611.

Blum, Linda M. "Possibilities and Limits of the Comparable Worth Movement." *Gender and Society* 1:4 (December 1987): 380–399.

Boaz, Rachel Floersheim. "Work as a Response to Low and Decreasing Real Income During Retirement." *Research on Aging* 9:3 (September 1987): 428–440.

Bode, Frederick A., and Donald E. Ginter. *Farm Tenancy and the Census in Antebellum Georgia*. Athens, GA: University of Georgia Press, 1986.

Bouvier, Leon F. "Planet Earth 1984–2034: A Demographic Vision." *Population Bulletin* 39:1. Washington, DC: Population Reference Bureau, 1984.

Carp, Frances M., ed. *Retirement*. New York: Behavioral Publications, 1972.

Church, George J. "Fixing Welfare." *Time* (February 16, 1987): 18–21.

Congressional Caucus for Women's Issues. Sara E. Rix, ed. *The American Woman 1987–88*. New York: W.W. Norton, 1987.

Congressional Research Service. *Hispanic Population of the United States: An Overview*. Washington, DC: Government Printing Office, 1983.

Corcoran, Mary, and Martha S. Hill. "Unemployment and Poverty." *Social Service Review* 54:3 (September 1980): 407–413.

Corcoran, Mary, Greg J. Duncan, and Martha S. Hill. "The Economic Fortunes of Women and Children: Lessons from the Panel Study of Income Dynamics." In *Women and Poverty*, edited by Barbara C. Gelpi, Nancy C.M. Hartsock, Clare C. Novak and Myra H. Strober. Chicago: University of Chicago Press, 1986.

Davis, Cary, Carl Haub, and JoAnne Willette. "U.S. Hispanics: Changing the Face of America." *Population Bulletin* 38:3. Washington, DC: Population Reference Bureau, 1983.

Desbarats, Jacqueline. "Ethnic Differences in Adaptation: Sino-Vietnamese Refugees in the United States." In "Refugees: Issues and Directions," edited by Dennis Gallagher. *International Migration Review* 20:2 (Summer 1986): 405–427.

Dooley, Martin, and Peter Gottschalk. "The Increasing Proportion of Men with Low Earnings in the United States." *Demography* 22:1 (February 1985): 25–34.

Dorris, Michael E. "The Grass Still Grows, the Rivers Still Flow: Contemporary Native Americans." *Daedalus* 110:2 (Spring 1981):43–69.

Duncan, Greg J. "The Volatility of Family Income Over the Life Course." Paper presented at the Annual Meetings of the Population Association of America. Chicago: April 30–May 2, 1987.

———. "Welfare Use in America." *ISR Newsletter* (Winter 1986–87): 5.

Duncan, Greg J., and Richard D. Coe. "The Dynamics of Welfare Use." In *Years of Poverty, Years of Plenty*, by Greg J. Duncan, Richard D. Coe, Mary E. Corcoran, Martha S. Hill, Saul D. Hoffman, and James N. Morgan. Ann Arbor, MI: Institute for Social Research, 1984.

Duncan, Greg. J., and Mary E. Corcoran. "Do Women 'Deserve' to Earn Less than Men?" In *Years of Poverty, Years of Plenty,* by Greg J. Duncan, Richard D. Coe, Mary E. Corcoran, Martha S. Hill, Saul D. Hoffman, and James N. Morgan. Ann Arbor, MI: Institute for Social Research, 1984.

Duncan, Greg J., and Saul D. Hoffman. "The Dynamics of Work Hours, Unemployment, and Earnings." In *Years of Poverty, Years of Plenty,* by Greg J. Duncan, Richard D. Coe, Mary E. Corcoran, Martha S. Hill, Saul D. Hoffman, and James N. Morgan. Ann Arbor, MI: Institute for Social Research, 1984.

———. "Recent Trends in the Relative Earnings of Black Men." In *Years of Poverty, Years of Plenty,* by Greg J. Duncan, Richard D. Coe, Mary E. Corcoran, Martha S. Hill, Saul D. Hoffman, and James N. Morgan. Ann Arbor, MI: Institute for Social Research, 1984.

———. "A Reconsideration of the Economic Consequences of Marital Dissolution." *Demography.* 22:4 (November 1987): 485–497.

Duncan, Greg J., and James N. Morgan. "An Overview of Family Economic Mobility." In *Years of Poverty, Years of Plenty,* by Greg J. Duncan, Richard D. Coe, Mary E. Corcoran, Martha S. Hill, Saul D. Hoffman, and James N. Morgan. Ann Arbor, MI: Institute for Social Research, 1984.

Duncan, Greg J., Richard D. Coe, and Martha S. Hill. "The Dynamics of Poverty." In *Years of Poverty, Years of Plenty,* by Greg J. Duncan, Richard D. Coe, Mary E. Corcoran, Martha S. Hill, Saul D. Hoffman, and James N. Morgan. Ann Arbor, MI: Institute for Social Research, 1984.

Duncan, Greg J., Richard D. Coe, Mary E. Corcoran, Martha S. Hill, Saul D. Hoffman, and James N. Morgan. *Years of Poverty, Years of Plenty.* Ann Arbor, MI: Institute for Social Research, 1984.

Easterlin, Richard A. "The New Age Structure of Poverty in America: Permanent or Transient?" *Population and Development Review* 13:2 (June 1987): 195–208.

England, Paula, and George Farkas. *Households, Employment, and Gender.* New York: Aldine, 1986.

Ennis, James E., and Richard Schreuer. "Mobilizing Weak Support for Social Movements: The Role of Grievance, Efficacy, and Cost." *Social Forces* 66:2 (December 1987): 390–409.

Espenshade, Thomas J. "The Economic Consequences of Divorce." *Journal of Marriage and the Family* 41:3 (August 1979): 615–625.

———. "Marriage Trends in America: Estimates, Implications, and Underlying Causes." *Population and Development Review* 11:2 (June 1985): 193–245.

Feldberg, Roslyn L. "Comparable Worth: Toward Theory and Practice in the United States." In *Women and Poverty,* edited by Barbara C. Gelpi, Nancy C. M. Hartsock, Clare C. Novak, and Myra H. Strober. Chicago: University of Chicago Press, 1986.

Ferman, Louis A., Stuart Henry, and Michele Hoyman, eds. "The Informal Economy." *Annals of the American Academy of Policital and Social Science* 493 (September 1987): 1–243.

Fitchen, Janet M. *Poverty in Rural America: A Case Study.* Boulder, CO: Westview Press, 1981.

Folger, John K., and Charles B. Nam. *Education of the American Population.* Washington, DC: Government Printing Office, 1967.

Fraser, Arvonne, and Kim Moutoux. *Forward Looking Strategies for the Advancement of Women to the Year 2000.* Minneapolis, MN: Hubert H. Humphrey Institute of Public Affairs, University of Minnesota, 1986.

Fuchs, Victor. "Redefining Poverty and Redistributing Income." *The Public Interest* 8 (Summer 1967): 88–95.

Fuller, Richard C., and Richard R. Myers. "The Natural History of a Social Problem." *American Sociological Review* 6:3 (June 1941): 320–328.

Gallagher, Dennis, ed. "Refugees: Issues and Directions." *International Migration Review* 20:2 (Summer 1986): 137–539.

Gelpi, Barbara C., Nancy C. M. Hartsock, Clare C. Novak, and Myra H. Strober, eds. *Women and Poverty.* Chicago: University of Chicago Press, 1986.

Glick, Paul C., and Arthur J. Norton. *Marrying, Divorcing, and Living Together in the U.S. Today.* Washington, DC: Population Reference Bureau, 1979.

Gomez, Rudolph, "Introduction." In *The Social Reality of Ethnic America,* edited by Rudolph Gomez, Clement Cottingham, Jr., Russell Endo, and Kathleen Jackson. Lexington, MA: D.C. Heath, 1974.

Gomez, Rudolph, Clement Cottingham, Jr., Russell Endo, and Kathleen Jackson, eds. *The Social Reality of Ethnic America.* Lexington, MA: D.C. Heath, 1974.

Gould, Julius, and William L. Kolb, eds. *Dictionary of the Social Sciences.* New York: Free Press for UNESCO, 1964.

Greenberger, Ellen, and Laurence Steinberg. *When Teenagers Work: The Psychological and Social Costs of Adolescent Employment.* New York: Basic Books, 1986.

Hagan, John, John Simpson, and A. R. Gillis. "Class in the Household: A Power-Control Theory of Gender and Delinquency." *American Journal of Sociology* 92:4 (January 1987): 788–816.

Harrington, Michael. *The New American Poverty.* New York: Holt, Rinehart & Winston, 1984.

———. *The Other America.* New York: Macmillan, 1962.

Hasenfeld, Yeheskel, and Mayer N. Zald, eds. "The Welfare State in America: Trends and Prospects." *Annals of the American Academy of Political and Social Science* 479 (May 1985): 1–206.

Hill, Martha S. "The Changing Nature of Poverty." In "The Welfare State in America: Trends and Prospects," edited by Yeheskel Hasenfeld and Mayer N. Zald. *Annals of the American Academy of Political and Social Science* 479 (May 1985): 31–47.

Hofferth, Sandra L., Joan R. Kahn, and Wendy Baldwin. "Premarital Sexual Activity Among U.S. Teenage Women Over the Past Three Decades." *Family Planning Perspectives* 19:2 (March/April 1987): 46–53.

Horton, Paul B., Gerald R. Leslie, and Richard F. Larson. *The Sociology of Social Problems.* 9th ed. Englewood Cliffs, NJ: Prentice-Hall, 1988.

Hoyman, Michele. "Female Participation in the Informal Economy: A Neglected Issue." In "The Informal Economy," edited by Louis A. Ferman, Stuart Henry, and Michele Hoyman. *Annals of the American Academy of Political and Social Science* 493 (September 1987): 65–82.

Jackson, Jacquelyne J. *Minorities and Aging*. Belmont, CA: Wadsworth, 1980.

Janson, Philip, and Karen Frisbie Mueller. "Age, Ethnicity, and Well-Being." *Research on Aging* 5:3 (September 1983): 353–367.

Kamerman, Sheila B. "Women, Children, and Poverty: Public Policies and Female-Headed Families in Industrial Countries." In *Women and Poverty,* edited by Barbara C. Gelpi, Nancy C. M. Hartsock, Clare C. Novak, and Myra H. Strober. Chicago: University of Chicago Press, 1986.

Kitano, Harry H. L. *Race Relations*. Englewood Cliffs, NJ: Prentice-Hall, 1985.

Kozol, Jonathan. *Illiterate America*. Garden City, NY: Anchor Books, 1985.

Larner, Jeremy. "Crisis in the Schools." In *Aspects of Poverty,* edited by Ben B. Seligman. New York: Crowell, 1968.

Leibowitz, Arleen, Marvin Eisen, and Winston K. Chow. "An Economic Model of Teenage Pregnancy Decision-Making." *Demography* 23:1 (February 1986): 67–77.

Lichter, Daniel T. "Racial Differences in Underemployment in American Cities." *American Journal of Sociology* 93:4 (January 1988): 771–792.

Lichter, Daniel T., and Janice A. Costanzo. "Nonmetropolitan Underemployment and Labor-Force Composition." *Rural Sociology* 52:3 (Fall 1987): 329–344.

MacKinnon, Catherine. *Sexual Harassment of Working Women*. New Haven, CT: Yale University Press, 1979.

McLanahan, Sara S. "Family Structure and Dependency: Early Transitions to Female Household Headship." *Demography* 25:1 (February 1988): 1–16.

McLeod, Jay. *Ain't No Makin' It: Leveled Aspirations in a Low Income Neighborhood*. Boulder, CO: Westview Press, 1987.

Merrick, Thomas W. "Population Pressures in Latin America." *Population Bulletin* 41:3. Washington, DC: Population Reference Bureau, 1986.

Merton, Robert K. "Introduction: The Sociology of Social Problems" In *Contemporary Social Problems,* edited by Robert K. Merton and Robert Nisbet. 4th ed. New York: Harcourt Brace Jovanovich, 1976.

————. *Social Theory and Social Structure*. 2nd ed. New York: Free Press, 1968.

Merton, Robert K., and Robert Nisbet, eds. *Contemporary Social Problems*. 4th ed. New York: Harcourt Brace Jovanovich, 1976.

Milkman, Ruth, ed. *Women, Work, and Protest: A Century of U.S. Women's Labor History*. Boston, MA: Routledge & Kegan Paul, 1985.

Milner, Jr., Murray. "Theories of Inequality: An Overview and a Strategy for Synthesis." *Social Forces* 65:4 (June 1987): 1053–1089.

Morris, Michael, and John B. Williamson. *Poverty and Public Policy: An Analysis of Federal Intervention Efforts*. Westport, CT: Greenwood Press, 1986.

Murray, Charles. *Losing Ground: American Social Policy, 1950–1980*. New York: Basic Books, 1984.

National Commission on Excellence in Education. *A Nation at Risk*. Washington, DC: Government Printing Office, 1983.

Nelson, Anne. "Women in Unions." In *The American Woman 1987–88,* by the Congressional Caucus for Women's Issues, edited by Sara E. Rix. New York: W.W. Norton, 1987.

Newitt, Jane. "Will the Baby Bust Work?" *American Demographics* 9:9 (September 1987): 32–35.

O'Connell, Martin, and David E. Bloom. *Juggling Jobs and Babies: America's Child*

Care Challenge. Occasional paper no. 12 in the series Population Trends and Public Policy. Washington, DC: Population Reference Bureau, 1987.

Ogden, Annegret S. *The Great American Housewife: From Helpmate to Wage Earner, 1776–1986.* Westport, CT: Greenwood Press, 1986.

O'Hare, William P. *America's Welfare Population: Who Gets What?* Occasional paper no. 13 in the series Population Trends and Public Policy. Washington, DC: Population Reference Bureau, 1987.

———. "The Eight Myths of Poverty." In *Social Problems 87/88* edited by Leroy W. Barnes. Guilford, CT: Dushkin, 1987.

———. "Poverty in America: Trends and New Patterns." *Population Bulletin* 40:3. Washington, DC: Population Reference Bureau, 1985.

Ortiz, Vilma. "Changes in the Characteristics of Puerto Rican Migrants from 1950 to 1980." *International Migration Review* 20:3 (Fall 1986): 612–628.

Palley, Marian Lief. "The Women's Movement in Recent American Politics." In *The American Woman 1987–88,* by Congressional Caucus for Women's Issues, edited by Sara E. Rix. New York: W.W. Norton, 1987.

Pampel, Fred C. *Social Change and the Aged.* Lexington, MA: D.C. Heath, 1981.

Pearce, Diana M. "Toil and Trouble: Women Workers and Unemployment Compensation." In *Women and Poverty,* edited by Barbara C. Gelpi, Nancy C. M. Hartsock, Clare C. Novak, and Myra H. Strober. Chicago: University of Chicago Press, 1986.

Philliber, William E. "Wife's Absence from the Labor Force and Low Income among Appalachian Migrants." *Rural Sociology* 47:4 (Winter 1982): 705–710.

Physician Task Force on Hunger in America. *Hunger in America: The Growing Epidemic.* Cambridge, MA: Harvard University School of Public Health, 1985.

Piotrkowski, Chaya S., and Mitchell H. Katz. "Women's Work and Personal Relations in the Family." In *Women: A Developmental Perspective,* edited by Phyllis W. Berman and Estelle R. Ramey. Washington, DC: National Institutes of Health, 1982.

Piven, Frances Fox, and Richard A. Cloward. "The Relief of Welfare." In *Crisis in American Institutions,* edited by Jerome H. Skolnick and Elliott Currie. 7th ed. Glenview, IL: Scott, Foresman, 1988.

Reich, Robert B. "What We Can Do." In *Crisis in American Institutions,* edited by Jerome H. Skolnick and Elliott Currie. 7th ed. Glenview, IL: Scott, Foresman, 1988.

Reid, John. "Black America in the 1980s." *Population Bulletin* 37:4. Washington, DC: Population Reference Bureau, 1982.

Remick, Helen, ed. *Comparable Worth and Wage Discrimination.* Philadelphia, PA: Temple University Press, 1984.

Ritzer, George. *Social Problems.* 2nd ed. New York: Random House, 1986.

Robertson, Ian. *Sociology.* 3rd ed. New York: Worth, 1987.

Robins, Philip K., and Katherine P. Dickinson. "Child Support and Welfare Dependence: A Multinomial Logit Analysis." *Demography* 22:3 (August 1985): 367–380.

Rosenfeld, Rachel Ann. *Farm Women: Work, Farm, and Family in the United States.* Chapel Hill, NC: University of North Carolina Press, 1985.

Roth, Dennis M. "Hispanics in the U.S. Labor Force: A Brief Examination." In *Hispanic Population of the United States: An Overview,* by the Congressional Research Service. Washington, DC: Government Printing Office, 1983.

Schreiber, Carol Tropp. *Changing Places: Men and Women in Transitional Occupations.* Cambridge, MA: MIT Press, 1981.

Schwager, Sally. "Educating Women in America." *Signs: Journal of Women in Culture and Society* 12:2 (Winter 1987): 333–372.

Scott, Hilda. *Working Your Way to the Bottom: The Feminization of Poverty.* London: Pandora Press, 1984.

Seligman, Ben B., ed. *Aspects of Poverty.* New York: Crowell, 1968.

Senderowitz, Judith, and John M. Paxman. "Adolescent Fertility: Worldwide Concerns." *Population Bulletin* 40:2. Washington, DC: Population Reference Bureau, 1985.

Shryock, Henry S., and Jacob S. Siegel. *The Methods and Materials of Demography.* Vol. 1. Washington, DC: Government Printing Office, 1973.

Skolnick, Jerome H., and Elliott Currie, eds. *Crisis in American Institutions.* 7th ed. Glenview, IL: Scott, Foresman, 1988.

Smith, James P., and Michael P. Ward. *Women's Wages and Work in the Twentieth Century.* Santa Monica, CA: Rand Corporation, 1984.

Smith, James P., and Finis R. Welch. *Closing the Gap: Forty Years of Economic Progress for Blacks.* Santa Monica, CA: Rand Corporation, 1986.

Smith, Joan. "The Paradox of Women's Poverty: Wage-earning Women and Economic Transformation." In *Women and Poverty,* edited by Barbara C. Gelpi, Nancy C. M. Hartsock, Clare C. Novak, and Myra H. Strober. Chicago: University of Chicago Press, 1986.

Smith, T. Lynn, and Paul E. Zopf, Jr. *Principles of Inductive Rural Sociology.* Philadelphia, PA: F.A. Davis, 1970.

Soldo, Beth J. "America's Elderly in the 1980s." *Population Bulletin* 35:4. Washington, DC: Population Reference Bureau, 1980.

Sørensen, Annemette, and Sara McLanahan. "Married Women's Economic Dependency, 1940–1980," *American Journal of Sociology* 93:3 (November 1987): 659–687.

Southeast Women's Employment Coalition. *Women of the Rural South: Economic Status and Prospects.* Lexington, KY: Southeast Women's Employment Coalition, 1986.

Statham, Anne, Eleanor M. Miller, and Hans O. Mauksch, eds. *The Worth of Women's Work: A Qualitative Synthesis.* Albany, NY: State University of New York Press, 1987.

Steinberg, Ronnie J. "A Want of Harmony: Perspectives on Wage Discrimination and Comparable Worth." In *Comparable Worth and Wage Discrimination,* edited by Helen Remick. Philadelphia, PA: Temple University Press, 1984.

Suter, Larry E., and Herman P. Miller. "Income Differences Between Men and Women." *American Journal of Sociology* 78:4 (January 1973): 962–974.

Thomas, Melvin E., and Michael Hughes. "The Continuing Significance of Race: A Study of Race, Class, and Quality of Life in America, 1972–1985." *American Sociological Review* 51:6 (December 1986): 830–841.

Tienda, Marta, and Shelley A. Smith. "Industrial Restructuring, Gender Segregation, and Sex Differences in Earnings." *American Sociological Review* 52:2 (April 1987): 195–210.

Tomaskovic-Devey, Donald. "Labor Markets, Industrial Structure, and Poverty: A Theoretical Discussion and Empirical Example." *Rural Sociology* 52:1 (Spring 1987): 56–74.

U.S. Bureau of the Census. *1980 Census of Population. Detailed Population Characteristics. United States Summary. Section A: United States.* Washington, DC: Government Printing Office, 1984.

———. *1980 Census of Population. General Social and Economic Characteristics.* Reports for states. Washington, DC: Government Printing Office, 1983.

———. *1980 Census of Population. General Social and Economic Characteristics. United States Summary.* Washington, DC: Government Printing Office, 1983.

———. "Child Support and Alimony: 1985." *Current Population Reports,* Series P–23, No. 152. Washington, DC: Government Printing Office, 1987.

———. *County and City Data Book, 1983.* Washington, DC: Government Printing Office, 1983.

———. "Educational Attainment in the United States: March 1982 to 1985." *Current Population Reports,* Series P–20, No. 415. Washington, DC: Government Printing Office, 1987.

———. *Estimates of Poverty Including the Value of Noncash Benefits: 1985.* Technical Paper No. 56. Washington, DC: Government Printing Office, 1986.

———. "Farm Population of the United States: 1985." *Current Population Reports,* Series P–27, No. 59. Washington, DC: Government Printing Office, 1986.

———. "Household After-Tax Income: 1985." *Current Population Reports,* Series P–23, No. 151. Washington, DC: Government Printing Office, 1987.

———. "Lifetime Work Experience and Its Effect on Earnings: Retrospective Data from the 1979 Income Survey Development Program." *Current Population Reports,* Series P–23, No. 136. Washington, DC: Government Printing Office, 1984.

———. "Marital Status and Living Arrangements: 1985." *Current Population Reports,* Series P–20, No. 410. Washington, DC: Government Printing Office, 1986.

———. "Money Income of Households, Families, and Persons in the United States: 1980." *Current Population Reports,* Series P–60, No. 132. Washington, DC: Government Printing Office, 1982.

———. "Money Income of Households, Families, and Persons in the United States: 1982." *Current Population Reports,* Series P–60, No. 142. Washington, DC: Government Printing Office, 1984.

———. "Money Income of Households, Families, and Persons in the United States: 1985." *Current Population Reports,* Series P–60, No. 156. Washington, DC: Government Printing Office, 1987.

———. "Money Income and Poverty Status of Families and Persons in the United States: 1985." Advance Data. *Current Population Reports,* Series P–60, No. 154. Washington, DC: Government Printing Office, 1986.

———. "Money Income and Poverty Status of Families and Persons in the United States: 1986." Advance Data. *Current Population Reports,* Series P–60, No. 157. Washington, DC: Government Printing Office, 1987.

———. "Population Profile of the United States: 1984–85." *Current Population*

Reports, Series P–23, No. 150. Washington, DC: Government Printing Office, 1987.

———. "Poverty in the United States: 1985." *Current Population Reports,* Series P–60, No. 158. Washington, DC: Government Printing Office, 1987.

———. "Projections of the Number of Households and Families: 1986 to 2000." *Current Population Reports,* Series P–25, No. 986. Washington, DC: Government Printing Office, 1986.

———. "Receipt of Selected Noncash Benefits: 1985." *Current Population Reports,* Series P–60, No. 155. Washington, DC: Government Printing Office, 1987.

———. "School Enrollment—Social and Economic Characteristics of Students: October 1983." *Current Population Reports,* Series P–20, No. 413. Washington, DC: Government Printing Office, 1987.

———. *Statistical Abstract of the United States: 1987.* Washington, DC: Government Printing Office, 1986.

———. "What's It Worth? Educational Background and Economic Status: Spring 1984." *Current Population Reports,* Series P–70, No. 11. Washington, DC: Government Printing Office, 1987.

———. "Who's Minding the Kids? Child Care Arrangements: Winter 1984–85." *Current Population Reports,* Series P–70, No. 9. Washington, DC: Government Printing Office, 1987.

———. Rosalind R. Bruno. "After-School Care of School-Age Children: December 1984." *Current Population Reports,* Series P–23, No. 149. Washington, DC: Government Printing Office, 1987.

———. Barbara B. Reagan, ed. "Issues in Federal Statistical Needs Relating to Women." *Current Population Reports,* Series P–23, No. 83. Washington, DC: Government Printing Office, 1979.

———. Cynthia M. Taeuber and Victor Valdisera. "Women in the American Economy." *Current Population Reports,* Series P–23, No. 146. Washington, DC: Government Printing Office, 1986.

U.S. Bureau of Labor Statistics. "Employment and Earnings: Characteristics of Families: Third Quarter 1987." *News* (October 26, 1987): Table 5.

———. "Families at Work: The Job and the Pay." *Monthly Labor Review* 106:12. Washington, DC: Government Printing Office (December 1983): 16–22.

———. "Most Occupational Changes are Voluntary." *News* (October 22, 1987): Table 4.

———. Nancy F. Rytina and Suzanne M. Bianchi. "Occupational Reclassification and Changes in Distribution by Gender." *Monthly Labor Review* 107:3. Washington, DC: Government Printing Office (March 1984): 11–17.

U.S. National Center for Health Statistics. "Advance Report of Final Natality Statistics, 1985." *Monthly Vital Statistics Report* 36:4. Washington, DC: Government Printing Office (July 17, 1987).

———. *The Feminization of Poverty and Older Women: An Update.* Washington, DC: Government Printing Office, 1985.

———. *Health, United States, 1985.* Washington, DC: Government Printing Office, 1985.

———. "Trends in Marital Status of Mothers at Conception and Birth of First Child: United States, 1964–66, 1972, and 1980." *Monthly Vital Statistics Report* 36:2. Washington, DC: Government Printing Office (May 29, 1987).

Valien, Preston. "Minority: Minority Group." In *Dictionary of the Social Sciences,* edited by Julius Gould and William L. Kolb. New York: Free Press for UNESCO, 1964.

Vaughn-Cooke, Denys. "The Economic Status of Black America: Is There a Recovery?" In *The State of Black America, 1984,* edited by James D. Williams. New Brunswick, NJ: Transaction Books, 1984.

Waite, Linda J. "U.S. Women at Work." *Population Bulletin* 36:2. Washington, DC: Population Reference Bureau, 1981.

Waite, Linda J., and Sue E. Berryman. "Job Stability among Young Women: A Comparison of Traditional and Nontraditional Occupations." *American Journal of Sociology* 92:3 (November 1986): 568–595.

Wallace, Claudia. "The Child-Care Dilemma." *Time* (June 22, 1987): 54–60.

Weitzman, Lenore J. *The Divorce Revolution: The Unexpected Consequences for Women and Children in America.* New York: Free Press, 1985.

Wharton, Amy S., and James N. Baron. "So Happy Together? The Impact of Gender Segregation on Men at Work." *American Sociological Review* 52:5 (October 1987): 574–587.

White, Richard. *The Roots of Dependency: Subsistence, Environment, and Social Change among the Choctaws, Pawnees, and Navajos.* Lincoln, NE: University of Nebraska Press, 1983.

Willborn, Steven L. *A Comparable Worth Primer.* Lexington, MA: Lexington Books, 1986.

Williams, James D. *The State of Black America, 1984.* New Brunswick, NJ: Transaction Books, 1984.

Williams, Terry M., and William Kornblum. *Growing Up Poor.* Lexington, MA: Lexington Books, 1985.

Wilson, William J. "The Black Community in the 1980s: Questions of Race, Class, and Public Policy." In *Majority and Minority,* edited by Norman R. Yetman. Boston, MA: Allyn and Bacon, 1985.

———. *The Declining Significance of Race: Blacks and Changing American Institutions.* 2nd ed. Chicago: University of Chicago Press, 1980.

Wilson, William J., and Kathryn M. Neckerman. "Poverty and Family Structure: The Widening Gap Between Evidence and Public Policy Issues." Paper presented at the Conference on Poverty and Policy: Retrospect and Prospects. Williamsburg, VA: Insititute for Research on Poverty and U.S. Department of Health and Human Services, December 6–8, 1984.

Yetman, Norman R., ed. *Majority and Minority.* Boston, MA: Allyn and Bacon, 1985.

Zimmerman, Elaine. "California Hearings on the Feminization of Poverty." In *Women and Poverty,* edited by Barbara C. Gelpi, Nancy C. M. Hartsock, Clare C. Novak, and Myra H. Strober. Chicago: University of Chicago Press, 1986.

Zopf, Paul E., Jr. *America's Older Population.* Houston, TX: Cap and Gown Press, 1986.

———. *Population: An Introduction to Social Demography.* Palo Alto, CA: Mayfield, 1984.

Index